RETIRING
IN
THAILAND

Sunisa Wongdee Terlecky & Philip Bryce

PAIBOON

PP

PUBLISHING

Published by

Paiboon Poomsan Publishing
582 Amarinniwate Village 2
Nawamin 90 (Sukha 1) Bungkum
Bangkok 10230
Thailand
Tel: 662-509-8632
Fax: 662-519-5437

Paiboon Publishing
PMB 256, 1442A Walnut Street
Berkeley
California 94709
USA
Tel: 1-510-848-7086
Fax: 1-510-666-8862

Info@paiboonpublishing.com
www.paiboonpublishing.com

Printed in Thailand

ISBN 9781887521796

Cover Design: Douglas Morton

Book designed and typesest by
72 Studio, Chiang Mai, Thailand
72studio@gmail.com

CONTENTS

Acknowledgements

Retiring In Thailand is now in your hands after much research and help from many people. Both of us are delighted to present this book to you.

We are grateful to our spouses. With their love, support, and encouragement, we were able to devote all the time and energy necessary to complete this project.

Special thanks goes to Mo Tejani, an author, retiree, and traveler who, as our consultant, has given us valuable input and helped make the book as informative as it can be.

We would like to express our warm thanks to all the retirees who granted us interviews and provided knowledge for each of the retirement locations.

We are grateful for the assistance of Dr. Narong Budhraja, director of Bangkok Hospital in Samui, who spent a great deal of time checking the content of the medical sections for accuracy.

Thanks to Harry DePietro who gave us an extraordinary story of his experience as a heart surgery patient in Bangkok.

And last but not least, a grateful thanks to Rich Baker, our editor, for his hard work in making our writing smooth and clear.

About This Book

With this book you get information from, and the perspectives of, both a foreigner and a native Thai. It is written to include the critical information you need to know before you embark upon retiring in Thailand. It is divided into five parts.

Part 1 introduces you to Thailand and provides general information about the country which will help you decide whether Thailand is the place for you to retire to.

Part 2 gives details on getting ready for living here: visa, healthcare, working, buying property, and money matters.

Part 3 provides helpful tips on how to live a successful life in Thailand, which is very important for new arrivals and is a friendly reminder for long-term retirees.

Part 4 lists popular retirement locations all over the kingdom and includes comments from numerous retirees in each particular place—so you can get sound advice directly from the 'locals.'

The final part of the book is a reference section that contains useful information and pointers for you to do your own research.

The two authors collaborated on different portions of the book. Philip researched and wrote the second part, while Sunisa gathered information and wrote all the other sections. Philip addresses the reader in Part 2, while the remainder of the book is from Sunisa's perspective.

The monetary units used are the Thai baht and the US dollar (except where stated otherwise). The exchange rate is 40 baht to one US dollar. Rates fluctuate around this average, but not by much. For up-to-date exchange rates, please check with a bank or on the Internet.

We hope that Retiring In Thailand is user-friendly, entertaining, and above all a valuable resource in your decision to live in the Land of Smiles.

Enjoy the book. Enjoy Thailand.

Introduction

You must be an adventurous soul to have picked up this book. Congratulations on giving yourself an opportunity to explore a new world you may never have considered before. We are very excited to provide you with information on how you can retire and live well in our favorite country, Thailand—the Land of Smiles.

There are likely to be many reasons why you are interested in this book. You may be reaching retirement age, want to retire early, or just stop working full time. You may be tired of working at a well-paid job that makes you unhappy with the quality of life you derive from it. You may be overworking in order to pay bills and maintain the lifestyle that you are accustomed to in your own country. You may be considering semi-retirement in order to work less and enjoy life more. You may be worried that the money you have in the bank, combined with your pension or social benefits, will not be enough for you to live off when you are older.

Whatever your reason, this book will open new doors for you. You will be offered alternatives that you may seriously consider later.

If you have been to Thailand before, you probably have a good idea about the country. But you may not be certain whether you want to live there or not. If you haven't visited Thailand, we recommend you travel there for a few weeks to see if it is a match for you. If you really like the country, we still suggest that you spend six months to a year renting a place to test the waters. Experience living in Thailand before you make any permanent decision.

Retiring In Thailand is a guide that gives you general information on retiring in the Land of Smiles. Our goal is to help you make decisions. It is not a travel guidebook. If you plan to see the country, we suggest one of the many travel guidebooks that are widely available.

We hope you will enjoy this book and find it useful and informative. We welcome all comments and suggestions—so we may improve our next edition and other future publications. Please send your comments to **retiringinthailand@gmail.com**. See you in Thailand!

Village boys entering the monkhood

MAP OF THAILAND

Thailand Facts

Geography-

Southeast Asia. Latitude 15 degrees north; longitude 100 degrees east. It occupies the western half of the Indochinese peninsula and the northern two-thirds of the Malay Peninsula. Bordered by Burma (Myanmar) to the north and west; Laos to the north and northeast; Cambodia to the east; and Malaysia to the south.

Capital- Bangkok (Krung Thep).

The Four Capitals-

Sukhothai Period 1238–1368 (9 kings)

Ayuthaya Period1350–1767 (34 kings)

Thonburi Period 1767– 1782 (one king)

Rattanakosin (Bangkok) Period 1782–present (9 kings)

Population- 65 million (2006).

Population, Bangkok Metropolitan Area- 9-10 million.

Government- Constitutional monarchy.

Head of State- King Bhumibol Adulyadej (1946 -).

Kingdom of Thailand-

Established in 1238 by King Khunsri Intrathit who proclaimed Sukhothai the capital. Known as Siam until 1939. The only Southeast Asian country never to have been colonized by a European power.

Area-

Land: 511,771 sq km (about the size of France or the State of Texas).

Water: 2,230 sq km.

Total: 514,000 sq km.

Number of Provinces- 76

Major Provinces-

Nakhon Ratchasima (Korat), Chiang Mai, Khon Kaen, Ubon Ratchathani, Phuket, Udon Thani, Songkhla.

Climate- Tropical monsoon, warm, hot, and humid.

Languages-

Thai, regional Thai dialects, hilltribes, and English.

Ethnicity- Thai 75%, Chinese 14%, others 11%

Religion- Buddhist 94%, Muslim 5%, Christian 1%

Currency- Baht

GDP Per Capita Income- $8,300 (2005 est.)

Country's Major Sources of Income-

Export of agricultural products, tourism.

Export Commodities-

Rice, tapioca, rubber, corn, jewelry, sugar cane, coconuts, soybeans, transistors, rubber, plastic, seafood.

Exports-

$105.8 billion (2005 est.): textiles and footwear, fishery products, rice, rubber, jewelry, automobiles, computers and electrical appliances.

Imports-

$107 billion (2005 est.): capital goods, intermediate goods and raw materials, consumer goods, fuel.

Industries-

Tourism, textiles and garments, agricultural processing, beverages, tobacco, cement, light manufacturing (jewelry and electric appliances, computers and parts, integrated circuits, furniture, plastics), automobiles and automotive parts; world's second-largest tungsten producer and third-largest tin producer.

Arable Land- 29%

Natural Resources-

Tin, rubber, natural gas, tungsten, tantalum, timber, lead, gypsum, lignite, fluorite, fish, arable land.

Import Commodities-

Computers, capital goods, intermediate goods and raw materials, consumer goods, fuel.

Labor Force

35.36 million; agriculture 49%, industry 14%, services 37%

Main Export Countries-

US, Japan, Singapore, China, Hong Kong, Malaysia

Main Import Countries-

Japan, US, China, Malaysia, Singapore, Taiwan.

GDP/PPP- $545.8 billion (2005 est.)

Inflation- 4.8%

Unemployment- 1.4% (2005 est.)

Life Expectancy

    Male: 69 years

    Female: 73 years

    All: 72.2 years.

Infant Mortality Rate- 19.5/1,000

Literacy Rate- 96%

Time- GMT + seven hours.

International Dialing Code- 66

Coastline- 3,219 kilometers.

Electric Current- 220 volts, 50 cycles.

Communications-

    Telephones: 6.7 million main lines (2004). Mobile cellular: 27 million (2005). Radio broadcast stations: AM, 204; FM, 334; short-wave, six (1999). Radios: 13.96 million (1997). Television broadcast stations: 111 (2006). Televisions: 15.19 million (1997). Internet hosts: 786,226 (2005). Internet users: 8.5 million (2005).

Transportation-

    Railways: 4,071 km (2002). Highways: 64,600 km (paved, 62,985 km; unpaved, 1,615 km). Waterways: 4,000 km principal waterways; 3,701 km with navigable depths of 0.9 m or more throughout the year; numerous minor waterways navigable by shallow-draft native craft. Ports and harbors: Bangkok, Laem Chabang, Pattani, Phuket, Sattahip, Si Racha, Songkhla. Airports: 111 (2002).

Home Sweet Home in Central Thailand

Happiness is an extended family

Temple guardian figure

PART 1
WHY THAILAND?

Many tourists have fallen in love with Thailand, the Land of Smiles, on their very first trip. Thailand is a medium-sized country about the size of France. It has so much to offer that it has drawn more repeat tourists than any other travel destination. It is one of the most exotic countries in the world. Thailand is full of beautiful, enchanting places for you to experience—and no matter what you want to do, Thailand is sure to have it for you.

Because of modern technology—the Internet, fast air travel, on-line banking, low-rate phone calls—people have more choices where to live and work. In recent years, many people have begun to think about their retirement and the prospect of living overseas after they quit full-time work. There are quite a few places that you may have heard of in Europe and Latin America where people have chosen to retire to. Some of you may be wondering why Thailand has now become the new destination of choice for retirees.

Low Cost Of Living

This is probably the most popular reason why Thailand is a good place for retirees.

Food in Thailand is not just tasty, it's also inexpensive. No place in the world can beat Thailand for delicious food, low prices, and great variety. You can enjoy tasty food for just $5 a day. If you occasionally want something more familiar, or just want some personal variety, it's cheap to cook your own favorite dishes at home. There are many supermarkets that stock both Thai and Western brands. You will most likely find all the ingredients you need to make the mouthwatering food you crave for.

Accommodation is available for all budget levels. It just depends on where and how you want to live. For example, one of our friends rents a three-bedroom house in Pai (a district in Mae Hong Son province in the north) for just $85 a month. Another friend, Dan, rents a large, three-bedroom house in a suburb of Bangkok for only $500 a month.

If you have the resources, you can live a lavish lifestyle. Bob Ellsworth rents an upscale condo in the Silom area of downtown Bangkok for $1,800 a month—which is the same as staying at a five-star hotel. There are luxurious condos and houses in Thailand that cost over a million US dollars. No matter what your budget or lifestyle choice, you will find it in Thailand.

Great Lifestyle

The low cost of living gives you the opportunity of a new lifestyle. There are so many activities (and alternatives) you can afford in Thailand that you can't at home.

In Thailand, many people can afford to have a full-time housekeeper for less than $200 a month. In the US, we have a cleaning lady that comes in every two weeks and works for six hours. We pay her $80. In Thailand we have a full-time maid and also a driver and a gardener. Back in San Francisco, we do our own driving and do most of the housework ourselves.

Many Western people are not used to having servants. So when you live in Thailand, you may have to learn how to deal with housekeepers and how to speak to them in the proper context. (You cannot be over-friendly with them; in the very hierarchical Thai society, it just doesn't work that way.) There are qualified people who are ready to work at a price you can afford. Ask around and get referrals for reliable domestic staff.

Spas and beauty treatments are extremely popular in Thailand. You will find some of the finest and most advanced health spas in the world, with excellent service at economical prices. I can afford to have facial treatments and a massage at least once a week. In the US I pay $120 for each microdermabrasion, but the same treatment costs only 1,000 baht ($25) in Bangkok.

For sport and outdoor enthusiasts, there is golf, sailing, scuba diving, snorkeling, dancing, and hundreds of other activities—for one-third of the price you pay at home. Just name the kind of activities you like, and you're almost certain to find them in Thailand.

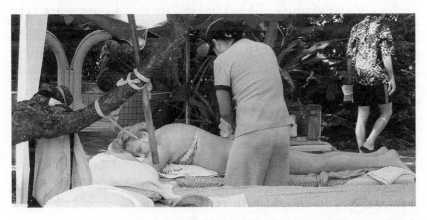

Pamper yourself with a spa massage right on the beach

Shopping Paradise

Thailand is a paradise for shoppers. I have given up shopping at the malls and department stores in the US and other countries. I know I can find everything I need in Thailand. I have the most fun shopping for clothes, textiles, jewelry, lacquerware, ceramics, furniture, pottery, and hilltribe crafts. You have to know where to shop, though, and you need to learn how to bargain a little. When you haggle with vendors, try to pay about two-thirds of the amount originally asked for. Don't overdo it because the sellers may become annoyed and think you are insulting them.

As in all countries, if you go to the tourist areas, you are not going to find the best deals. Try to go where Thai people shop. Ask your Thai friends to show you how and where you can shop inexpensively

Learn how to shop like a Thai, and you can live like Thai people do.

Affordable Healthcare, Dental Care, Cosmetic Surgery

Thailand has one of the best medical services in Asia. Private and government-run hospitals give efficient and quick service to locals and visitors alike. Thai doctors and nurses are very well trained, and the dentists are among the best in the world. And the fees are very reasonable. Health tourism is a booming business in Thailand. There are even medical and dental tours from countries like Korea and Japan.

You can purchase most medications from aspirin to antibiotics to Viagra at Thai pharmacies without a prescription. Prices are about half what you pay in the West. However, you need to be careful when you purchase medicine in Thailand. Check the generic and brand names. Make sure it's the right kind. Preferably you should talk to a pharmacist who can speak

4

English. Ultimately, you should consult a doctor in Thailand or at home to make sure that the medicine is safe for you.

Cosmetic surgery is very popular among Thais—especially nose enhancements. I met some of my high-school classmates at a reunion in 2005 and noticed that half of them looked quite different. Most told me they'd had a nose job. Thai people envy the larger Caucasian nose because they think it's sexy and attractive. You can have your nose fixed for less than $500.

Besides facial surgery, many of my Thai women friends have had breast enlargements. This costs between $1,000 to $2,000.

Doing Business

Thailand has a well-developed infrastructure and a free-enterprise economy. The government has officially encouraged foreign investment for many decades, but it does not always make it easy for foreigners to own their own business in Thailand. However, Thailand is better than many other countries in this respect.

If you want to retire from the job you have in your own country, but still want to work in Thailand, it's possible to do so. You can investigate the possibility of starting a business so you can still have a regular income or just to keep you from boredom. You will have to deal with the Thai bureaucracy, but it is not that bad compared to other developing countries.

If the nature of your work doesn't require you to be in a particular place, you are a good candidate for setting up a business in Thailand. A graphic designer we know has his business in Bangkok and remains in contact with his clients in the US by phone and the Internet. For more information on doing business see the book *How to Establish a Success-*

ful Business in Thailand by Philip Wylie, also published by Paiboon Publishing.

Travel To Other Asian Countries

Thailand is located in the center of Southeast Asia. A short flight will take you to Burma, Laos, Cambodia, Malaysia, Indonesia, and Singapore. If you live in Thailand you can easily take longer trips to other Asian countries like India, Nepal, Japan, or China. If you like to travel and see other exotic countries, Thailand is the most convenient place to use as a base. You may become quite busy discovering the diverse cultures and people of the region.

You'll probably want your friends and family to visit you in Thailand. It will give them a chance to have an adventure of their own. There are countless travel agencies that can help you plan your trips.

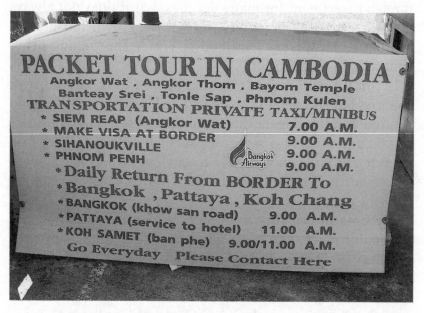

Many exotic locations are just a short bus or plane ride from Thailand

Low Crime Rate

Thailand is generally a very safe place to live. The crime rate in Bangkok remains far lower than that in many American cities—or of any other city of its size and population. Like anywhere else, you will still need to take precautions. If you don't do drugs, engage in child prostitution, deal with local people in illegal activities, or overtly flash your wealth, you will be safer than almost anywhere else in the world. Thai people are pleasant and welcome foreigners. The many crime stories and gruesome incidents in the local newspapers almost always involve Thais only.

Exciting Cities, Rustic Villages, Tropical Islands

Thailand is one of the most diverse countries in the world. Living in a big city in this country can be as convenient and exciting as living in New York, London, or Paris—at a much cheaper cost.

If you prefer tranquility, choose a smaller town or a quiet beach or island. In many of the remote areas you will find that the price of land and cost of living is cheaper than in the popular parts of the country.

Friendly, Fun-Loving People

When you retire, you might want to live in a place where you are surrounded by pleasant people. Thais are famous for their friendliness, hospitality, and fun-loving nature. They are a generally happy people who love to smile. That's why the country is nicknamed the Land of Smiles. Thais enjoy life and are laid-back. The value of *sanuk* ('having fun') is most important. Thais love to drink, sing, and especially eat. There are no excuses for having a party in Thailand!

You will feel welcomed by the Thais. In everything they do, the people will make you feel comfortable and at ease. Excellent service is something Thailand is famous for.

Thais are especially friendly to foreigners. They love to talk and ask questions and practice their English; so get ready to converse with them (in either English or Thai). Try to learn, and hopefully master, some of the Thai language.

Sometimes you may think that people are not so friendly. They might be looking at you with a frown. Don't worry, it might just be a case of shyness. Just give a little smile and you will get one in return. This ice-breaking technique works nearly every time.

Beautiful Beaches, Magnificent Mountains

Many of the world's most beautiful beaches are found in Thailand. Tourists from all over the world spend long hours on planes just to enjoy the sun, sand, and surf in Thailand. If you live in Thailand, you won't have to travel across time zones to partake in your favorite water sports. You can relax on white-sand beaches and swim in turquoise seas almost whenever you want.

Find your ideal beach in Thailand

The hill country of the north of Thailand is spectacular and attracts people who love nature and the great outdoors. You can explore the mountains and stunning natural scenery on wheels, or on four legs or two. Go mountain biking or rent a jeep for a tour of the north; go trekking or take a jungle trip on the back of an elephant.

Nightlife, Entertainment, Leisure

You never have to worry about nightlife and entertainment in Thailand. The Land of Smiles has few competitors in this category. You just have to set and adhere to an entertainment budget.

For those who like nightlife, music, and dancing there are bars and pubs galore, nightclubs, discotheques, concert halls, teahouses, lounges, and karaoke bars.

For food and drink lovers, there are unlimited opportunities for dining. You will experience not only delicious and economical Thai food, but culinary treats from all over the world. Thailand is famous for its award-winning gourmet restaurants with international cuisine. In the main urban areas like Bangkok, Pattaya, and Chiang Mai, there are Italian, Mexican, French, American, German, Russian, Greek, Indian, Middle-Eastern, Scandinavian, British, Japanese, and Chinese restaurants. And numerous others besides. Chinese restaurants are found all over the country. Japanese food has been popular for quite a while among the Thais. Korean and Vietnamese food is also becoming fashionable. American and Continental breakfasts are available in many hotels and coffee shops.

If you miss junk food, there are McDonald's, KFC, Pizza Hut, and Subway outlets on almost every street corner in Bangkok. Ice-cream parlors and coffee chains are found in malls all over the country. After Starbucks invaded, Thais started drinking more coffee, and there are now Thai companies like Black Canyon selling good quality coffees.

Buses service all areas of Thailand, are inexpensive and run very often

Health food is becoming more popular with the Thais. You can now purchase organic fruits and vegetables. Thailand has an abundance of Oriental and Western gastronomic pleasures.

Thailand has numerous theme parks, zoos, wildlife sanctuaries, national parks, museums, theaters, and cinema complexes.

Sports lovers can spend their time at the golf course, tennis or squash court, exercising at the gym, or playing soccer or rugby. There's even an ice-hockey league in Bangkok. Almost any sport or outdoor pursuit can be found in Thailand—including some you've never even heard of or thought would be possible here.

You will find all of the above list of activities and opportunities in all the bigger cities. In smaller towns, you may find some but not others.

Study The Cultures Of The East

Thailand has a rich cultural heritage. Its neighbors also have exotic cultures of their own. Living and retiring in this region will give you the opportunity to immerse yourself in these diverse cultures. You will see Buddhist monks and temples everywhere you go. Thailand is a place where you can gain knowledge of Buddhism, other Eastern philosophies, and practice yoga or meditation. You can enrich your life by combining the best of East and West.

Easy To Get To And Get Around

Bangkok's new Suvarnabhumi International Airport provides a gateway to Southeast Asia, and the old Don Muang Airport is also used for domestic flights. These air hubs connect directly to North America, Australia, Europe and other parts of Asia, with daily flights by the world's major airlines.

You can also enter Thailand by road or rail from Singapore and Malaysia.

Getting around the country is convenient and inexpensive. Thailand has low-cost airlines that fly to all regional cities. Rail travel is also efficient, inexpensive, and comfortable by Asian standards. Air-conditioned bus is the most popular

Northern Thailand is abundant with many different hill tribes

11

form of transport among Thais. The buses are economical and quite reliable—but not always safe. Every province and town has its own bus system.

Public transport is the cheapest way to get around. In Bangkok, public buses cost only a few baht. There are taxis, *tuk-tuks* (three-wheeled, 'open-air' taxis), motorcycle taxis, riverboat taxis and ferries, the 'skytrain,' and the recently opened, state-of-the-art subway system.

A Harmonious Melting Pot And Salad Bowl

The Thais are proud to show off their culture, and they graciously welcome visitors. Although one of the world's most important Buddhist countries, Thailand allows complete freedom of religion.

Thailand is a gay friendly country, and has a very large gay population of its own. A survey conducted by *Time Asia* magazine found that Thais are the most gay-friendly people in Asia. This could derive from the belief in *karma*: one is born to a certain station, and condition, in life because of one's conduct in past lives. Being gay is accepted by the Thais. There is no violent prejudice against gay people (as there is in some Western countries). That kind of irrational hatred is not understood in Thailand.

Because what is now Thailand is the center of Southeast Asia, many different peoples lived there for centuries—long before the present country was formed. The people of Thailand are a mix of Chinese, Khmer, Mon, Lao, Malay, Indian, and numerous other races. That's why you will see many kinds of faces and skin tones among the Thais. This is perhaps a factor in the overall physical attractiveness of the people.

Thailand is a melting pot of cultures and peoples. Now, with Caucasians, Japanese, and Africans entering the racial mix, the country is more like a huge salad bowl.

The Thai people love peace and are happy to live harmoniously with people of all races.

A New Definition of Retirement

The accepted definition of retirement has been "the end of working." When people reached the age of 65 (in America) they quit working and retired. The dictionary defines retirement as "withdrawal" – not only from one's work but also withdrawal into privacy or seclusion.

Today retirement is taking on a new meaning that appears to be a more exciting definition of how many of us will live out our later years. People now look at retirement as an opportunity at a new beginning. Beginning a new career, a new phase of learning, an opportunity to do volunteer work and give back to their community, and a time to set new goals and start new activities.

In the past, when a person retired they were worn out from physical labor. Now the job market has changed and our work is less physically demanding plus people are living longer.

Currently more people who reach retirement age will want to continue, or need to continue working full or part-time. For some people retirement means a change in the type of work they have been doing with no thought of slowing down, and this could be at age 45 or 50 not necessarily at 65.

In America the "Baby Boomer generation", people born between 1946 and 1964, encompass a group of over 77 million on the verge of reaching retirement age. When compared to their parents' generation this group will be in better health, will live longer and will need more money to retire. In addition, this generation will need to make more choices but luckily they have access to a plethora of information to make those choices.

In many industrialized nations turning age 50 means you have only lived half of your adult life. According to the American Association of Retired Persons (AARP), when people reach retirement age they seek four things to provide a satisfying life: economic security, good health, personal fulfillment and work. And the most far-reaching change in the perception of retirement is the inclusion of work in this mix.

Many people reaching retirement age see themselves continuing to work, some as a necessity and some as a way to achieve their personal fulfillment. Scores of people are looking forward to starting a new career or starting that new business they have always dreamed of.

Economic security at retirement age used to mean social security and a pension. Today it has changed to social security, personal savings and earnings from working during retirement. In addition, considering the high cost of living during their retirement years is an important factor for people when determining their economic security. Many people are researching their options for living outside of their home country and Thailand is coming up more often as a search response.

Health care cost is another important factor in retirement planning. Limited health insurance coverage and extremely high health care costs are impacting the new retirement strategies. People are opting to get in shape and eat more healthy food but eventually all of us will need to rely on the health care system in our country. People turning 50 now are getting an education on the limited health care coverage and high cost of aging as the caregivers for their aging parents. According to AARP a one year's stay in a nursing home can cost as much as $55,000 in America. In Thailand the cost of health care is much lower than in western countries yet the level of care is comparable.

In the old way of thinking by age 50 most people were expected to have settled down and would be experiencing the loneliness that was to come as their children were leaving home. The fact is that many people reaching 50 are experiencing the opposite with the most upheavals ever in their lives. Starting second families, caring for their parents and grandchildren, starting new careers and facing home relocation decisions. If you are in this age group and feeling unsettled about your life decisions you have plenty of company.

Many people are exploring all of the new options available to them that will define their own personal retirement solution. How and where to live, what new challenges and directions to explore, plus developing a road map to getting there are all part of the new "retirement" adventure.

In the new world view the word retirement will come to mean new choices and new beginnings plus the freedom to fulfill your dreams, rather than a time to withdraw and wait for the end to come.

A Brief History of Expats in Thailand

Although many European and some American expats were living in Bangkok prior to World War II, it was the British that had the most impact. The children of the Thai royalty were educated in Britain and there were many British advisors working in Thailand. The British Chamber of Commerce was founded in 1946 with 17 founders and 3 'associate' (non-British) members.

A major influx of expats in Thailand resulted because of the American military involvement in Vietnam between 1964 and 1975. Pattaya became the "rest and relaxation" destination of choice for war weary servicemen. Thailand is now home to at least 500 Vietnam War veterans that decided to stay in the "Land of Smiles."

15

Many veterans chose to remain because their life was simpler and their retirement benefits bought more in the less expensive economy of Thailand. Also, many veterans have Thai wives and children, which was another motivation to remain.

But the majority of expats in Thailand came as visitors for business or leisure purposes and then decided to plant their roots here. This can be seen in the history of clubs and associations that have been established in Thailand. The Pattaya Expats Club was established in 2002 but the Rotary Club of Pattaya was founded way back in 1972.

The new veterans are the ones that boast about their number of years living in Thailand. Many stories are told about the "good old days" before the ATM machines and multinational coffee shops, when somtam (Thai papaya salad) cost only 10 baht.

As more expats join the ranks of westerners choosing to live long term and also retiring in Thailand they join a long tradition of people who are enjoying the benefits of the best that Southeast Asia has to offer.

How Two Retirees Are Spending Their Lives In Thailand

Richard's Fun And Spiritual Life In Bangkok
Richard Rubacher is a retired American. He is 70 and single.

"I came to stay in Thailand in 2000. In this country I am surrounded by beauty that bubbles from the cityscape of Bangkok, the countryside, the villages, and from its people who perform senseless acts of beauty and random acts of kindness.

"For many of my expat friends from around the world, Thailand is a tonic for the soul.

"The spirit of fun pervades Thai people. An example is in the nicknames given to girls. I know a nurse named Shrimp. Hello Nurse Shrimp. A waitress friend is named Vegetable. There is Beer, Ice, Cocoa, Frog, Pumpkin (my first Thai girlfriend) and Shy (she was reluctant to make an appearance on earth).

"In the magical kingdom I became friends with the 'Forrest Gump of Thailand.' I practice the Thai Gump's far-out method of conflict resolution.

"I became friends with the 'Spiritual Banker of Thailand.' He shows you how to open a spiritual bank account and make regular deposits through meditation. Your life becomes enchanting because you are trained, through meditation, to see, feel, and experience life from the eyes of 'Beauty.' I learned how to mediate for the first time here in Thailand.

"I met a motorcycle taxi driver in the resort of Pattaya. During rides he gives you therapy and tells you about the mysteries of this mysterious land. Ask him what you to want to know about Thai culture. The taxi therapist knows.

"My friend Joker John and his Thai wife Suzy introduced me to a five-year-old Thai girl. No one in her family speaks English. Joker and Suzy had little Dana as a houseguest and spoke English to her. After three days she began speaking English. They showed her how to use a computer and introduced her to an English-language course. Now she's a wiz on the computer and she works the mouse with ease. She's on the Internet, searching for other five-year-old cyber-learners to practice English.

"I have Thailand fever. A serious case of it.

"For relaxation, I frequent my favorite places—massage parlors. I go to the 'naughty' massage parlors and the 'nice' ones. In either place, I experience the Thai Touch.

"Lucky me. I have a Thai girlfriend. She also has the Thai touch.

"I was in a state of denial about my eyesight. I kept buying stronger lenses to see. Finally, I went for an eye check-up. The diagnosis was cataracts in both eyes. Vision was 20/100 in each eye. I was told to have the cataracts removed at Rutnin Eye Hospital in Bangkok. Guess what? Post-surgery my vision in one eye is 20/25 and 20/30 in the other. When I go to California on my next visit, I will take the doctor's certificate to the Department of Motor Vehicles to have my driver's license changed. I can drive *without* glasses. In the States you do not get the same kind of *loving care* that Thailand provides.

"My apartment has one bedroom, a bathroom, kitchen, and three balconies. It's completely furnished, has an Olympic-sized swimming pool, a fitness center, and a private snooker club—all for $500 a month. That includes electricity, water, and two phone lines (one for the computer). When something needs fixing, I go to the office on the second floor. In five minutes a maintenance man knocks on my door. No charge for the repairs. I'm in the center of Bangkok, a ten-minute walk to the 'skytrain.' The price in San Francisco would be $3,000; in Sacramento $1,700; in New York City $4,500.

"Shopping for groceries in the supermarket is a fun experience. When you can't find a certain item, you just ask one of the helpers, found in every nook and cranny. Instead of telling you what aisle, she'll give you a personal escort to where the item hangs out—accompanied, of course, with the Thai smile.

"Come to this magical land and you too will be afflicted with Thailand fever. It's contagious."

Kanjana In Bangkok

Kanjana Srisongkram 39, married, with no children.

“I live part of the year in Los Angeles and part of the year in Bangkok. From November to February I go to Thailand to escape the cold and wet weather and enjoy the coolest time of year there. I also go there for business during the rainy season around July and August.

"I have a house with five bedrooms in a very good area of Bangkok that I bought for 6 million baht ($150,000) in 2004. It's about a half hour from either of the old and new Bangkok airports, and half an hour to the downtown Sukhumvit area. It's close to The Mall at Bangkapi and many other big stores.

"Every morning after I wake up, Nong, the housekeeper, has my Thai breakfast (at least four dishes) waiting on the dining table. My family pays her 7,000 baht ($175.00) a month and she comes in six days a week. She does everything that you would expect of a good housekeeper, including the cooking.

"Within a three-minute walk of the house, there are five restaurants and about a half dozen food stands. If I decide not to eat Nong's food, I can have a nice meal outside for about a dollar. And the food sellers are open all day and all night, which is quite common in the big cities.

"I became good friends with the girls in one of the three beauty parlors that are close to the food stalls. They give me great service because I always tip them $3 to $4 every visit. Other Thai people don't tip that much, or at all. What service do I get there? Manicure and pedicure for $4, hair wash and blow dry for $2, full body massage and spa for $12.00. I drop by at least twice a week.

"My dentist and dermatologist are also close by. It's very easy to make appointments to see them. Specialty clinics are found almost everywhere and you can drop by anytime. Five years ago, when I had fibroids in my uterus, I was in San Francisco and needed to have a laporoscopy and an ultrasound. I was told I had to wait to get an appointment with my gynecologist for three months. My pain was killing me, so I decided to fly to Thailand. I got a professor at Chulalongkorn University to treat me in less than a week.

"The quality of the medical professionals in Thailand is comparable to Western standards, but the cost of doctors' visits are unbelievably low. So I always have my check-ups and medical procedures done in Thailand. I still have my health insurance in the US for the time I live there just in case of an emergency.

"Having lived in big cities all my life, Bangkok is a perfect place for me. My husband (from California) and I are both salsa and tango dancers. We dance at Club La Rueda on Sukhumvit Soi 18 for salsa, and for tango we go to Club Fogo Vivo, a Brazilian restaurant at the Intercontinental Hotel. Each visit costs less than $5 per person. If you don't order drinks, you can have lots of fun very cheap.

"My husband loves to have a massage. He used to have his Swedish massage in Los Angeles. It was a good deal at $85.00. In Bangkok, he can have the same type of massage in a nice studio for $30.00. I prefer traditional Thai and foot massage, which is much cheaper. You'll pay about 200 to 250 baht ($5 to $6) for a two-hour traditional massage and 250 to 300 baht for a one-hour foot massage.

"Thais can see almost all of the new Hollywood movies the same week they premiere in the USA. Movie theaters and video stores are found all over Bangkok. You can see the same movies for one-third of the price you pay at home. I love going to movies in Thailand because I can watch Thai ghost movies besides the other foreign films.

"Actually, I do get tired of being in Bangkok sometimes (even with massage, spas, and dancing). The nice thing about Bangkok is that it's just a few hours' drive to a great beach. We can drive to the resort town of Hua Hin or the island of Koh Chang and spend a few days relaxing. We also take short trips to Laos or Burma.

"For the lifestyle that I describe above, my husband and I spend about $2,000 a month. The trips outside Thailand add to the cost because of airfares and other expenses. You can live much cheaper if you have a different lifestyle. If you can speak Thai or have Thai friends and family, you can get lots of incredible deals."

Are You Ready To Retire In Thailand?

Here are some factors that will 'pre-qualify' you and help you decide whether or not you are a retiree candidate for Thailand.

- You have to be open to new adventures. Thailand is an exotic place for Westerners. There will be many new things for you to experience. It's also a unique country in Asia, with its own distinct culture quite different from that of its neighbors.
- You should love to travel. There are countless things for you to see and do in Thailand.
- You have to be able to adapt to a new lifestyle and be tolerant of others. Your life and the people around you will be very different from what you are used to at home.
- You have to be enthusiastic about new things in a new and different culture. Thailand has its own ways and its own culture. You will have to learn to adjust. Many foreigners are shocked when they discover that things are done in a certain way in

21

Thailand. You have to be open-minded. You will need to look at things differently.

- You should be able to make and enjoy new friends. This is important for retirees. You will not see your family and friends back home for a while. You will need new companions so you won't feel bored or lonely.
- You ought to be willing to learn the basics of the Thai language. Learning the Thai alphabet really helps with pronunciation, and is not that difficult to memorize. Try to become fluent, or at least competent, in the types of phrases you'll need in your everyday life.
- You have to be healthy enough mentally and physically. Living abroad is hard for most people at first. You will need to be strong in both body and mind to make the most of your time.
- You have to accept your status of being a foreigner in Thailand. You won't be able to vote, and the Thais are not usually interested in listening to your point of view on the country's politics or economy. If you are a Caucasian, please get used to being called a *farang*. It's not usually meant as an insult. It's just ingrained in the way Thais refer to Westerners.
- You should appreciate a slower pace of life if you choose to retire in one of the smaller towns. Boredom is not something you often find in the Land of Smiles, but when you are away from the cities, you will find life moves more slowly. Make sure you are involved in enough leisure activities to avoid boredom.
- You have to be optimistic. Those who don't know Thailand may try to talk you out of moving there.

Do as much research as possible before you go. Don't let negative issues like prostitution, the insufferably hot weather, or dirt and disease turn you off. Thailand is rich in beauty and culture, and famous for its friendly people.

- You will have to deal with a different type of bureaucracy. It takes longer to get simple things done in Thailand. You will have to get used to its ways.

- You must be financially stable without needing to work. If you want to work part-time or 'semi-retire' in Thailand, make sure you are up to date on the continually changing (and seemingly arbitrary) laws regarding work permits or business ownership, and have a good fall-back plan for your future should you decide to return to your country.

Thai culture respects elders

PART 2
PLANNING YOUR
RETIREMENT IN
THAILAND

For many people, the decision about when and, to some degree, where to retire is largely a financial one. This chapter covers the information you need to know to help you plan for retirement and manage your money while following the various rules of your home country and Thailand. It specifically addresses US and UK citizens. Those of other nationalities may be subject to similar regulations, but they should check with the relevant tax and social security authorities in their own country for full details on what rules apply to them.

All costs are shown in local currency and US dollars. The assumed rate is 40 baht to one US dollar, and 68 baht to one UK pound sterling.

Information For US Citizens
And Permanent Residents

Social Security

As an American citizen or permanent resident, you are eligible to collect social security while living in Thailand. You can get social security retirement benefits as early as age 62, but if you retire before your full retirement age, your benefits will be permanently reduced, based on your age. If you retire at age 62, your benefit would be about 20 percent lower than if you waited until you reach full retirement age of 65 to 67, depending on date of birth.

When you reach retirement age, if you are living in Thailand, you can apply by phone (1-800-772-1213) or Internet (http://www.ssa.gov) or visit the US Embassy (American Citizens' Services) in Bangkok to apply. The government can deposit money into your US or Thai bank account.

Social security in America is a hot political issue. By 2017, the social security administration predicts there will not be enough people paying into the system to maintain the current level of payments, and by 2040 it may be exhausted.

I'm 35 years old. If nothing is done to improve social security, what can I expect to receive in retirement benefits from the program?

Unless changes are made, at age 69 in 2040 your scheduled benefits could be reduced by 26 percent and could continue to be reduced every year thereafter from presently scheduled levels.

I'm 26 years old. If nothing is done to change social security, what can I expect to receive in retirement benefits from the program?

Unless changes are made, when you reach age 60 in 2040, benefits for all retirees could be cut by 26 percent and could continue to be reduced every year thereafter. If you lived to be 100 years old in 2080 (which may be common by then), your scheduled benefits could be reduced by 30 percent from today's scheduled levels.

To estimate what your future social security benefit, visit the social security website at http://www.ssa.gov/planners/calculators.htm where you will find a social security calculator. In this calculator, you can enter your previous and expected future income and the calculator will estimate you social security payments, disability benefit, and survivor benefits at different retirement ages. You can also request a statement from the social security administration if you do not already have them mailed to you regularly.

The following tables shows a few examples using the simple calculator. All calculations are in 2006 dollars.

56 years old

Current Earnings	Stop Work At	Retire At 66	Retire At 70	Disability
40,000	Retirement age	$1,234	$1,697	$1,122
40,000	Now	$1,113	$1,469	$1,167
80,000	Retirement age	$1,853	$2,510	$1,748
80,000	Now	$1,739	$2,296	$1,790

Notice that for a 56-year-old, retiring now versus working for another six years makes relatively little difference.

46 years old

Current Earnings	Stop Work At	Retire At 62	Retire At 66	Retire At 70	Disability
40,000	Retirement age	$922	$1,361	$1,720	$1,186
40,000	Now	$671	$953	$1,182	$1,234
80,000	Retirement age	$1,354	$1,972	$2,476	$1,807
80,000	Now	$1,075	$1,527	$1,893	$1,853
120,000	Retirement age	$1,525	$2,193	$2,733	$2,106
120,000	Now	$1,259	$1,788	$2,217	$2,130

For a 46-year-old, retiring now reduces your potential full payment by about 40 percent. Notice also that for higher wage earners, the benefit levels off at about $100,000 per year.

The calculator will give you a choice of displaying your estimated benefit payment in current dollars or estimated inflation-adjusted dollars at retirement age. The latter will be a substantially higher number, but I advise against using that number for planning. Even though you may get that many dollars in so many years, remember that everything else you need to buy will have inflated at the same rate, so your real purchasing power will likely be based on the current dollar value, not the inflation adjusted value.

In the normal course of events, if you die, your spouse or children under 18 will receive survivor benefits. However, if your spouse is not a US citizen, he/she may not be eligible for this benefit. If he/she has lived in the US for at least five years, he/she may be eligible and other restrictions may apply.

28

If your spouse is not eligible for survivor benefits, your ex-spouse may be eligible to receive them if the spouse has not re-married.

If your income is above a certain level you have to pay tax on a portion of your social security benefit. Certain forms of exempt income such as IRA and 401K are included when you determine how much of your social security benefit is taxable. However, non-taxable distributions from a Roth IRA won't affect the tax on your social security benefits.

Medicare

Medicare is the US health insurance program for people aged 65 or older. Unfortunately Medicare is not available for people living abroad.

IRA/401K Tax Deferred Retirement Accounts

Most working people in America contribute to tax deferred retirement savings accounts such as 401Ks and IRAs. Contributions to these accounts are from 'before tax' money, so they reduce your tax liability during the year of contribution. Also, the account balance is generally higher than it would be if using 'after tax' money, so if the account appreciates in value, the dollar amount of appreciation will be higher. Distributions (i.e. withdrawals) are taxable as normal income, but since you are likely to be in a lower tax bracket at retirement age, there is a substantial tax benefit to saving in these accounts.

Ordinarily, you can start withdrawing money from your IRA and 401K accounts at age 59 and a half. If withdrawing prior to 59 and a half years of age, the IRS would normally charge a 10 percent penalty. There is however, a little-known IRS rule called "Substantially Equal Periodic Payments" (SEPP), also known as 72(t), which allows you to withdraw money from an IRA account at any age without penalty.

SEPPs are periodic withdrawals or distributions that you set up for five years or until you turn 59, whichever is later, and they must meet the IRS requirements to be exempted from the early withdrawal penalty. You should seek professional tax advice about this.

Age At Start Of SEPP Distribution	Retirement Account Balance	Annual Distribution*	Account Balance At Age 59*	Annual Distribution[1]
45	100,000	$5,519 (17,000 baht per month)	$79,392	$2,577
45	250,000	$13,798 (42,000 baht per month)	$198,479	$6,443
45	500,000	$27,597 (85,000 baht per month)	$396,959	$12,887
50	100,000	$5,806 (17,000 baht per month)	$84,299	$2,924
50	250,000	$14,515 (44,000 baht per month)	$210,747	$7,310
50	500,000	$29,030 (89,000 baht per month)	$421,495	$12,887
55	100,000	$6,201 (19,000 baht per moth)	$90,854	$3,378
55	250,000	$15,502 (47,000 baht per month)	$227,136	$8,446
55	500,000	$31,004 (95,000 baht per month)	$454,272	$16,892

*Using Amortization Method   1- Using Required Minimum Method
Based on a 4.53 percent interest rate and single life expectancy.

Substantially Equal Periodic Payments (SEPP)

The rules for 72(t) distributions require you to receive SEPPs based on your life expectancy to avoid a 10 percent tax penalty on any amounts you withdraw. Payments must last for five years or until you are 59 and a half, whichever is longer. Further, the SEPP amount must be calculated using one of the IRS approved methods that include:

- **Required Minimum Distribution Method:** This is the simplest method for calculating your SEPP, but it also produces the lowest payment. It simply takes your current balance and divides it by your single life expectancy or joint life expectancy. Your payment is then re-calculated each year with your account balance as of December 31 of the preceding year and your current life expectancy. This is the only method that allows for a payment that will change as your account value changes. Even though this may provide the lowest payment, it may be the best distribution method if you expect wide fluctuations in the value of your account.
- **Fixed Amortization Method:** With this method, the amount to be distributed annually is determined by amortizing your account balance over your single life expectancy, the uniform life expectancy table, or joint life expectancy with your oldest named beneficiary.
- **Fixed Annuitization Method:** This method uses an annuity factor to calculate your SEPP. This is one of the most complex methods. The IRS explains it as taking the taxpayer's account balance divided by an annuity factor equal to the present value of an annuity of $1 per month beginning at the

taxpayer's age attained in the first distribution year and continuing for the life of the taxpayer. For example, if the annuity factor for a $1 per year annuity for an individual who is 50 years old is 19.087 (assuming an interest rate of 3.8 percent), an individual with a $100,000 account balance would receive an annual distribution of $5,239 ($100,000 divided by 19.087 = $5,239). This calculator uses the Annuity 2003 Mortality Table, which is a non-sex-based mortality table and is acceptable for the IRS. Your annuitized SEPP is based on your life expectancy only, and is not based on the age of your beneficiary.

It is important to remember that while 72(t) distributions are not subject to the 10 percent penalty for early withdrawal, all applicable taxes on the distributions must still be paid. Further, taking any early distributions from a retirement account reduces the amount of money available later during your retirement.

Account Balance
The account balance used to determine the payment must be determined in a reasonable manner. For example, with a first distribution taken on July 15, 2003, it would be reasonable to determine the account balance based on the value of the IRA from December 31, 2002 to July 15, 2003. For subsequent years, the same valuation date should be used.

Reasonable Interest Rate
This is any rate less than 120 percent of the Federal Mid-Term rate for either of the two months immediately preceding the month in which the distribution begins. For January 2005, 120 percent of the Federal Mid-Term rate was 4.53 percent.

From the above examples, you can see some interesting facts. Clearly, account balance is the most important factor determining the distribution amount. Using the numbers from the amortization method, notice that the age you start withdrawing makes a relatively small difference. For example, if you have $250,000 in your retirement account and you start withdrawing at 45 years old, you would get $13,798 (42,000baht per month). At 55 years old you would get $15,502 (47,000 baht per month). The difference is only about 13 percent. Your account balance at age 59 would be $198,479 (45 years old) and $227,136 (55 years old) which again is 13 percent.

However, remember that with adjustment for inflation, the real purchasing power of this distribution is less over time. Remember that all of this information is with reference to SEPP (i.e. payments before age 59 and a half). After 59 and a half you are free to withdraw money whenever you like, without the 10 percent penalty, but you are still liable for tax.

Investing For Retirement

I am not a financial consultant, so I will not attempt to advise you how to invest your money, except to say that any reliable financial information will tell you to diversify your portfolio and that the older you get, the less risky investments you should take on.

I tend to watch my mutual funds daily, and as of this writing have had a good couple of years. However, I've noticed the happiness I feel when my portfolio goes up does not compensate for the fear and loss I feel when it all goes down. I would sleep better at night if I sold everything in favor of fixed-income investments, but for some inexplicable reason I haven't done it yet.

Since IRA and 401K accounts are owned by you, you can will them to anyone. If you plan to leave them to your Thai spouse or children, remember to let your financial institution know.

Some financial institutions will deposit money into your Thai bank account, but many will not. You should check with your institution, and if necessary, open a US bank account that does allow you to initiate wire transfers to Thailand via phone or the Internet. Withdrawals from your IRA and 401K accounts would then go through the intermediary bank account.

Taxes

The following should not be used as a substitute for professional tax advice. It is intended as general information and pointers to relevant resources. Please consult with a tax professional for tax planning and preparation.

There are several important and potentially beneficial tax implications for American citizens and permanent residents living abroad, the main one being that you may qualify to exclude from income up to $80,000 of your foreign earnings. The IRS website contains valuable information at: http://www.irs.gov.

Here are a few excerpts from the IRS site. I suggest you follow the above link and review the IRS information carefully. Make frequent reviews of tax laws as they will most certainly change in the future.

US Citizens And Resident Aliens Abroad—Filing Requirements

If you are a US citizen or resident alien living or traveling outside the United States, you are generally required to file income tax returns, estate tax returns, and gift tax returns and pay estimated tax in the same way as those residing in the United States. Your income, filing status, and age generally determine whether you must file a return.

Foreign-Earned Income Exclusion—
What Is Foreign Earned Income?

Foreign-earned income is income you receive for services you perform in a foreign country during a period your tax home is in a foreign country and during which you meet either the bona fide residence test or the physical presence test.

Tax Home

Your tax home is the general area of your main place of business, employment, or post of duty, regardless of where you maintain your family home. Your tax home is the place where you are permanently or indefinitely engaged to work as an employee or self-employed individual. Having a 'tax home' in a given location does not necessarily mean that the given location is your residence or domicile for tax purposes.

Bona Fide Residence Test

You meet the bona fide residence test if you are a bona fide resident of a foreign country (or countries) for an uninterrupted period that includes an entire tax year. You can use the bona fide residence test to qualify for the exclusions and the deduction only if you are either a US citizen or a US resident alien who is a citizen or national of a country with which the United States has an income tax treaty in effect.

You do not automatically acquire bona fide resident status merely by living in a foreign country or countries for one year.

Questions of bona fide residence are determined according to each individual case, taking into account such factors as your intention or the purpose of your trip, and the nature and length of your stay abroad. You must show the Internal Revenue Service (IRS) that you have been a bona fide resident of a foreign country or countries for an uninterrupted period that includes an entire tax year. The IRS decides whether you qualify as a bona fide resident of a foreign country largely on the basis of facts you report on Form 2555 (http://www. irs.gov/pub/irs-pdf/f2555ez.pdf). The IRS cannot make this determination until you file Form 2555.

Physical Presence Test

You meet the physical presence test if you are physically present in a foreign country (or countries) 330 full days during a period of 12 consecutive months. The 330 qualifying days do not have to be consecutive. You can count days you spent abroad for any reason. You do not have to be in a foreign country only for employment purposes. You can be on vacation time. The physical presence test applies to both US citizens and resident aliens.

The physical presence test is based only on how long you stay in a foreign country or countries. This test does not depend on the kind of residence you establish, your intentions about returning, or the nature and purpose of your stay abroad. However, your intentions with regard to the nature and purpose of your stay abroad are relevant in determining whether you meet the tax home test explained under "Tax Home In Foreign Country" in Publication 54. (http://www. irs.gov/publications/p54/index.html).

In my interpretation of these two tests, I believe the physical presence test is more appropriate for retired people so long as you spend at least 330 days per year outside the US. The rules for the bona fide residence test seem a little vague, to say the least. I believe it is targeted at people on a temporary assignment in a foreign country for more than one year who expect to return to the US.

Foreign-Earned Income Exclusion

If you meet certain requirements, you may qualify for the foreign-earned income and foreign housing exclusions and the foreign housing deduction.

If you are a US citizen or a resident alien of the United States and you live abroad, you are taxed on your worldwide income. However, you may qualify to exclude income up to $80,000 of your foreign earnings. In addition, you can exclude or deduct certain foreign housing amounts.

When Social Security And Medicare Taxes Apply Outside Of The US

In general, US social security and Medicare taxes continue to apply to wages for services you perform as an employee outside of the United States if one of the following applies:

- You are working for an American employer.
- You perform the services on or in connection with an American vessel.
- You are working for a foreign affiliate of an American employer under a voluntary agreement entered into between the American employer and the US Treasury Department.

If you work in or own a business outside the US and are younger than full retirement age, notify the nearest US embassy or consulate or social security office right away. If you do not, it could result in a loss of benefits.

Tax Planning

For tax planning and preparation, you may want to seek professional advice from a certified public accountant experienced in foreign tax matters. Such people can be found in Thailand, but their services are not cheap (usually $100-$300 per hour), so it pays to do your homework first. A low cost, or even free resource is the IRS website, and TurboTax™.

If you work or have sources of income anywhere in the world, you are required to report it on your US tax returns. If you use TurboTax, and you specify your address as a foreign country, it should prompt you to enter your foreign-earned income and residency status. If it does not, search for a Form 2555 ("Foreign-Earned Income") or Form 2555 EZ ("Foreign-Earned Income Exclusion") on the TurboTax site. I have found that by declaring my foreign-earned income, I can reduce my overall US taxes. This may not apply to everyone, but I recommend you try it and see what effect it has on your bottom line.

Note that currently you cannot file taxes electronically if living abroad, so plan to send your paper return before the April 15 deadline. Also, the IRS will not deposit refunds into a non-US bank account. If you ask for a refund check, be sure your bank will accept it. If not, the US embassy may cash it, but I recommend direct deposit to a US bank account.

Sometimes it is useful for planning purposes to estimate your tax liability in various different possible scenarios; say living and working in the US half the year and Thailand half the year, or living in Thailand full time and living off investments and saving. A great way to estimate your taxes for free is TurboTax.

I often create hypothetical tax returns using a fake name and social security number to see what my tax liability would be in different situations. TurboTax doesn't charge you anything until you print or file a return, which clearly you will not do for a fictitious one. I usually choose the *Ultimate*™ package from TurboTax.

Because of the low cost of living and excellent health services, retiring in Thailand on a modest retirement income can be far more attractive than staying in the US. Remember that

TurboTax will only give you information for the current tax year (previous year). If the tax laws change, the information could become invalid.

Foreign Bank Accounts
Any US citizen or permanent resident who has a financial interest in, or signature authority, or other authority over any financial account in a foreign country—if the aggregate value of these accounts exceeds $10,000 at any time during the calendar year—must file a "Report of Foreign Bank and Financial Account" (FBAR), form number TD F 90-22.1 with the IRS. The FBAR is due by June 30 of the year following the year that the account holder meets the $10,000 threshold. Failure to file an FBAR when required may potentially result in civil penalties, criminal penalties, or both. This form is intended to track criminal financial activity and does not affect your taxes.

Information For UK Citizens

State Pensions*
The State Pension is a pension scheme run by the State. It is split into two main parts: basic State Pension and additional State Pension

How Much Money Will The State Pension Give Me?
Everyone is likely to be entitled to different amounts depending on how many years they have paid, been treated as having paid, or been credited with, National Insurance (NI) contributions
You can get a forecast as to how much State Pension (which can be either your basic State Pension, your additional State

*provided by http://www.thepensionservice.gov.uk

Pension, or both) you might expect to receive (reflecting your position today and given in today's values). The older you are (up until you retire), the more accurate this estimate is likely to be.

Get A State Pension Forecast Online

A State Pension forecast tells you how much money you are likely to get when you claim a State Pension. It provides personalized information that can help you plan how much money you may need to save for retirement. You can also ask 'What if?' questions to see how changes in your circumstances, such as retiring later, could affect your financial situation. In most cases your forecast can be provided online while you wait at—
https://secure.thepensionservice.gov.
uk/statepensionforecast/

When Can I Get My State Pension?

The earliest you can get your State Pension is when you reach State Pension age. This age is currently different for men and women, although women's State Pension age will gradually increase between 2010 and 2020 to become the same as men's. At the moment, your State Pension age will be:

- Men: 65 years old.
- Women: 60 years old if you were born on, or before, 5 April 1950; 65 years old if you were born on, or after, 6 April 1955. (For women born on or after 6 April 1950 but on or before 5 April 1955, it is 60 years old plus one month for each month (or part month) that your birth date fell on or after 6 April 1950.)

Did You Know? There Is No State Retirement Age

Your State Pension age is a legally stated age at which you can start claiming your State Pension. People often assume that State Pension age is the age for retirement and leaving work.

You can carry on working and either draw your State Pension or put off claiming it to earn extra State Pension.

Your retirement is not bound by law, but is the time when you choose to leave work—this can be earlier, the same time as, or later than when you reach your State Pension age. It can also be earlier, the same time as, or later than when you reach your normal retirement age under a private pension scheme.

Will I Get My State Pension Automatically?

No. To receive the State Pension, you must claim it. You can make your claim upon approaching your State Pension age, or you can choose to claim it later and receive a higher State Pension or a one-off taxable lump sum.

UK State Pensions While Living In Thailand

Pension forecasts for overseas customers are dealt with by HM Revenue and Customs. Find out more on their website: http://www.hmrc.gov.uk/cnr/osc.htm

Queries about National Insurance contributions for overseas customers are dealt with by HM Revenue and Customs.

The Pension Service International Pension Center (IPC) deals with queries about United Kingdom benefits payable to overseas customers. You can contact the IPC on +44 191 218 7777 or fax +44 191 218 7293. Or you can write to the International Pension Center, Tyneview Park, Newcastle Upon Tyne, NE98 1BA, United Kingdom, or go to http://www. thepensionservice.gov.uk/contactus/contact-pod-form.asp.

Social Security Abroad — A UK Government Guide

The following contains relevant excerpts from http://www. hmrc.gov.uk/pdfs/nico/ni38.pdf.

National Insurance Contributions

National Insurance (NI) helps to pay for some social security benefits, including State Pensions. There are six classes of NI contributions. The class you pay in the UK depends on whether you are employed, self-employed, or pay voluntary NI contributions.

Class 1

You must pay these if you work for an employer and your earnings are at, or above, the Lower Earnings Limit. The amount you pay depends on what you earn (up to a maximum NI contribution an employee can pay). Your NI contribution is deducted from your wages. Your employer also has to pay NI contributions for all employees who earn at, or above a set limit.

Class 1A

These contributions are paid only by employers who provide employees with certain benefits in kind for private use—for example, cars and fuel.

Class 1B

These contributions are paid only by employers who enter into a Pay As You Earn (PAYE) Settlement Agreement with the Inland Revenue for tax.

Class 2

These contributions have to be paid in respect of each week in which you are self-employed. You pay the same amount however much you earn. In the UK, you can pay these NI contributions by quarterly bill, or by direct debit, which allows you to pay NI contributions every four or five weeks in arrears (depending on the number of Sundays in the tax month) directly from your UK or Channel Islands bank or building society account.

Class 3

These are voluntary contributions and can be paid if you want to protect your right to some social security benefits and you are not liable to pay Class 1 or Class 2 NI contributions. You pay them like Class 2 NI contributions, or as a lump sum at the end of the tax year.

Class 4

Class 4 NI contributions are for self-employed people whose net profits are over a certain amount. These are normally paid by self-employed people in addition to Class 2 NI contributions. They are collected with income tax, and do not count towards benefits.

How Much You Pay

The amounts charged normally change at the beginning of each tax year (6 April). Details are given in Leaflet GL23— "Social Security Benefit Rates." You can get this from your social security office or from the DWP website at: www.dwp. gov.uk/publications/dwp/2004/gl23_apr.pdf

NI Contribution Classes And UK Benefits

The class of NI contributions you pay affects the benefits you can get.

Other benefits are non-contributory. This means that you do not have to pay any NI contributions to get them—but you must meet the rules that apply to them.

From April 2000, benefits for widows and widowers are dependent on your late spouse's Class 1, 2, or 3 NI contributions.

Basic State Pension can also be based partly or wholly on the husband's NI record if this increases the value of your entitlement. From April 2010, basic State Pension can be based on the NI record of either partner, whichever reaches State Pension age first.

If you are divorced and have not married again, you may be able to claim benefits based on your former spouse's NI contributions.

See the following table detailing the various benefits according to the class of NI contributions that apply to your specific situation

Benefit	Class 1	Class 2	Class 3
Contributions-Based Jobseeker's Allowance	Yes	No	No
Incapacity Benefit	Yes	Yes	Yes
Bereavement Benefits	Yes	Yes	Yes
Basic State Pension	Yes	Yes	Yes
Additional State Pension	Yes	Yes	No

If You Are Employed Abroad

When must you pay Class 1 NI contributions? When you are employed abroad, Class 1 NI contributions must be paid

44

for the first 52 weeks you are there, if you meet the following conditions:

- Your employer has a place of business in the UK, and
- You are 'ordinarily resident' in the UK, and
- Immediately before starting the employment abroad you were resident in the UK.

Ordinarily Resident
You are ordinarily resident in a particular country if you:
- Normally live there, apart from temporary or occasional absences, and
- Have a settled and regular mode of life there.

You may be ordinarily resident in:
- A place from which you are temporarily absent, or
- Two places at once, in some circumstances.

When you go abroad, there are a number of factors which are considered in deciding whether or not you are ordinarily resident in the UK. The Inland Revenue's Center for Non-Residents (Newcastle) will consider the circumstances of individual cases if you have any doubts about whether you are ordinarily resident or not. Contact them, giving as much information as possible.

Paying NI Contributions While You Are Abroad

Class 1 NI Contributions
Class 1 NI contributions are payable by you and your employer just as if you were employed in the UK. The rates are the same and your employer will deduct your contribution

from your salary and pay it to the Inland Revenue on your behalf.

If you are in any doubt about the status of your employer or require information on how to pay your share of Class 1 NI contributions, write to the Inland Revenue Center for Non-Residents at Newcastle.

Class 2 NI Contributions

After the first 52 weeks, you may wish to pay either Class 2 or Class 3 NI contributions on a voluntary basis to protect your entitlement to State Pension and bereavement benefits. Although these benefits are payable anywhere abroad, they are not normally increased when pension rates go up in the UK.

From 6 April 2000, Class 2 NI contributions are less expensive than Class 3 NI contributions. You can pay them if you are employed or self-employed abroad and if you satisfy the following conditions:

- You have lived in the UK for a continuous three-year period at any time before the period for which NI contributions are to be paid, or
- Before going abroad you paid a set amount in NI contributions for three years or more (this will be checked when you ask to pay Class 2 NI contributions), and
- You were an employed or self-employed earner immediately before you went abroad, or
- You would normally be employed or self-employed, but were unemployed immediately before you went abroad.

If you want to pay Class 2 NI contributions while you are abroad, fill in and return application form CF83. If you are liable for Class 1 NI contributions, do not apply to pay

Class 2 NI contributions until your UK liability has ended. Voluntary payment of Class 2 NI contributions does not give cover for healthcare abroad in any circumstances.

Class 3 NI Contributions

You can pay voluntary Class 3 NI contributions to protect your right to State Pension and, if you are married, your spouse's right to bereavement benefits. Although these benefits are payable anywhere abroad, they are not normally increased when pension rates go up in the UK. In addition, these contributions do not count towards Incapacity Benefit.

You can pay Class 3 NI contributions whether you are working abroad or not, but not for the period you are liable to pay Class 1 NI contributions. You can pay Class 3 NI contributions abroad:

- If you have paid Class 1 NI contributions for the first 52 weeks of your employment abroad, or
- You satisfy either of the following conditions:
- You have lived in the UK for a continuous three-year period at any time before the period for which NI contributions are to be paid.
- Before you went abroad, you paid a set amount in NI contributions for three years or more (this will be checked when you ask to pay Class 3 NI contributions).

If you want to pay Class 3 NI contributions while you are abroad, fill in and return the application form CF83. If you are liable for Class 1 NI contributions, do not apply to pay voluntary Class 3 NI contributions until your UK liability has ended. Voluntary payment of Class 3 NI contributions does not give cover for healthcare abroad in any circumstances.

Deciding Whether To Pay Voluntary NI Contributions

You can generally choose to pay Class 2 or Class 3 NI contributions while abroad if you wish to protect your entitlement to some social security benefits. There are some points to bear in mind when deciding what NI contributions you wish to pay.

It is important to note that Class 2 or Class 3 NI contributions should be paid by the due date, that is within 42 days of the end of the tax year they cover. Late payments may affect your right to benefits. There are also time limits for payment and financial penalties for late payment.

How Much Do You Pay?

The UK NI contribution rates are the same abroad as in the UK. Leaflet GL23—"Social Security Benefit Rates" tells you the latest rates.

How To Pay Voluntary NI Contributions Abroad

You can choose to pay Class 2 or Class 3 NI contributions by direct debit, annual payment (this allows you to pay NI contributions for a complete tax year, once a year, in arrears, direct to the Inland Revenue National Insurance Contributions Office) or via an agent (you can get someone in the UK to pay your NI contributions for you).

Check with the Inland Revenue's Center for Non-Residents (Newcastle) before paying your NI contributions.

Other Ways Of Covering Your NI Record

There are two other ways in which your NI record can be maintained: Credits and Home Responsibilities Protection.

Whilst in the UK, you may be able to get credits instead of having to pay NI contributions. If your opportunity to work is limited because you are looking after a child or a sick or disabled person, Home Responsibilities Protection

48

can make it easier to get a basic Retirement Pension. See Form CF411—"How To Protect Your State Pension If You Are Looking After Someone At Home." Home Responsibilities Protection will apply to you abroad if you meet the same rules as for people in the UK.

Additional Information

If you marry while you are abroad and you have been paying any class of NI contribution, write to the Inland Revenue's Center for Non-Residents (Newcastle). Give the date you married and your own NI number and that of your spouse.

For further information on all State Pension issues, see leaflet NP46—"A Guide To State Pensions" or write to the center at Newcastle.

Pensions

If you move abroad to work before you reach State Pension age, you may not build up entitlement to a State Pension (the basic State Pension and any additional State Pension) for those years. However, this depends on your particular circumstances (for example, whether it is a UK company you work for, or a foreign one).

If you go to live abroad permanently, you will not get a yearly increase in your State Pension (including your additional State Pension) unless you live in a country the UK has an agreement with that allows for these increases (known as 'upratings'). For information on which countries these are, and how UK State Pensions are paid to people abroad, see leaflet GL29—"Going Abroad And Social Security Benefits" or the website: www.dwp.gov.uk/resourcecentre/social_fund. asp. Their general website: www.thepensionservice.gov.uk.

Retirement Pension Forecast

You can ask for a forecast of what pension you can expect to get when you reach State Pension age. The pension forecast will tell you what your pension is currently, and whether or not it can be improved.

You will not need a pension forecast if you are within four months of State Pension age.

If you are abroad, or are planning to go abroad in the near future, and not within four months of State Pension age, you should write to the Inland Revenue's Center for Non-Residents (Newcastle). They will send you form CA3638 to fill in and return. Or you can download this from www. inlandrevenue.gov.uk/cnr/osc.htm#6.

Cover For Healthcare

You cannot get back from the UK National Health Service money you have paid for medical treatment abroad. The UK has healthcare arrangements with some countries, but not Thailand.

You are strongly advised to take out private travel insurance. Healthcare abroad can be very expensive if you are not insured. The expense of bringing someone back to the UK in cases of illness or death is never covered. Make sure you have adequate insurance wherever you are going. Ask your travel agent, insurance company, or broker.

UK Tax Consideration Of Living In Thailand

The following is referenced from HM Revenue and Customs Service, Center for Non-Residents at Newcastle; http://www.hmrc.gov.uk/cnr/index.htm

General Non-Resident Tax FAQ

In what circumstances would I become non-UK resident if I left the UK?

50

Normally if you leave the UK permanently or for three years or more or to work abroad full-time, you will become not resident and not ordinarily resident in the UK if your absence from the UK covers a complete tax year (i.e. 6 April to 5 April), and you spend less than 183 days in the UK during the tax year, and your visits to the UK do not average 91 days or more per tax year over a maximum of four years. (For visits to the UK, days of arrival and departure are not normally counted as days spent in the UK.)

What do I need to do, as I am going to live or work abroad?

Inform your Tax Office and ask for a Form P85 and Leaflet IR138.

When I go to live or work abroad, will I continue to pay UK tax?

If you remain resident in the UK for UK tax purposes, normally you will be taxable on your income arising in the UK and overseas. If you become non-resident, you will normally only be taxable on your income arising in the UK.

Can I choose to pay tax in the UK on UK source income rather than in my country of residence?

No. If a double taxation treaty is involved, the country in which you pay tax will be determined as a matter of fact and not choice.

Will I have to pay tax in the country to which I go to live or work?

The country to which you go to live or work may tax you on your worldwide income. This will depend on its own laws. You may need to ask the tax authority there for advice.

Why am I paying tax in the UK on my income when I am no longer resident there?

Income arising in the UK will remain liable to UK income tax. However, depending on your nationality and where you live, you may be eligible to make a claim for repayment of UK income tax.

What happens if I decide to let my UK home or property whilst I am living or working abroad?

You will be taxable on any profit you make in letting your property. Normally the rent should be paid to you after deduction of UK income tax at the basic rate, but you may apply for the rent to be paid to you without deduction of tax. Ask your tax office for Form NRL1. If gross payment of rent is approved, you will still be liable to tax on your net profit. A "Self Assessment" tax return will be issued to you to enable you to account for the tax due.

When I go to live abroad, I will begin to receive a pension from my former employer. How will this be treated for UK tax purposes?

Normally the pension will be taxable in the UK. It may also be liable to tax in the country in which you live. If so, you may be able to get relief under the terms of any double taxation treaty between the UK and the country in which you live.

I have a bank/building society account in the UK. Will tax still be deducted from interest if I am non-resident in the UK?

Not if you are not ordinarily resident in the UK and the bank or building society at which you have the account operates accounts paying interest without deduction of tax to individuals not ordinarily resident in the UK. You would need to download Form R105, or ask your bank or building society for a copy, to apply for gross payment of interest. This does not mean that the interest is no longer chargeable to UK tax, although where you are treated as not resident for the whole tax year—and provided that the account is not held in connection with a trade, profession, or vocation carried out through a branch or agency in the UK—the liability to tax on interest from a UK bank or building society is limited to the tax deducted at source, if any. There is further information in Leaflet IR138—"Living Or Retiring Abroad" and also in "Self-Assessment" helpsheet IR300—"Non-Residents And Investment Income (PDF). If tax has been deducted from the interest, you may be eligible to claim a refund, whole or partial, under any double taxation treaty between the UK and your country of residence, or a refund up to the level of your personal allowances, if you are entitled to claim these. Is it necessary for me to claim exemption for my UK National Insurance Retirement Pension, as this is not taxed?

No tax is taken from your National Insurance Retirement Pension, but it still remains liable to UK income tax and is therefore included in any tax liability calculation. Claiming exemption under a double taxation treaty frees up the allowances the National Insurance Retirement Pension is using, so that the allowances can be set against other liable income.

In what circumstances will I be treated as a UK resident for UK tax purposes?
Broadly, you will be treated as resident for a tax year if:
- You are in the UK for 183 days or more in the tax year, or
- You visit the UK regularly and your visits average 91 days or more a tax year over a period not exceeding four years, or

- You come to the UK for a purpose that will mean you are in the UK for at least two years.

However, this is a complex subject and your residence position depends on your own personal circumstances. If you require more details, you should contact the Center for Non-Residents at Newcastle.

Non-Resident Landlords

The Non-Resident Landlords Scheme is a scheme for taxing the UK rental income of non-resident landlords.

The scheme requires UK letting agents to deduct Basic Rate tax from any rent they collect for non-resident landlords. If non-resident landlords don't have UK letting agents acting for them, and the rent is more than 100 pounds sterling a week, their tenants must deduct the tax. When working out the amount to tax, the letting agent/tenant can take off deductible expenses.

Letting agents and/or tenants don't have to deduct tax if HM Revenue and Customs (HMRC) tells them not to. HMRC will tell an agent/tenant not to deduct tax if non-resident landlords have successfully applied for approval to receive rents with no tax deducted. But even though the rent may be paid with no tax deducted, it remains liable to UK tax. So non-resident landlords must include it in any tax return HMRC sends them.

Non-resident landlords can apply to receive their rent with no tax deducted on the basis that either:

- Their UK tax affairs are up to date, or
- They have not had any UK tax obligations before they applied, or
- They do not expect to be liable to UK income tax for the year in which they apply, or

- They are not liable to pay UK tax because they are Sovereign Immunes (these are generally foreign Heads of State, governments, or government departments).

Capital Gains For UK Taxpayers

I am not resident in the UK. Am I liable to capital gains tax?

(i) If you are not resident in the UK but are ordinarily resident there, you are liable to capital gains tax for each year that you are ordinarily resident.

(ii) If you are not resident/not ordinarily resident in the UK, then you may or may not be liable to capital gains tax, depending on the date that you left the UK, the period of time you were resident in the UK before your departure, and the length of time you expect to live abroad.

I carry on a trade through a branch or agency in the UK, but I am not resident/not ordinarily resident. Am I liable to capital gains tax when I dispose of assets held for the purpose of this trade?

Yes, you are liable to capital gains tax on these disposals.

I became not resident/not ordinarily resident in the UK before 17 March 1998. Am I liable to capital gains tax on the disposal of assets?

You are not liable to capital gains tax on any disposal of assets you make during the tax years for which you are wholly not resident and not ordinarily resident, providing they are not assets held for the purpose of a trade, profession, or vocation carried on through a branch or agency in the UK. If you return to the UK, you will be liable on gains from any disposals during the tax year of return. However, see the answer below concerning possible concessional treatment.

I understand that non-residents are now treated differently for capital gains. When did this happen and what are the changes?

The changes are effective from 17 March 1998. Before that date, if you were not resident and not ordinarily resident in the UK, you were not liable to capital gains tax on disposals of assets that were not held for the purpose of carrying on a trade, profession, or vocation through a UK branch or agency. If you left the UK on or after 17 March 1998, you fall within the new rules for capital gains.

How long do I need to be abroad to avoid being liable to capital gains tax?

This depends on when you left the UK:

(i) If you left the UK on or before 16 March 1998, see the answer above.

(ii) If you left the UK on or after 17 March 1998, you would need to be not resident and not ordinarily resident in the UK for at least five full tax years between the year you left the UK and the year of your return.

I am leaving the UK. Will I be liable to capital gains tax if I sell my home before or after I leave the UK?

In most cases you will not pay tax on any gain you make when you dispose of your only residence. You may be liable to capital gains tax if you leave your home or have a second property. You will find more information on this topic in our help sheet IR283—"Private Residence Relief." This can be obtained from the telephone order line on 0845 9000 404; or if outside the UK, +44 870 1555 664.

I live abroad and let my property in the UK. I am thinking of selling this property. Will I be liable to capital gains if I sell this before I come back to the UK?

If you are liable to capital gains tax, then this will include the gains you make on disposal of your let property. If your let property was at some time your home, please refer to helpsheet IR283—"Private Residence Relief."

I am leaving the UK shortly. Am I liable to capital gains tax in the year I leave the UK?

Yes, but if you cease to be resident or ordinarily resident in the UK, you may, by concession (extra statutory concession D2), not be liable to capital gains tax on gains arising to you from disposals made after the date of your departure. However, you can only qualify for this concession if you were neither resident nor ordinarily resident in the UK for the whole of at least four of the seven tax years immediately preceding the tax year in which you leave the UK.

Money Matters

Opening a bank account in Thailand is usually a simple affair. Typically all you need is a passport, although same banks may ask for a letter from your embassy verifying you are the person on the passport, or a work permit. If you have trouble at one branch, try another; they all seem to operate on different rules.

Any personal account (i.e. not a business account) will include an ATM card. You can typically set the daily limit on your ATM withdrawals to any amount you want.

A Thai bank account is necessary if you plan to get a marriage or retirement visa. The requirements for this visa are that you have a balance of at least 400,000 and 800,000 baht respectively when applying for the visa extension. This is a significant amount of money and it would be nice to get interest on it.

Thai banks offer almost no interest on savings accounts— about half a percent, which is well below inflation.

Tax On Foreign (Outside Thailand) Income While Living In Thailand

You are not required to declare or pay tax on foreign income, including social security and pension distributions in Thailand if you are not a Thai citizen or permanent resident.

Foreign Exchange

Since most of us will likely have the majority of our income and savings in our home-country currency, we are very susceptible to foreign exchange rate fluctuations. Over the last five years, the dollar has steadily fallen against the baht, while the pound has held fairly steady. Unfortunately, there is no way to predict the future for exchange rates. The only sure way to lock in your savings to the current baht rate is convert your money to baht, which few people would advise.

Preparing For Your Move To Thailand

Once you have moved to Thailand, you may find it too expensive or inconvenient to return to your home country frequently. Check how you will withdraw money from retirement and bank accounts when living abroad, and set up everything in advance.

If you are required to sign documents and have your signature notarized, you can usually get this done at your embassy in Bangkok, for a fee and a long wait in line.

If you are planning to do online wire transfers (see below), I recommend you do at least one transfer while inyour home country just to check everything is working.

I suggest you visit or call all your financial institutions, explain that you are moving to Thailand, and ask them how you will access your accounts and withdraw money while away. I find that occasionally, the person I talk to doesn't always know the whole story, so I call a couple of times to check I get the same information.

Wire Transfer

Wire transfer is the preferred way to transfer money to Thailand. Wire transfers usually get the best exchange rate, are very secure, and provide proof of transaction—which is required for some visa and other services.

In the electronic age, just about all banks support some level of online banking, but this does not automatically mean you can initiate wire transfers to your Thai bank account via the Internet. Some banks, such as Citibank in the US, do allow wire transfers to Thailand via the Internet, but many do not. Banks with a strong international presence such as Citibank and HBSC have branches in Bangkok.

If you are concerned about Internet security, as you should be, ask your bank if they have a secure ID system. Through my bank in the US, I have a secure ID card, an electronic gizmo that changes the pass code every few seconds. When I log into my account, I enter the code from the secure ID device and the bank verifies it, so it is impossible to break into the account without that device. This is particularly important if you use Internet cafés to log into your accounts, since you can never know if the Internet café is logging activity on their computers.

Wire transfers typically take up to five days to go through, so plan ahead if you have a big expense coming up.

In an attempt to control the rising Baht exchange rate and discourage speculation in the Thai currency, in 2006 the Bank of Thailand announced it intended to withhold 30%

of income foreign currency transfers for one year unless the receiver of the transfer could prove the money was for a long term investment in Thailand. However, to my knowledge this rule was never implemented and I have never heard of anyone actually having any money withheld from a transfer.

ATMs

ATM withdrawals are convenient and the exchange rate may be competitive with wire transfer, but many banks charge steep fees for using someone else's ATM machine. Smaller local banks are less likely to charge high ATM fees because they don't have many ATMs in their home country, so no one would use their services if the fees were high.

Many banks block ATM withdrawals in certain countries they consider high fraud risk. Close to the top of this list is Thailand, so don't always expect your ATM card to work at a machine. As a general rule, you should always have a minimum of two ways to get access to your money. If you are having trouble at an ATM machine, you may still be able to withdraw from the card at the bank teller, so long as you have your passport.

Beware of ATM fraud. Check your ATM card is safe often. Check your account often for fraudulent activity. Don't let people see you entering your PIN into ATM machines.

Some machines eat cards. For this reason I always prefer to use a machine at a bank, not one outside a 7-Eleven or at a station or other random location. Also, occasionally the machine may not give up the money even though it deducted the amount from your account. This happened to me once. Fortunately, it was at a bank's machine, so I told the bank about my problem, they investigated, and the charge on my account was reversed. If it had been a machine at a convenience store or mall, who knows?

Banking is easy in Thailand

ATM machines in Thailand are used for a multitude of banking transactions including paying bills and sending money to individuals and businesses. If you live in a remote location, you may find it convenient to shop on the Internet or by phone for things you cannot buy locally. Almost no Thai business will accept credit-card purchases over the phone, but most will take bank transfer, which can be done from an ATM machine if you have a Thai bank account.

Credit Cards
Most big tourist hotels and many high-end shops and restaurants will accept credit cards, but outside of Bangkok and a few popular tourist areas, cash and bank transfer is the only way to buy most things.

Credit-card withdrawals can be made at a bank. You will need to show your passport. Most credit-card companies will charge up to 2.5 percent for a cash advance.

Be sure when mailing a replacement for a foreign credit or ATM card it is sent registered post or traceable courier.

PayPal™

If you are involved in online shopping and transactions, you may have a PayPal account. Beware, PayPal does not like Thailand and frequently freezes the accounts of people if they log in from a Thai IP address. Frozen accounts usually cannot be unfrozen without returning to the US.

PayPal is not governed by the same laws that govern banks, and they can do just about anything they want with your money. See http://paypalsucks.com for some entertaining horror stories.

PayPal ATM card only charges a $1 fee at any ATM worldwide, but beware of frozen accounts. PayPal will not let you withdraw money from a Thai bank account.

Cash And Travelers' Checks

Needless to say, travelers' checks are safer than cash, and they often get better exchange rates than cash. If exchanging cash, $100 bills get a better rate than smaller denominations. I have no idea why.

Checks

Your Thai bank should accept checks from abroad. The key word here is 'should.' In my experience, I've just got a blank stare. Your embassy may cash government checks.

How Much Money Do I Need
To Retire In Thailand?

Many visitors to Thailand, at almost any age, dream of throwing in their lot back home; saying goodbye to the mortgage, bills, taxes, winters, and the ex; and moving to paradise. Some people just do it and hope for the best, but most of us like to plan when we can afford it.

There are some obvious and less obvious things to consider when calculating how much money you need to retire.

Clearly your age and life expectancy are the main factors, since that determines how many years you have to support yourself. Assuming you plan to leave your spouse and children with something when you die, you will also have to consider their needs, too.

Your general health and family history is a big factor, since it will determine how much you will need to budget for healthcare.

Your lifestyle is critical to how much you need to retire. I know people who can live in Thailand on less than 20,000 baht per month, but the average is 60,000-80,000 and could be much higher if you like to travel or spend a lot of money on 'entertainment.'

Lifestyle is one the few retirement factors you can control directly. Many people in Western societies are caught in a never-ending circle of spending and debt. Society and desire encourage us to buy a bigger house, a faster car, another trip to Thailand! We pay with credit cards and loans and feel satisfied until we realize we have to work another 20 years to pay for everything.

Living in Thailand offers the opportunity to change your lifestyle for something simpler, more sustainable, and, in my opinion, more rewarding. Material possessions are usually not so important since, outside of Bangkok at least, most people don't have many. In Thai society, personal relationships with family and friends are often more important than material things.

Many people, when moving to Thailand, find they can be happy with a modest place to live, a small motorcycle, and not much else. Travel within Thailand and around Southeast Asia is cheap and fun; eating out is hardly more expensive than cooking at home; outdoor activities are available all year round and mostly free. Think about your lifestyle choices and if you can be happy with less.

And then there is the girlfriend factor. One of the most popular reasons old white guys like myself gravitate to Thailand is the availability of beautiful, young Thai ladies. They may be great for your happiness and libido, but usually come with a price tag—and the size of the price tag is generally proportional to the 'beautiful' and 'young' part.

In the highly recommended book, *Thailand Fever*, my friend Chris Pirazzi describes the intricacies of Western-Thai relationships, which can be summarized succinctly by the T-shirt slogan, "No Money, No Honey." In Thailand, you will quickly find it takes a whole village to raise a child, and if that child is a pretty girl, it usually takes a foreign guy to pay for it—including livestock. Not that I am saying don't date pretty younger women; I married one and it's the best thing I ever did. Just be aware what you are getting yourself into and take your time before you commit.

Where possible, I recommend having some kind of ongoing income besides savings. Besides the obvious benefit of having more money coming in, some kind of work often helps people lead a more fulfilling and satisfying life—and makes them more aware of how much money they are spending. In my experience, foreigners in Thailand that do not work, often fall into self-destructive lifestyles involving drinking, sex, and drugs. However, please remember that working without

64

a work permit or working on a retirement visa is strictly prohibited and can result in expulsion from Thailand or even jail.

Back to the question of how much does it take to retire in Thailand? An informal poll was taken in the Thaivisa.com forum asking how much money people think you would need to retire at 50. Of the 86 people that responded, 38 percent said over 40 million baht, about 1 million dollars! Another 43 percent said between 10 and 30 million (more reasonable if you are prudent and lack serious health issues).

There are several retirement calculators available online, most of which assume you are living in the US or Europe. However, they should provide a useful starting point.

All of these retirement calculators require some pretty big assumptions. You need to guess how long you will live. How much you need to spend on capital purchases such as a house or car, and how much you need to spend every month on living expenses.

How much you need to spend on healthcare is difficult to estimate, as is budgeting for emergencies. You will also need to estimate the return on your investments. Try to be realistic or even a bit conservative when making your assumptions, or you could find yourself penniless in your old age—and Thailand has no social security net except the family.

If you are relying heavily on investments for your retirement, I suggest you put some of that money in a low-risk investment such as interest-bearing accounts, certificates of deposits, or government bonds. Then do retirement calculation based on a worst-case scenario where your higher risk investments lose greater than 50 percent and you get seriously ill. Together with a more optimistic (but realistic) calculation, this should give you an upper and lower boundary on how much money you need and what kind of lifestyle you can afford.

Estimating The Cost Of Retirement In Thailand

As discussed, the cost of living in Thailand varies greatly depending on your lifestyle, health status, and possibly other expenses like debts back home, alimony, and child support.

This example is for a 45-year-old man with a wife (low maintenance) and two children. He owns the land and house he lives in, two motorcycles (which are paid for in cash), and likes to live well and enjoy the things he moved to Thailand for but not extravagantly.

Item	Average Cost Per Month
Food and drink (at home)	20,000
Meals and entertainment (eating out)	10,000
Utilities (electricity, water, gas)	2,000
Internet/phone	3,000
Transportation (local, motorcycle)	1,000
Household expenses[1]	5,000
Miscellaneous (clothing, laundry, etc)	5,000
Visas and visa trips	5,000
Medical[2]	5,000
Travel/fun	10,000
TOTAL	66,000

1- Including maintenance. Housing costs can vary quite dramatically, even after the house is built. Repairs and new furniture could make that estimate unrealistic. If you do not own your own house, you can assume 10,000-20,000 baht per month for rent in most parts of the country.
2- Expect the healthcare cost to increase significantly as you and your spouse have children and get older.

In reality, I probably spend about 80,000 baht a month to live in Thailand, but I think that will go down a little when my house is truly finished, but go up in 10 to 20 years as health becomes more of an issue.

This next example is a 40-year-old male, single and living very simply in a village in northern Thailand. He spent almost nothing to move to Thailand, lives in a rented house, drives a rented motorcycle, does not drink or smoke, and, to the best of my knowledge, does not have a girlfriend.

Item	Average Cost Per Month
Rent	2,500
Maid, laundry	600
Utilities (electricity, water, gas)	600
Internet/phone	1,000
Transportation (local, motorcycle rent)	2,900
Food and drink (home and restaurant)	2,500
Visas and visa trips	1,000
TOTAL	11,100

The following examples are provided by http://www.banksite.com/calc/retire. These estimates do not include social security benefits, so you may be able to subtract your estimated social security benefit from your estimated cost of living.

Required Monthly Income At Retirement (Current Baht, Dollars)	Years To Retirement	Life Expectancy After Retirement	Amount Needed At Start Of Retirement
40,000 baht, $1,000	0	25	$229,000
40,000 baht, $1,000	15	25	$447,000
40,000 baht, $1,000	0	40	$314,000

40,000 baht, $1,000	15	40	$654,000
80,000 baht, $2,000	0	25	$458,000
80,000 baht, $2,000	15	25	$954,000
80,000 baht, $2,000	0	40	$629,000
80,000 baht, $2,000	15	40	$1,308,000

For the above calculations, annual yield on investments is assumed to be 7.5 percent. Historically equities (stocks and stock funds) get about 10 percent annual yield, but for someone planning to retire with no additional source of income it may be risky to put all your investments in equities, so I have assumed a 50/50 split between equities and fixed income at 5 percent. Annual inflation is assumed at 5 percent, since in the US we seem to heading that way. See http://inflationdata.com/Inflation/Inflation_Rate/DecadeInflation.asp for historical data.

Maintaining Financial Ties To Your Home Country

Even if you live permanently outside your home country, it is likely you will have an ongoing need to continue some financial links there for emergencies, family ties, visits, and other reasons.

Bank accounts, credit cards, and drivers license from your home country will usually require you have a real address (not a PO Box) in the same country. If you do not have an address there, ask a family member or close friend if you can use their address to forward important mail to.

Maintaining a credit card or two is very useful for emergencies, since most International hospitals will take major credit cards.

Visas, Work Permits, Permanent Residence, Taxes And Living In Thailand

To live in Thailand long term, unless you plan to use the 30-day visa on arrival, you will need one of the following visas:

- Transit visa.
- Tourist visa.

68

- Non-immigrant visa (includes business, marriage, and retirement).
- Diplomatic visa.
- Official visa.
- Courtesy visa.

Of these, the tourist and non-immigrant visas are appropriate to most people.

Thai visas are confusing. I lived in Thailand for three years on various types of visa and it wasn't until researching this book that I fully understood all the full implications, so pay close attention to the following and I will attempt to explain.

PLEASE NOTE, Thai visa rules seem to change every few months and each immigration office, consulate and embassy has their own set of rules and interpretations which can change hourly! The following information is intended as a general guide and is accurate at the time of writing only. Please check with Thai immigration or the thaivisa.com forum for up to date information about Thai visas.

Visa rules as of June 2006 are described in the following document:

http://www.lawyer.th.com/National_Police_Office_Order_Oct_2006.pdf

Tourist Visa

A tourist visa is valid for up to 90 days (per entry) and costs 1,000 baht ($25) per entry and must be applied for at a Thai consulate outside Thailand. Application is simple and is not dependent on financial status or age.

Upon arrival in Thailand, Immigration will stamp your passport allowing you to stay for 60 days. The stamp is referred to as the "extension of stay." The extension of stay can be extended at any Immigration office inside Thailand for an additional 30 days for 1,900 baht.

You must leave Thailand when your extension of stay expires; the fines for overstaying have been recently been increased from to 500 baht per day in violation and can result in *persona non gratis* status.

When applying for a tourist visa, you can apply for up to four entries, although some Thai consulates, especially in Asia, may issue less than four. Penang, in Malaysia, usually allows only three. An unused entry on your visa entry allows you to come back into Thailand at any border Immigration checkpoint and get another 60-day stamp without the necessity of re-applying for a new visa.

Non-Immigrant Visa

Non-immigrant visas are intended for people planning to stay a long time in Thailand, either for work ('B' visa) family ties ('O' visa) or retirement ('O-A' visa). Non-immigrant visas are either single-entry or multiple entries.

Single-Entry Visa

A single-entry visa is valid for three months from the date of issue and allows a stay for a single period of up to 90 days, after which you must depart, although it may be extended at local Immigration for a further 30 days for 1,900 baht. A further visit will require a new visa, which can only be obtained outside Thailand. The cost of a single-entry visa is $50.

Multiple-Entry Visa

A multiple-entry visa is valid for 12 months from the date of issue and allows you to enter Thailand on as many occasions as required for stays of up to 90 days each (unless extended into an O-A visa) within the validity of the visa.

70

When the 90-day stamp you received at Immigration when crossing the border into Thailand has expired, you must leave Thailand. However, a trip outside of Thailand to any border is sufficient and you can return to Thailand immediately and get a further 90-day stamp. Because it is a multi-entry type, this procedure can continue throughout the validity of the visa (usually one year). The start date of the validity is when the visa is inserted in your passport at the Thai consulate abroad. It is not the date of first entry into Thailand.

Your first 90 days will start with a date stamp in your passport upon arrival in Thailand. Each entry's expiry date (89 days later) can be extended at an Immigration office in Thailand for 30 days at a cost of 1,900 baht, although most people choose to do visa runs. If you make your last entry into Thailand immediately before your one-year multi-entry visa expires, you will actually get one year plus 90 days plus another 30-day extension in Thailand for 1,900 baht—nearly 16 months from when the visa was first issued in your passport.

A multi-entry non-immigrant visa *does not* allow you to stay in Thailand for one year, a very common misunderstanding. It only allows you to visit Thailand multiple times within a one-year period, with stays of up to 90 days.

Only a retirement extension, or a spousal extension, allows you to stay in Thailand for one year, and is only available in Thailand as an addition to an 'O' visa (thus turning it into an 'O-A' visa). The cost of a single-entry visa is $125.

To apply for a non-immigrant visa, you must have one of the following reasons to apply: business or conference; research; mass media; missionary; teaching and education; family reunion; settlement after retirement; or medical treatment.

71

Staying in Thailand using single- and multi-entry visas

	Cost Single-Entry	Cost Multiple-Entry
Visit to Penang including transport, hotel, food, etc	6,000 baht	6,000
Non-immigrant visa	2,000 baht ($50)	5,000 baht ($125)
One extension of stay at local Immigration office	1,900 baht	
Four visa runs (2,000 baht each)		8,000
TOTAL	9,900 baht ($250) for 120 days (83 baht per day)	19,000 baht ($475) for 485 days (40 baht per day)

There are three ways to extend a non-immigrant visa: marriage to a Thai citizen; retirement if over 50; and business. This can usually be done inside Thailand if you have the appropriate type of visa.

Marriage And Marriage Visas

Non-Immigrant O; Marrying A Thai

A sizeable percentage of foreigners decide to stay and retire in Thailand because they meet the girl (or boy) of their dreams here. The number of seemingly available and very attractive

Thai ladies in this country is sometimes overwhelming, and I'm sure the cause of many motorcycle accidents.

If you want to marry a Thai citizen, you will need proof from your embassy that you are legally able to marry. The legal marriage registration can be performed at any district office (*amphur*) in Thailand.

First, you must visit your embassy in Thailand. If you have previously been married, you must provide the original divorce decree or death certificate. If you have not been married, your embassy will verify that. Request an affidavit (US) or affirmation of freedom to marry (UK), which must be completed and notarized at the embassy. The embassy will usually charge about 4,000 baht for this service.

This affidavit or affirmation must be translated into Thai by a licensed legal translator, of which there are many close to the embassies. Translation fee is typically about 5,000 baht.

The translated affidavit or affirmation must then be stamped by the Legalization and Naturalization Division, Department of Consular Affairs, Ministry of Foreign Affairs(www.mfa.go.th) at 123 Chaeng Wattana Road, Laksi District, Bangkok 11120. (Tel. 02 575-1056 -59, 02 981-7171.) There are two fees available: 400 baht per document, taking up to two full days; or 800 baht per document for the same-day service.

The translation service may be able to take care of this for you for a small fee and mail it to you if you are not resident in Bangkok.

Then, at any future date, you can go to get married at any *amphur*. You will need to bring the translated, stamped affidavit or affirmation; passport; and ID card of your future spouse. You do not need witnesses as in the US or UK, and marriage at the *amphur* is free.

Once you are married, everything you or your spouse acquires (except land [see later chapter]) is joint property of the marriage. Everything you owned before the marriage remains 100 percent yours. This is significant in the case of divorce. You may want to seek professional legal advice about prenuptial agreements and wills prior to marriage.

It is normal in Thailand for the man to give a dowry to the family of the bride. This would normally be 20,000 to 100,000 baht for a village girl with little education and no career, up to 2,000,000 baht or more for a college-educated girl from a middle- or upper-class family.

Many Western men are tempted, or lured, into settling close to their wife's hometown or village. Be aware that this can be problematic, as the extended family—which typically includes at least half the village—will view a foreigner as a walking ATM machine. Your wife will receive daily visits from family and friends in need, asking for 'loans,' which, even if refused, can become a strain on the marriage and quality of life.

Spousal Extension To Non-Immigrant Visas

A non-immigrant O or B visa can be extended for up to one year. Applying for a non-immigrant visa is described above.

You can apply, with your Thai wife, at any main Immigration office, but the approval will come from Bangkok. Application will include:

- Application Form TM.7 available at: http://www.thaivisa.com/forum/index. php?showtopic=41308.
- Original and copy of passport with validity not less than 18 months.
- Two 4 x 6 cm photos.

- Marriage certificate (if married outside Thailand, you must provide a letter of guarantee from your embassy).
- 1,900 baht fee.
- Evidence of a combined family income (husband or wife or both working) of not less than 40,000 baht per month. Evidence is usually in the form of previous 3 months paid tax receipts. If money is earned abroad you will need proof such as pay stubs, tax receipts and proof of bank transfers into Thailand. Note that in the past, you could show proof of 400,000 baht in a Thai bank account but this rule was changed in National Police Office Order No. 606/2006, http://www.lawyer.th.com/National_Police_Office_Order_Oct_2006.pdf, however, if you applied for a marriage extension under the old rule, you can renew it under the same old rule.
- Up to date bank book.
- If working in Thailand, a work permit and evidence of tax payment are required.
- Documents indicating Thai nationality or permanent residence of the wife, such as identification card, census registration, address/residence identification, or passport (in case the wife is a permanent resident).
- The applicant accompanying his spouse to the Immigration Bureau to certify all the documents. The couple must be able to confirm they are still husband and wife. You may be asked to bring a friend (preferably Thai, with an ID card) who has known you and your spouse for a significant time, to verify that you are living together as husband and wife.

They may also ask to see the following:
- Wife's house register and identification card.
- Birth certificates of children (if any).
- Map of the house.

At the time of the initial application, you should receive an extension of stay for about 45 days and will be told to return to the same office on that date. Assuming the extension is approved, you will be stamped for an extension of stay for one year minus one day from your current entry into Thailand. For example, if you entered Thailand on January 10 and applied on April 20, your final approval would be about June 5 and would be extended until January 9 the next year. (Note: you should not reduce the money in the bank below 400,000 baht during the application period.)

If your extension of stay expires and the final extension has not yet been approved, you must return to the Immigration office again to receive another short extension. If you have a work permit, the permit must be extended in conjunction with each visa extension.

After your first extension, you can extend the visa for another year. You will need to show the same financial information for renewal (i.e. a minimum of 400,000 baht in the bank or 40,000 baht per month income).

The Immigration office sometimes refuses one-year marriage extensions for the smallest of reasons. It pays to be well prepared with documentation and have more than the minimum 400,000 baht.

Retirement Visa—Non-Immigrant O-A
A retirement visa is available for people 50 or over and allows for a single stay of one year with an extension inside Thailand. There are two ways to apply for a retirement visa:

- In your home country, apply at a Thai consulate for a non-immigrant visa category O-A. This is a non-O visa pre-approved for retirement.
- Obtain from any Thai consulate a non-immigrant visa category O, single or multiple entry (single is cheaper). When applying, state the reason for the visa as "To plan for permanent retirement." When entering Thailand, permission to stay will be given for 90 days. During the last 30 days of your permitted stay, apply at your local Immigration office for an annual extension for the purpose of retirement.

To apply using either method, you will need the following:
- Three copies of application form TM.7 available at: http://www.thaivisa.com/forum/index.php?showtopic=41308.
- Original and copy of passport with validity not less than 18 months.
- Three passport-sized photos of the applicant taken within the past six months.
- 500 baht fee.
- Letter from your embassy saying you wish to retire in Thailand. Make a copy of the letter; you can use it in future extensions. Immigration will accept a copy, but they want to see the original.
- Verification stating that the applicant has no criminal record, issued from the country of nationality or residence. The verification shall be valid for not more than three months and should be notarized by your embassy if applying in Thailand. If applying for an O-A visa in your home country, you will need a letter from the police stating you have

no criminal record and you are not wanted by the police.

- Proof of a sum of 800,000 baht (or equivalent in another major currency) in a Thai bank bearing your name, or an income of not less than 65,000 baht per month or a combination of the two. For example: 400,000 baht in the bank and 32,500 baht per month income. Money in the bank must have been in your bank account for at least 3 months prior to application to prove that the money wasn't borrowed to get the visa extension. You will need to show a bank statement or bank certified letter, not just your bank book. If applying for an O-A visa in your home country, you will need to show the equivalent amount of money in a bank in your home country. A bank statement will usually suffice.
- If the applicant is in poor health or is sensitive to colder climates or has resided in Thailand for a long period, and is 50-59 years old, special circumstances may be given. The applicant must submit medical certificates and proof that he/she has lived in Thailand for a long time.
- Note: A medical certificate is no longer required for a retirement extension

The first time you get a retirement extension, your current visa (90 days) will be extended by about nine months, for a total of one year. Thereafter, the renewal is for one complete year periods and can be extended in Thailand at any Immigration office for 1,900 baht providing you maintain 800,000 baht in a Thai bank account or can show evidence of an income of 65,000 baht per month, or a combination of both.

The source of these funds must come from abroad, so when transferring money to your Thai bank account, it is necessary that you get a Foreign Exchange Transfer Form (FETF), formerly known as a *Thor Thor 3*, from your bank.

If you are using foreign income as part of your financial proof, you must obtain from your embassy a notarized document indicating your annual income. This can be provided by the US embassy for a fee of 1,200 baht. At the US Embassy American Citizens' Services desk, fill in an "income" form and submit it for notarizing. It may be wise to take tax returns and other proof of income, but apparently, this is not usually requested by the US.

The UK and Australian embassies are more likely to review income sources. (Note: you will still have to show a "reasonable" amount in a Thai bank account, probably at least 200,000 baht.)

You should not allow your bank balance to fall below 800,000 baht (assuming you are not using foreign income) until your retirement extension is approved. Once approved, I have read that unless you have funds coming from abroad, it is preferable to periodically withdraw money from this account for living expenses or Thai Immigration may suspect you are working, which is strictly prohibited.

Unfortunately, being married to a Thai citizen does not reduce the 800,000 baht or 65,000 baht per month requirement.

Foreign single women are treated the same as foreign single men. Only when a foreign woman is married to a Thai man are the rules different. She does then not need to show independent financial security.

A foreign man wishing to retire in Thailand with his (foreign) wife would be granted an O-A visa, but his wife would only be granted an O visa. Only one 800,000 baht would be needed, but she would have to make border runs.

If you and your non-Thai wife are both over 50, it probably makes sense to apply separately, each for an O-A visa. This would save any border runs, but would need 800,000 baht in separate bank accounts, or income, in order for both to qualify.

You are not allowed to work while on this type of visa. Also, you must report to Immigration every 90 days to verify your current address or face a fine of 5,000 baht plus 200 baht per day.

With all the required documents in hand, and the bank certification dated within a day or two, the applicant goes to the Immigration office, the one-year retirement visa is sometimes issued immediately, or is ready a day or two later.

(Note: the bank certificate of account balance for 800,000 baht must show that the money came into the bank from another country. The bank will need to be able to follow the paper trail, or transfer. Ask the bank for a copy of the wire transfer document to keep as proof of international transfer, which would be required in order to re-transfer the money out of Thailand, later.)

The overriding criterion is to satisfy the Immigration officer that you have sufficient money to live in Thailand comfortably, without the need to rely on Thailand for support. Being able to demonstrate more than the minimum amount goes a long way. If you have the bare minimum and no other income, they may refuse. But if you can show the minimum plus even a small regular pension, this will often suffice. They know a pension is ongoing.

Ernie K., Pattaya

"Here are the facts, plain and simple. I just extended my retirement visa at the Pattaya Immigration office in Jomtien. You have to do the following:

80

"Make a money transfer to a Thai bank from a foreign account. No matter how much pension income you have, Immigration wants to see the bank account. Just before you go for your extension, you will have to go to your bank and tell them you need a letter to Immigration for extending your visa. It's a pre-printed form. They need your passport with the visa stamp in it, which they will copy, and your bank book. In about ten minutes you'll have your letter, signed by the bank officer. It cost me 200 baht.

"Get the letter copied, along with your passport and your bank book, making sure to copy the first page and all the pages with entries. I suggest you get the letter the day or so before you go for your extension; it has to be timely.

"In addition, you will need a letter from a doctor or a clinic. I went to a clinic on Central Road in Pattaya, with my lady as interpreter, and said I needed a letter for Immigration stating that I did not have any of the five dreaded diseases. The doctor pulled out a form, asked if I was healthy, looked at my passport and visa, and for 200 baht copied the number down on the form, along with my name, and handed it to me. No examination, no check-up. The form was written in Thai, but I assumed it was what I needed, and it was.

"Next, the American Embassy. It's crowded and there's no place to park, I suggest you take public transportation, or a cab. Inside there are two windows. I got in line and asked the lady for the form I needed, then went into the adjoining room and filled it out. Basically it asks you to enter your monthly income. It's self explanatory and very simple. I took all the W-2 forms, SS forms for the current year, and past three years. She didn't ask for any of that. I handed in the form and in less than ten minutes the lady called my name. I went to the window and she asked me if the statements on the form I filled out were the truth to the best of my knowledge, to which I answered yes. She had me sign the letter from the

81

embassy stating that I was a US citizen, with x amount of income every month from the US government and/or other sources. It goes on to say you are applying for an extension of a current Thai visa and any assistance you can provide, etcetera. I signed it in her presence; she signed it, stamp dated it, and that was that; 1,200 baht.

"Make one or two copies of the original. Keep the original for next year. They will accept a copy but they want to see the original.

"Now you're ready to go to Thai Immigration. The one on Soi 5 in Jomtien was a snap. After I got everything together it took less than a half hour, but wherever you go, go early Monday. They shuffle you around between three different officers, mostly women, but they were very polite, and most helpful. It cost 1,900 baht for the extension. And you have to report back every 90 days."

Exit And Re-Entry Permit

Once you have a retirement or marriage extension, simply leaving Thailand will cancel your current visa, and your extension. You would have to start again in order to get another retirement extension.

Safeguard your extension by obtaining an exit and re-entry permit so that your current extension will continue on your return to Thailand. A one-time exit and re-entry permit is 1,000 baht. A multi-use exit and re-entry permit is 3,800 baht. Both permit types expire on the same anniversary date of the one-year extension

The application form for a re-entry permit into the kingdom is available at: http://www.thaivisa.com.

Business Visa (Non-Immigrant B) And Work Permit

If you plan to work in Thailand, you are legally required to have a work permit. A necessary prerequisite for a work permit is a non-immigrant 'B' visa. A necessary prerequisite of both is a job offer from a Thai company. If you do not have a job offer from a Thai company, you can start your own company, usually with the help of a lawyer. To be able to acquire a work permit for its employees (you), a company must be majority owned by Thai nationals (i.e. 51 percent Thai shareholders, meaning you can own only a maximum of 49 percent). For more information about starting companies in Thailand, please see "*How to Buy Land And Building A House in Thailand.*"

Applying for a non-immigrant B visa and a work permit is a relatively complex process, involving many Thai documents, and is usually handled by a lawyer. Typically, a lawyer will charge about 10,000-15,000 baht for the initial application (not including company set-up) and 4,000 baht for work-permit extension, which is required every three months (unless extended).

A full package including company set-up, visa, and work permit, is typically about 40,000 baht. Check that your lawyer is experienced in visa and work permit applications. If you are unsure of local legal services, seek out the larger national law firms such as Siam Legal or Sunbelt Asia.

It is possible to apply for a visa and work permit yourself for about 2,000 baht in filing fees, but unless you read and write Thai very well, you will need a substantial amount of help.

You can apply for a non-immigrant B visa in your home country or any Thai consulate outside Thailand. If you are already in Thailand, the simplest way is to go to the Thai

Consulate in Penang, Malaysia. The requirements for getting a non-immigrant visa are:

1. The applicant has been offered a job or starts a Thai company to employ himself/herself.
2. The company requests that the applicant be given a non-immigrant visa so the company may apply for a work permit for him/her.
3. The company knows the person to be dependable, upstanding, and law abiding, and that they will respect the laws and customs of the Kingdom of Thailand.

The consulate or consular officer will ask for copies of the registration documents and financial statements from the company.

Obtaining A Work Permit

The employee (you) must provide the following documents:
- Passport (copies of every page). Each copy must be signed by the employee.
- Non-immigrant visa.
- Departure Card TM.6.
- Education certificate (signed copy).
- Transcript (signed copy; see note below).
- Certificates or licenses held by the applicant (signed copy; see note below).
- CV or resume describing in detail the applicant's past positions, duties, performance, length and place of employment.
- Photos, three in quantity, 5 x 6 cm in size (not passport photos) with full face and taken wearing business attire (no hat, and some jurisdictions

require suit and tie). The picture must have been taken within six months of the application.

Thai government officials may require these documents to be certified by your country's embassy this requires bringing your degree, resume, license, or certificate to your embassy to declare it is a true and original document. You are required to pay an authentication fee to your embassy. In addition, they can require you to translate these documents into the Thai language.

The employer (or your company) must provide the following documents:

- Commercial Registration Department certificate showing that the organization for which the applicant is going to work has been duly registered as a juristic person, giving the name of the managing director and/or director, and its objectives and registered capital (see note below).
- Shareholders list certified by the Commercial Registration Department (see note below).
- Factory License (if required) issued by the Factory Department, Ministry of Industry (see note below).
- VAT Certificate *Phor Phor 20* (see note below).
- Withholding Tax *Phor Ngor Dor 1* (if renewing work permit, see note below).

Thai government officials require that all documents have the seal of the company stamped on every page and the true and authorized signature(s) of the managing director and/or directors next to the seal. In addition, government officials have in the past requested official copies of registration, shareholders, licenses, and certificates to have been issued

85

by their respective agencies within the previous 90 days of your application for the work permit.

Getting A Work Permit Approved

A job description is often the determining factor in the approval or denial of a work permit. Unless the written job description requires skills that a Thai is not likely to possess, the application will not be approved.

Your lawyer should write professional and accurate job descriptions in order for you to gain quick approval.

The Labor Department often seems to want to reduce the number of permits actually issued to help demonstrate that they are protecting Thai jobs. Therefore, if your company applies for three permits, they may only approve one or possibly two. You need professional help to ensure all of your applications will have a successful outcome.

Once the application is submitted for your work permit, you must not let your visa expire. The Labor Department's system links the non-immigrant visa ("extension of stay") you listed on your application to the work permit paperwork.

The work permit, once approved, allows you to work at the noted company and location. If you change employers or place of work, you must make a new application. Also, within ten days of resignation or if you are terminated or laid off, you must return your work permit to the Labor Department. It is your responsibility to return your work permit booklet; don't count on your company doing it.

Tax ID Card

Once your work permit has been arranged, your company must apply for a Thai taxpayer identification card. This ID card has a tax ID number which you will need to list on tax documents.

Renewing Your Visa And Work Permit

Your work Permit expires when your "extension of stay" does. The extension of stay is the date stamped in your passport when you entered Thailand.

You must renew your stay before you can renew your work permit. If you have an unexpired multiple-entry visa, simply cross any border and then return. If you have a single-entry or expired multi-entry visa, you must visit a Thai consulate abroad (usually Penang) to obtain a new visa. You will need to provide the consulate with copies of your work permit and new recommendation letter from your company, the company registration documents, and financial and tax reports. Renewing your work permit for one year typically costs about 3,000 baht not including a 100 baht application form 'fee'.

Changing Visa Types

It is possible to change some visa types such as non-immigrant B to O. Visa changes can only be done in the headquarters of Immigration on Soi Suan Plu in Bangkok. There is a department exclusively dealing with visa changes on the second or third floor (the organization and layout of these offices are in a continual state of flux, changing from one year to the next).

Visa Runs

Penang, Malaysia
Royal Thai Consulate-General
1 Jalan Tunku Abdul Rahman
10350 Penang
Tel. (60-4) 226-8029, 226-9484; Fax. (60-4) 226-3121

Most long-term foreign residents in Thailand will become all too familiar with Penang, Malaysia. The Thai Consulate

General in Penang is the closest consulate to Thailand that offers multiple-entry visas, and is relatively easy to get to with cheap flights, train, and bus services from Bangkok and Hat Yai. The consulate will be closed on all Thai and Malaysian holidays, so remember to call ahead (60 942268029 or 60 42269484) or go to http://www.bank-holidays.com/ to check whether they will be open when you arrive.

Typically, the Penang consulate will issue multiple-entry tourist and non-immigrant visas. However, they sometimes stop issuing multiple-entry tourist visas for no particular reason, then resume.

A well-established visa support business has developed in Penang, mostly in Chulia Street, George Town. If you take a bus to Penang, you will be greeted by representatives of many visa-processing agents. These people typically work out of the many bookshops and money changers along Chulia Street and are not legally associated with the Thai Consulate, but have been helping foreigners get visas for years and are very good at it. For a few hundred baht, they will fill in the forms and take your passport to the consulate, wait in line, and bring it back, usually in a day or so. Paying a little extra usually guarantees passport returned the next morning.

In my experience these agents are generally very honest and reliable. At first you may feel uneasy about handing your passport to a stranger who meets you off a bus, but everyone does it and these guys know how to work with the consulate. They almost always get the visa without a hitch.

The consulate only accepts visa applications in the morning. Unfortunately, most overland arrivals (train, bus, or minibus) get into Penang just before, or after, lunch, so unless you're quick or you get an early flight, your first day is usually wasted. If using an agent, hand your passport over as soon as you arrive. He will fill out the forms and check your paperwork is in order, which can be quite extensive if applying for a non-immigrant visa.

I have found the Maybank ATMs do not accept ATM cards with more than six-digit pin codes, which my US card has. There is, however, a Citibank and HSBC halfway between George Town and the ferry pier (to Butterworth on the mainland, where the train station is) which work fine.

Most people on a limited budget stay in George Town, which has budget to mid-level accommodation from about 200-2,000 baht per night (cockroaches are free!) If you want to go upmarket, try one of the resorts on the tourist side of the island at Batu Ferengi.

Even if you do not stay in Batu Ferengi, it is worth a visit to kill time and shop in the night market. Residents of Penang are always puzzled why so many foreigners want to get in and out of the place as quickly as possible. By comparison with Thailand, Malaysia virtually begs people to live there, yet no one wants to stay.

Fake goods in Malaysia—such as designer knock-offs and DVDs—are of far higher quality and cheaper than Thailand. Brand-name electronics in the Komtar area of George Town are usually cheaper than Thailand.

Kuala Lumpur, Malaysia
Royal Thai Embassy
206 Jalan Ampang
50450 Kuala Lumpur
Tel. + 03 248-8222, 248-8350; Fax. + 03 248-6527

Flights from Bangkok to KL start at about 1,800 baht on Air Asia. Application forms are available after 9.15. The consular section is across a small courtyard and the doors open at 9.30. Passports are collected from the gatehouse at 11.30 the following day. The queue starts in the courtyard and not in the street. Multiple-entry visas are not available in KL.

Kota Bharu, Malaysia
Royal Thai Consulate-General
4426 Jalan Pengkalan Chepa
15400 Kota Bharu, Kelantan
Tel. (60-9) 744-5266, 748-2545; Fax. (60-9) 744-9801

Vientiane, Laos
Royal Thai Embassy
Route Phonekheng
Vientiane
P.O. Box 128
Tel. 214-5813, 214-5856; Fax. 66 1 411-0017

The overnight sleeper train from Bangkok to Nong Khai costs about 700 baht. At Nong Khai take a *tuk-tuk* to the Friendship Bridge. Ignore the drivers trying to sell you a visa. At Thai Immigration your passport and departure card are required. Cross the Friendship Bridge by bus. At Laos Immigration you need your passport, plus two passport photos, and the entry fee of about $30 (payable in baht).

In Laos the currency is the kip, but they accept baht and US dollars everywhere. Take a bus (40 baht) or *tuk-tuk* (100 baht) to Vientiane. Accommodation is easy to find. Chindamay Guesthouse on Tha Setthathirat is cheap.

Return to Bangkok can be booked at any travel agent. There is a bus that is cheaper and slightly faster than the train, but far less comfortable.

There are no ATMs in Laos, only banks to change money, so take cash.

Phnom Penh, Cambodia
Royal Thai Embassy
196 Preah Norodom Boulevard
Phnom Penh
http://www.mfa.go.th/web/1300.php?depid=186
Sangkat Tonle Bassac
Khan Chamcar Mon
Phnom Penh
Tel. 855 23 726 306-10 (Auto Line); Fax. 66 0-2575-0509,
855 23 726 303

Singapore
Royal Thai Embassy
370 Orchard Road
Singapore 0923
Tel. 65 235-4175, 737-2158; Fax. 65 732-0778

Airfares to Singapore are often cheaper than domestic fares
inside Thailand, although the cost of staying in Singapore is
significantly higher than other parts of Southeast Asia. However, if you are shopping for electronics, you could almost
save the cost of the trip on a computer or camera.

Visit Sentosa Island by cable car and visit the shopping
centers on Orchard Road. Budget hotels in a central location
cost about 2,500 baht per night.

Border Runs
If you have a multiple-entry visa, when your current stay
expires, you will need to leave Thailand at any border and
return for a new extension of stay. The following locations
are popular 'border run' destinations for foreigners resident
in Thailand.

Ranong To Myanmar (Burma)

Many companies offer visa runs to Ranong from Phuket, Krabi, Surat Thani, Koh Samui, and other places in the south. It's a 10-20 hour round-trip and costs about 1,000-2,000 baht with minibus, food, and boat included.

You will first be taken to the Immigration office, where they will stamp you out of Thailand. However, you are still in Thailand, so you must take a short taxi ride to the longtail boat (five minutes) for the crossing to Myanmar. The trip across the river to Myanmar takes about 30 minutes.

Including the several Immigration checkpoints in Thailand and Myanmar, you can be back in Thailand in about two hours. However, you still need to officially re-enter Thailand at the Immigration office where you checked out. This office nominally closes at 5 p.m. (although I have seen it stay open much later for people who are coming back late). If you are not on a tour, plan to be in Ranong by 3 p.m. at the latest if you plan to be back in Thailand the same day.

Hat Yai To Sadao, Malaysia

Flights to Hat Yai from Bangkok can be as low as 400 baht (plus taxes). From Hat Yai take a taxi to Sadao (Malaysian border) and then back to Hat Yai town; a round-trip of about six hours.

Kota Bharu, Malaysia

Royal Thai Consulate
4426 Jalan Pengkalan Chepa
Kota Bharu
Kelantan

The overnight sleeper train from Bangkok to Sungai Kolok costs about 650 baht. Sungai Kolok Station is short walk to Immigration. Show your passport and departure card, then walk over the bridge to Malaysian Immigration and take a taxi to Kota Bharu for about 300 baht. Several guesthouses around Kota Bharu are aimed at backpackers. It is necessary to be respectful of the Muslim population here. Women should dress modestly. Alcohol is scarce and expensive.

The return journey can be booked in any travel agency in Kota Bharu, or you can take a taxi back to Sungai Kolok and buy a train ticket before boarding (slightly risky as trains may be fully booked; but there is accommodation in Sungai Kolok).

(If you are intending to go to Kota Bharu, it would be a shame not to visit the nearby Perhentian Islands. Take a taxi from Kota Bharu to Kuala Besut Pier for about 300 baht. The islands are absolutely gorgeous; the beaches are stunning and the crystal-clear waters are full of amazing marine life. Scuba diving here is very affordable.)

Mae Sai To Myanmar (Burma)
Mae Sai is the most convenient border run from Chiang Mai, Chiang Rai, and other places in the north. Leaving Chiang Mai at 9 a.m. gets you to Mae Sai by 1 p.m. A short *song-taew* ride from the bus station gets you to the border.

Get an exit stamp from the Immigration office, pass the checkpoint, and cross the bridge into Myanmar. At a small office on the right-hand side of the bridge, an Immigration officer takes your passport and $10 or 400 baht, and gives you a receipt.

If you have time, continue over the bridge and into the market town, which is well stocked with cheap Chinese goods, CDs and DVDs (a great selection for 70 baht each).

Returning, pick up your passport from Myanmar Immigration and cross back into Thailand. Note that Immigration will ask for proof you have at least 10,000 baht for a tourist visa or 20,000 baht for a non-immigrant visa, either in cash or a Thai bank book. If you dress nicely, they may not ask.

The return bus leaves at 3:30 p.m., so be back in Mae Sai by 3 p.m. because the *songtaew* journey to the bus stop takes at least 15 minutes. There are later buses changing in Chiang Rai.

Mae Sot To Myanmar

Mae Sot is reported to be an easy border crossing. Take a *tuk-tuk* to the border, stamp out, walk across the bridge, hand your passport and 500 baht to the police on the other side, no photos required. Walk back across the bridge and stamp back into Thailand. Don't use this border if you're even one day overstayed in Thailand as the police stop all buses looking for illegal Burmese workers and will detain you for a few hours and may fine you.

Chiang Saen To Myanmar

Located 60 kilometers from Chiang Rai. The boat to Myanmar is 500 baht. You will get a tourist visa entering Myanmar for 250 baht.

Chiang Khong To Laos

You will need a visa for Laos prior to arrival; the cost is about 700 baht. The minibus from Chiang Mai is 190 baht each way, and the boat is 20 baht. Leave Chiang Mai at 10 a.m. and you're back by 6 p.m.

Aranyaprathet To Poipet, Cambodia

Aranyaprathet is the nearest border point and the most convenient from Bangkok and Pattaya. The train from Hualamphong Station in Bangkok to Aranyaprathet costs about 50 baht and takes four hours. From the Aranyaprathet train station, take a taxi to the border. You can also take a bus from Mor Chit Bus Station in Bangkok. Many travel agencies offer a visa-run minibus service.

At the border, ignore the people who want to help you fill out the forms. Stamp out, walk 50 meters to the other side, then get in line for a visa. Pay 1,100 baht and stamp into Cambodia. Join the next line to stamp back out. Walk 50 meters back to Thailand. Take at least two passport photos with you. Hurry back to the train station, as the 6 a.m. train from Bangkok turns around about 90 minutes after it arrives. You'll be back in Bangkok or Pattaya around 8 p.m.

Chong Chom To Cambodia

The border is approximately 70 kilometers south of Surin. Bus and taxi services are available from Surin to Chong Chom and the trip takes about 1 hour. The Cambodia visa is 1,200 baht plus a 300 baht exit fee! Walk 50 meters across the border, stamp in, and come back. Take two passport photographs.

Permanent Residence In Thailand

You can apply for permanent residency in Thailand if you have lived in Thailand and held a non-immigrant visa for at least three years. You will be required to show similar documents to the ones used to apply for the non-immigrant visa and also take an interview which includes a test of your ability to speak, read, and write Thai.

The cost of permanent residency is 191,400 baht or 95,700 baht if you are married to a Thai citizen. This is clearly a rather expensive alternative to retirement visa, which, at 1,900 baht for 40 years amounts to only 76,000 baht.

There is a quota of 100 persons per year from each nationality for permanent residence status.

Thai Citizenship

It is possible for a foreigner to gain Thai citizenship. The application is similar to permanent residence, but a higher level of spoken and written Thai is required. It is not necessary to be married to a Thai citizen.

General Thoughts On Visas

Like most countries, Thailand does not allow foreigners to just come and live here indefinitely (unless permission is given in the form of a residence permit). A visa is temporary by its very nature and can be terminated at any time by Immigration. It should not be considered a right, or a way to gain permanent residence in Thailand for life.

You should not state that you are leaving your country to live in Thailand, either to the Thai authorities, or to any Thai embassy or consulate—because to qualify for most visas you must have a permanent home address outside Thailand. Any 'B', 'O,' or 'O-A' visa is actually only a renewable temporary visa. There is no such thing as a permanent visa. You would need a permanent residency permit or citizenship in order to eliminate the need for a visa.

Please remember, if you have permission to stay for a long period (i.e. a retirement visa, marriage visa, or work permit), you must report to an Immigration office every 90 days to confirm your address—or pay a 5,000 baht fine plus 200 baht a day. Some immigration offices will allow 90 day reporting by mail. You should check with your immigration office because some do not. I have heard that if there is the smallest mistake in the documentation when reporting by mail, the report will not be accepted and you will not know about the problem until you next renewal when it can become a big problem.

Do not send your passport to another country unaccompanied for a new visa; it is illegal and the consequences are very serious.

If you wish to take your Thai friend or spouse to your home country, they will need either a tourist visa or an immigration or fiancé visa.

Thai applicants for tourist visas for the USA, European countries, and Australia require evidence of strong ties to Thailand—such as a job, money in the bank, land, or family commitments. Simply being married to a citizen of another country does not guarantee a tourist visa, as I can personally testify. The USA is notoriously difficult for tourist visas for all nationalities since the "9/11" terrorist attacks. I went to the US Embassy in Bangkok with my wife for a tourist visa; we provided proof she had money in the bank, owned land, had children in Thailand, yet she was refused. I have read similar reports from many people.

Bringing Your Household Items To Thailand

You have six months from your entry into Thailand to bring in your household items from your home country. After you have been granted a permit to stay for a year in Thailand, your belongings will not be taxed. However, if your permit to stay is for less than one year, these items will be taxed 20 percent import duty plus 7 percent value-added tax. The period of six months starts from the date that you initially entered Thailand on the retirement visa, regardless whether you leave or re-enter Thailand after that date. However, the deadline is somewhat flexible. If your personal items are due to arrive in Thailand more than six months after the entry date, you should inform Customs about this at least two months before the six-month deadline.

Working In Thailand

Why is there a section on working in a book about retirement? Well, we consider retirement to be a change in lifestyle as we noted early in this book in A New Definition of Retirement. We are not assuming any particular age or work status. Working in your home country is something you have to do to survive; in Thailand it may be something you want to do to enjoy life.

I probably don't need to tell you that earnings in Thailand are a fraction of those in the West for a similar job. However, if your overall lifestyle on a modest income is better in Thailand than it would be back home, it may be the right choice for you.

Typical jobs for foreigners in Thailand including teaching; bar, restaurant, or hotel work; import-export; or Internet-based freelance work.

For more information on doing business see the book *How to Establish a Successful Business in Thailand* by Philip Wylie, also published by Paiboon Publishing.

Regardless of what type or work you do, you are required by Thai law to have a work permit if you plan to actively participate. If you are simply investing in, say, a bar, you do not technically need a work permit, but many foreign bar owners have got into trouble with the law simply by sitting at their own bar and talking to their staff or customers.

To be safe, I recommend you get a work permit; it will cost about 4,000 baht per month (including taxes and lawyer fees) and has the advantage that you can get a three-month or one-year visa. (See the visa section and ask your lawyer for more information about work permits in Thailand.)

If you are caught working without a permit, you could be fined, deported, or even jailed. And don't think that just because you are not getting paid, that you don't need a work permit. Several tsunami volunteers were deported for

98

'working' without a work permit! Making routine repairs or bringing food and drinks to tables have landed many foreign restaurant owners in serious trouble.

There is an extensive list of occupations that foreigners are prohibited from, including the following: labor; work in agriculture, animal breeding, forestry, fishery, or general farm supervision; masonry, carpentry, or other construction work; wood carving; driving motor vehicles or non-motorized carriers, except for piloting international aircraft; shop attendant; auctioneer; supervising, auditing, or giving services in accounting, except occasional international auditing; gem cutting and polishing; hair cutting, hairdressing, and beautician work; hand weaving; mat weaving or making of wares from reed, rattan, kenaf, straw, or bamboo pulp; manufacture of manual fibrous paper; manufacture of lacquer ware; Thai musical instrument production; manufacture of niello ware; goldsmith, silversmith, and other precious metal work; manufacture of bronze ware; Thai doll making; manufacture of mattresses and padded blankets; alms bowl making; manual silk product making; Buddha image making; manufacture of knives; paper and cloth umbrella fabrication; shoemaking; hat making; brokerage or agency work, except in international business; dressmaking; pottery or ceramics; manual cigarette rolling; legal or litigation service; clerical or secretarial work; manual silk reeling and weaving; Thai character type-setting; hawking; tourist guide or tour organizing agency; architectural work; civil engineering work.

Remember that you may be required to declare your foreign-earned income in your home country and pay tax on it. See the previous section on taxes for your home country.

Teaching

The most obvious and popular occupation for foreigners in Thailand is teaching, usually English, although other subjects such as math, science, and computers often pay better.

In the more established schools and universities, you will need a teaching credential such as a degree or TEFL (Teaching English as a Foreign Language) or CELTA (Cambridge Certificate in English-Language Teaching to Adults). You can get a CELTA and other qualifications in Thailand for about $1,400.

Pay for teachers usually ranges from 500 to 1,500 baht per day or 20,000 to 50,000 baht per month depending on subject, location, and your qualifications.

Language schools are very common in Bangkok and most major cities. Outside of the big cities you may need to start your own school. You can also volunteer in the government schools to help the local kids.

Bars, Restaurants And Hotels

These type of jobs (or investments) are very popular in Bangkok and the tourist spots. The advantage is that you can start something yourself without any experience as an employer. In my observation, it is possible to make a living in these types of businesses, but just barely.

Many people open bars, restaurants, or guesthouses without doing a realistic expense and income analysis. Sales expectations are overly optimistic, if done at all, and the real costs of getting into business are not calculated.

Before you invest money in one of these types of businesses, look at what the local competition is doing. How many customers do they have, and how much do they spend? Don't forget. If you check such things in the high season and everyone looks busy, it could be a false analysis; they may not see a customer for days at a time in the low season.

Make a realistic estimate of income and expenses over the whole year and think about rent, food, utilities, staff, and police pay-offs (yes, this is Thailand). Remember, you are new and you will not have the returning customers to rely on. If you are realistic in your planning, you will probably find you will barely make ends meet; not that that necessarily means don't do it. I have many friends who have bars, restaurants, and bungalows and are making a living. It's hard work for very little money, but at least they are their own boss and living in Thailand. Also, be careful not to drink away the profits!

If you are planning to build business premises, you should be even more careful about your financial planning. Unless you live in a part of the country such as Pattaya, Phuket, or Koh Samui—where it is possible to charge higher prices to higher-end customers—it may be very hard to recover the cost of building and ongoing maintenance from budget-conscious customers. It may be wise to rent a place first and get some local experience before you commit to a major expense.

Theme-based businesses seem to do well. Resorts that focus on scuba diving or, more recently, yoga and meditation often seem to be full all year round.

Import-Export

Many items in Thailand, especially handicrafts, are far cheaper than in the West. Some foreigners make a reasonable living, or at least cover the cost of their trips to Thailand, by buying such items in Thailand and selling them abroad. On the small scale this may mean buying a few hundred or thousand dollars' worth of handicrafts or jewelry and selling it in local markets back home. If you plan to do this, try to find items that you can sell for at least five times what you paid for them. Clearly, small and light is an advantage if you are carrying them with you on the plane.

Check the limits for importing commercial goods into your country unless you want to run foul of the Customs service.

I have talked to several people who make a modest living in this way. Usually they prefer smaller, cheaper items that can be bought for a few baht in Thailand. If you are interested in larger, more valuable items, you will probably need the help of an import-export company, of which there are many in Bangkok.

In the age of e-bay, it is relatively simple to sell items over the Internet and ship directly to the customer from Thailand. This has the advantage that, in many cases, you do not need to buy the item until you have sold it. Successful selling on e-bay is all about getting good feedback, so make sure you are selling high-quality goods and ship them in a timely manner and are responsive to customer e-mail.

I would not advertise the fact that you are in Thailand, because many people will be wary of fraud. If your items are very obviously sourced in Thailand, you could use statements like "from our suppliers in Thailand"—but avoid saying that you are based in Thailand.

When mailing items abroad, you will have to declare the value to Customs. Small items valued at under a certain figure will not have a Customs fee, but other items valued over a certain amount will. Customs fees must be paid by the receiver, so your customers must be aware of that. On small items such as CDs, it is actually about the same price to mail from Thailand to the US as it is from places within the US itself. Be sure to send them registered mail from any post office so it won't go missing

Internet-Based Business

Thanks to the Internet, the world is quickly becoming a much smaller place. For several years I have been doing contract computer programming for clients in America from my house in Thailand. Many people are finding they can do jobs like programming, customer support, or graphic design from halfway around the world. Usually, you would already be well established in your field of expertise, with a list of steady, reliable clients that you can count on for more work. It is quite hard, but not impossible, to attract new clients from a long distance.

In Thailand even the small towns have internet cafes

This kind of work is the 'holy grail' for expats; earning a Western pay check while living in Thailand. However, it is not without its disadvantages. You will still have schedules to meet and bosses to keep happy. And if things go wrong, 'that guy 5,000 miles away in Thailand' is an easy target for the ax! I have found that people chained to their desks back in the office can be quite jealous of someone in the enviable position of working from home in paradise. It pays to keep a low profile about your work status and not rub it in their faces—something I must confess is very hard for me to avoid.

Several people have been quite successful with Thailand-related web businesses, such as tourism and information websites, or accommodation booking. To be successful, you need to get your website noticed by the major search engines. This subject is a book in itself, and many have been written. However, here are the basics:

Search engines mostly work by counting the number of links pointing to your site. Try to get similar but non-competitive sites to point to your site. High quality links (i.e., links from popular sites) are best. Initially, it will be difficult to get webmasters to exchange links with you because you are unknown. Search the web for free sites to place links such as classified advertising boards, forums, and directories. List your site with all the popular directories, such as dmoz.org and yahoo. Put some useful, and ideally unique, information on your site, such as a travel guide to your area of the country, or interesting stories from travelers. It usually takes a long time for the search engines to notice your site, and you may want to pay for commercial advertising to get things started.

Remember that paid advertising does not usually improve your search rank and should never be considered a substitute for the time-consuming work of promoting your site by spending a lot of time on the web.

Income Tax In Thailand

If you are working in Thailand, you are required to pay tax. You may also be required to declare your Thai income in your home country. The following is the tax rate in Thailand.

Net Taxable Income (In Baht)	Tax Rate
1 to 200,000	5%
200,001 to 500,000	10%
500,001 to 1,000,000	20%
1,000,001 to 4,000,000	30%
4,000,000 and above	33%

Renting Out Property Abroad

Many people generate income by renting out their properties abroad. Remember that rental income will usually be considered taxable income in that country, but not in Thailand (unless you are a citizen).

Unfortunately, it seems the majority of long-distance rentals eventually run into problems with tenants not paying the rent or damaging the property. And, unless you have someone close to the property taking care of things, trips back home to evict non-paying tenants and repair property can cost more than rental income.

Communications And Internet Access

Fortunately for the traveler or resident with limited Internet needs, every town and virtually every village in Thailand has an Internet café offering dial-up to high-speed Internet at a few baht per minute.

If you are a more frequent user of the Internet, you may want to get connected from home. There are several ways to connect to the Internet from your house, depending largely on your proximity to the main telephone office.

Dial-Up

If you can get a telephone line to your house, you can use a dial-up service such as csloxinfo or ji-net. You will need a telephone line from TOT or TT&T. The connection charge is about 3,700 baht plus the cost of cable, and the subscription fee is about 200 baht per month (TOT). Local calls and special access numbers such as 1222 are three baht per call, unlimited time. So, if you call once a day, your phone bill will only be about 400 baht per month.

The unlimited services seem very attractive at about 350 baht per month, but unfortunately are unreliable and very slow. The packages that give a fixed number of hours are inconvenient if, like me, you sit at your computer all day, but at least they are reasonably fast and connections are far more reliable than unlimited services.

An ISP (Internet Service Provider) such a csloxinfo or ji-net charges about 350 to 600 baht per month, so your monthly dial-up cost may be about 500-1,000 baht per month. Ji-net is cheap but very unreliable; on most days it is impossible to connect. The free TOT service is more reliable and often faster. Csloxinfo (limited hours) is more expensive but seems to connect well most of the time and the speed is quite good for dial-up.

TOT provides a free connection using login 'totonline@ totonline.net' and password 'totonline' But this service usually disconnects you after about one hour, presumably so you have to make a new phone call. However, if you want cheap, occasional Internet from home and do not care about a bit of inconvenience, it is a good choice, and also a good back-up when the paid services are not working.

As you would expect, dial-up is slow and connections are unreliable. Expect to get about 20kbps. Any average web page such as yahoo.com takes up to 10 seconds to load. It takes about a minute to connect.

Mobile Phone—GPRS

You can connect to the Internet using a GPRS-enabled mobile phone or a GPRS adapter for your computer. If using a GPRS phone, the phone and your computer should have blue tooth capability so the computer can connect to the phone.

DTAC and AIS (mobile phone services) both offer a GPRS service with unlimited connection time for about 1,500 baht per month on a one-year contract. Data rate is about the same as dial-up, but connecting time is much faster—usually only a few seconds—and reliability may be better depending on your proximity to the phone tower.

Using GPRS also has the big advantage that it will work anywhere in Thailand that gives you a signal, so it is ideal if you travel a lot. SIM card readers for laptop computers are easily found in computer shops.

DSL—High-Speed Internet Via Phone Line

DSL is the best choice for higher speed and more reliable Internet, but is usually only available in larger towns or within about ten kilometers of the telephone company office. DSL packages for individuals start at about 700 baht per month (TOT phone lines). Advertised data rates start at 256kbps down and 128kbps up, and you should be able to get 200kpbs down on most days.

IPSTAR Satellite Internet

IPSTAR provides Internet access from anywhere in Thailand via a satellite dish. The advertised data rates start at 256kbps down and 128kbps up, but you will almost never see that speed. On an average day you may get 40kbps down, which is still twice that of a good day on dial-up

IPSTAR currently costs about 5,000 baht to set up and 1,800 baht per month for the lowest speed, so it is the most expensive and possibly least reliable of all the connection methods. Reliability is fairly bad, and you will probably need a phone line for back-up if you need the Internet every day. Clouds, rain, and wind are a big problem for IPSTAR. However, if you want reasonable speed and you are in the countryside, this is probably your only choice.

I used IPSTAR for about 2 months but found the phone line far more reliable and cancelled the contract. Most of my friends have had the same experience.

Computers And Electronics—Power Supply
Voltage in Thailand is 240 volts. Most devices like laptop computers and mobile phones will work on anything from 100 to 240V. However, if you are bringing items from the US, check that they will work with 240V. Look at the power adapter or on the case, close to the power plug.

I am in the computer business, yet I have managed to blow up one printer and one desktop computer because I forgot to check the power rating. If your item will not take 240V, you can buy a 240-110V step-down transformer at most electrical shops. Remember to check the amp rating if you are using a transformer.

Heat
I don't need to remind you that Thailand is a hot country. Unlike humans, who can jump in a cold shower cool off, your electronics will just sit and bake. Computers, printers, modems, and other electronic devices are designed for an air-conditioned office environment. They may run excessively hot in non-air-conditioned rooms in Thailand, which could cause unreliability or permanent damage.

I recommend pointing a fan at any electronic item that feels warm to the touch when running. I always have fans pointing at my laptop and my satellite modem.

Vermin

I am constantly digging crushed jing-joks (lizards) out of my printer. Being a writer in Thailand isn't as glamorous as it appears! I also have a large colony of flying insects inside my loudspeakers. Covering electrics with a bug proof cover of some kind may help.

Driving In Thailand

If you drive or own a vehicle, you must get a Thai driving license. Your driving license from your home country or an international driving license is only valid in Thailand for three months from entry into the kingdom.

If you live in Thailand and drive without a Thai license, your insurance will most likely be invalid in case of a claim, and the police may fine you.

Getting a Thai driving license requires the following:

- International driving license (unless you plan to take a driving test).
- Passport with a non-immigrant visa.
- Passport photo (2.5 cm).
- Medical certificate from any small clinic (costs about 100 baht).
- Letter from Immigration confirming your address in the area. You will need to show Immigration your rental agreement or house registration book.
- 105 baht for a car license or 55 baht for a motor-bike license.
- Minimum age of 18.

It is best if you already have an International Driving Permit, otherwise you will have to take a written test and a driving test, in your own vehicle. If you do not have an international license, a driving license from your home country may be acceptable.

Your first license will be valid for one year. After the first year, you will be entitled to a license for five years.

Concerns About Retiring In Thailand

Many people who come to Thailand have an adventurous spirit and have often traveled widely already. Many, like me, love Thailand and the Thai people and want to spend the rest of our days here. As we get older, we need more stability in our lives; knowledge that we have sufficient money to live to a reasonable age; good healthcare; and a sustainable lifestyle.

When I ask long-term Thai residents what is their main concern looking to the future, retired in Thailand, the answer is almost always the same: uncertainty.

Thailand has a fairly stable system of government and is reasonably foreigner friendly, offering long-term marriage and retirement visas with relatively few strings attached. However, it hasn't always been that way, and there is no guarantee it will stay that way in the future.

It is always possible Thailand could elect a government that is more hostile to foreigners. Long-term visas could become harder or impossible to get. Any number of things could happen, and as foreigners we have no rights and no voice in the running of the country.

Dying in Thailand

If you plan to spend the rest of your life in Thailand, that inevitably means you plan to die here. You should tell your spouse or a close friend what should happen to your body when you die. Some health insurance plans include repatriation of remains. In Thailand, the dead are usually cremated at the local *wat*. A death must be reported to your embassy, so make sure somebody close to you knows where to contact.

Last Will And Testament

It is important that you have a last will and testament written in both English and Thai and notarized, usually by a lawyer. If you do not have a will, your assets in your home country will likely not be accessible to your Thai family, and your assets in Thailand may not be available to your family back home, especially if you have land and a house in the name of a company.

For more information on legal matters see Paiboon Publishing's book Thai Law for Foreigners.

Healthcare In Thailand

Clinics, Doctors' Offices, And Polyclinics

Most minor ailments can be treated at a local clinic, doctors' office, or polyclinic. The latter offer a full range of services, including laboratory facilities and tests. The doctor's fee will usually be around 100-200 baht, and the total bill, including medication may be no more than 500 baht. Most towns, some villages, and all cities will provide a good selection of general practitioners.

Many towns and cities will also have a number of specialists in fields such as dermatology; obstetrics and gynecology; ear, nose and throat.

In parts of the country with a large foreign population, you will typically not have any problem speaking English to a doctor. In more remote locations, you may want the help of a Thai friend if your Thai isn't good enough to describe your symptoms and understand the treatment.

Hospitals

For major illnesses and serious accidents, you can visit either a private or a government hospital. Private and government hospitals are available in every major city in Thailand, but tertiary care (cancer care, neurosurgery, organ transplant, for example) may only be available in Bangkok, Chiang Mai (Chiang Mai University Hospital), and in Songkhla (Prince of Songkhla University hospital).

Most hospitals offer a walk-in service, where you can see a general practitioner or a specialist with or without an appointment. Hospital outpatient visits may cost a little more than clinics. Many hospitals offer a 24-hour emergency service.

Private Hospitals

With over 400 private hospitals—including many internationally accredited hospitals such as Bumrungrad, Bangkok Hospital, Samitivej, Lanna Hospital Chiang Mai, Bangkok Phuket Hospital, and many others—Thailand is recognized as one of the leading centers for medical tourism in the world. In 2005, nearly 1.3 million foreigners came to Thailand for medical treatment, with over 400,000 treated at Bumrungrad Hospital in Bangkok alone.

The reasons why so many foreigners seek medical treatment in Thailand are simple: world-class medical facilities and treatment at a fraction of that in the West.

All this bodes well for people considering retirement in Thailand; all the benefits of the medical tourists with the advantage of easy availability of follow-up care and without the 20-hour flight home while still recovering.

Bangkok, Chiang Mai, Pattaya, Phuket, Koh Samui, and other places have multiple competing international hospitals with Western-trained doctors and foreigner-friendly staff and services. International hospitals have state-of-the-art facilities and equipment and almost no waiting for appointments. The quality of care is comparable to the US, Europe, and Australia.

In addition to the well-known international hospitals, every major city and nearly every big town has a good choice of private and government hospitals. The doctors who work in the fancy international hospitals also work in other private and government hospitals; the latter charging far less than the former, but without café latte in the lobby!

Most private hospitals will want to verify that you have the means to pay the bill before admitting you. If they are unable to verify this, they may send you to a public hospital. Public hospitals are not free, even for Thais' (unless covered by social security), but will usually treat first and ask for money later in an emergency.

Public (Government) Hospitals

Public hospitals tend to be overcrowded and often a little run-down, but may be a good choice if you are on a limited budget or without medical insurance. These hospitals should not automatically be considered inferior to private hospitals. Often, the same doctors work in both the private and public sectors, and some of the government hospitals are as well, or better, equipped than private ones.

Thai hospitals will generally take any patients, Thai or not. There is a patients' bill of rights in Thailand, enacted April 16, 1998, which states, among other things, that a patient is entitled to receive full medical services regardless of status, race, nationality, religion, social standing, political affiliation, sex, age, and the nature of the illness. In government hospitals you may not find that all the doctors and nurses speak perfect English.

An acquaintance of mine has anemia and occasionally requires a total blood transfusion. The cost in Bangkok Pattaya Hospital for this treatment is about 50,000 baht; very reasonable by US standards. However, this man does not have insurance and lives on a limited budget. He was able to get the same treatment at Queen Sirikit Navy Hospital in Sattahip, Chonburi for a staggeringly cheap 2,000 baht!

Another friend recently had a hernia operation. The price quote from Taksin Hospital, a large private hospital in Surat Thani, was 54,000 baht for the surgeon's fee and 10,500 baht per night for the room. Uninsured and on a limited budget, he opted for the government hospital in Nathon, Koh Samui. The surgeon's fee was 16,000 baht and he paid 1,500 baht per night for an equivalent room to Taksin, but with a sea view. The operation went well, but the patient was unhappy with the follow-up care. He had a secondary infection, and when he went back to the hospital, the doctor was uninterested in his condition, prescribed some antibiotics, and sent him away without an explanation of what to do next.

If admitted to a private hospital, you will typically get a private, air-conditioned room with TV, video, and refrigerator. The room will likely have an extra bed, as it is normal in Thailand for a family member to stay with the patient for their entire stay. Similar facilities may be available in public hospitals, but you will have to pay extra. Some hospitals do not provide any food service, so it is sometimes necessary to have someone accompany the patient throughout their stay.

Patient Records
Following any significant medical diagnosis or treatment, you should request copies of your medical records in Thai and English together with X-rays and other diagnostic information. This may be necessary for insurance claims and future reference.

Emergency Services

Emergency ambulance services differ from those found in most Western countries. All hospitals have ambulances, but they are mostly used to transfer patients in advance. Emergency numbers are only useful if you can speak Thai. If you need help, contact the Tourist Police.

In the event of an accident, an ambulance is not always called. In many cases, a passing motorist or taxi will take the injured to hospital.

In Bangkok and some other places, charity foundations operate pick-up-truck crews who race each other to the scenes of accidents and emergencies. They have a dubious reputation (somewhat improved in recent years) and their staff are not always well trained. They have been known to do more harm than good to accident victims.

If you have insurance, you should carry your insurance card at all times. If not, carrying a major credit card should ensure some level of treatment.

Medevac

If you live outside of a big city, some emergency and serious conditions may require medical evacuation (medevac). If a significant distance is involved, you may require air transportation. This can be arranged by most hospitals or insurance companies. (Note: the insurance company will want to make arrangements if it is liable for covering the cost.)

If the patient is conscious, a commercial flight may be possible, usually accompanied by a nurse or paramedic. If the patient is unconscious, a charter air ambulance may be required together with a doctor, nurse, and aid. This typically costs about 300,000 baht within Thailand; much more for international flights.

Quality Of Medical Services In Thailand

Most long-term expats in Thailand consider the standard of care in Thailand comparable and in some ways better than that available in their home country. Many doctors, especially those working at private hospitals, received at least part of their training in the West. Larger hospitals, particularly those that cater to medical tourism, are as well equipped as their US or European counterparts.

However, the comment I hear over and over again from foreigners living in Thailand is the convenience and availability, and of course low cost, of medical care in Thailand.

Waiting times to see a doctor are often minutes versus hours. X-rays, blood work, and other lab-test results are often available within an hour. Appointments for outpatient treatment or even major operations are usually available within days, versus weeks or months in the West. You can make an appointment to see a specialist without a time-wasting and expensive referral. Rooms are comfortable and so affordable that patients tend to stay longer in hospital under the supervision of trained staff rather than discharge themselves early to save money.

However, there are some significant differences in the way doctors in Thailand work versus their Western counterparts. Doctors in Thailand, especially surgeons and senior consultants, are considered just a few steps below royalty by their Thai patients. Doctors are not used to being questioned or even asked for information by their patients, and are almost never criticized or second-guessed. As a result, your doctor may feel defensive if probed for a detailed explanation of your condition, and might be reluctant to discuss alternate treatment options. If in doubt, seek a second opinion by yourself.

Thai patients usually consider receiving medication a necessary part of any visit to a doctor, regardless of the condition. As a result, Thai doctors are enthusiastic about prescribing medication. Over-prescribing is a problem not just in Thailand, but in many other Asian countries, and also in the West.

Testimonials On Healthcare In Thailand

Dominic Taylor, Chumphon

"On May 6, my wife went to an expensive hospital in Chumphon to give birth. The baby was born, but with severe complications. When I eventually found a doctor who could speak some English, he told me my son was being transferred to the local government hospital for observation, as they did not have the facilities to do anything, but not to worry as it was a routine matter.

"I presented myself at the government hospital to be told my baby was very ill and they would do all they could. They allowed me into the ICU and I could see he was being taken care of very well.

"The following day, the doctor at the expensive place told my wife he had been to visit our son, not to worry, and I was making a big deal over nothing. This continued for three days, when I was called back to the government hospital.

"The doctor I met there was a true professional. She took me to a side room and explained [in superb English] that my son would be dead within 24 hours. She had plenty of time to answer questions. I had suspected this outcome and, quite frankly, the other staff had already tried to prepare for the worst. My son died the same day.

"The point I am making is be very careful which hospital you choose. Price does not always reflect quality. I would not wish what happened to us on my worst enemy. Be careful.

"Thanks for the wonderful care and support we received from those amazing doctors and nurses at the government hospital. Money is the last thing on my mind at this time, but I leave the reader with this: the expensive private hospital still charged me 30,000 baht; the government hospital was free."

Jon S., Bangkok, 2004

"I had been suffering back pain for several years. It had progressively become worse. I visited a doctor in Bumrungrad Hospital, Bangkok for the first time in September 2002. Bumrungrad is one of the best hospitals in Thailand. Although relatively expensive for Thais, it is comparatively cheap for Westerners.

"I arrived at the hospital without an appointment. I saw a doctor within 45 minutes. He sent me for X-rays—a nurse escorts you to the X-ray department. I waited 25 minutes, had the X-rays, and then returned to the doctor. He reviewed these and said they were indicative of a disc problem, but to make certain it would be better to have an MRI scan. This was booked for the following evening. They took me down to the MRI machine to see it in operation. Apparently, many patients get claustrophobic inside, and they want to see what you think; you can ask to be sedated.

"I arrived the next evening half an hour before the appointment. You get changed and wait. You are taken into the MRI room and laid onto a sliding bed. Earphones with music are put on you, and you are given a panic button. The bed slides into the machine. It is very claustrophobic. If you press the button, they pull you out. You are in the machine for 30-45 minutes.

"I came the next day to see the doctor. The results of an MRI are amazing. It's like a series of photos down through your body, and is understandable even to the untrained. He showed me where my disc had herniated and was pushing out against a nerve. He suggested I try physiotherapy and certain

118

exercises and see how that went. The alternative was surgery, and it seemed premature for that.

"The cost for the X-rays, consultation, and MRI was about 14,000 baht ($350). An MRI scan is 10,080 baht. You can also keep the scans for a second opinion.

"My back does not improve. I am back in March 2004. By now the pain is nearly constant, waking me at night. I am limping; the only relief is to lie down. Back to see the doctor for X-rays and another MRI. We tried two weeks of physiotherapy. They managed to stop the pain for a few minutes at a time. They injected Novocain into my buttock and back of my leg, and that switched the nerve off for about 30 minutes and it was bliss.

"So we were at the point of surgery. I spoke to a doctor friend in the UK and he seemed to confirm their diagnosis. I tried to get some prices out of BUPA, UK. The operation alone would probably be around 8,000 pounds ($14,000) not including tests and aftercare.

"So I took the plunge and signed into Bumrungrad. I had to wait a week to get a bed and the necessary surgeon. I went in on a Friday afternoon. I chose a private room.

"The surgeon and the original doctor visited me and explained what they would be doing. The surgeon spent two years in a Chicago hospital, spoke English very well, and seemed very competent.

"I had the operation in the morning and it took about an hour and 40 minutes. When I came round, I felt rough. I had a morphine drip in my arm and a dispenser in my other hand. I could push the button and it injected more morphine up to a certain level.

"They took me back to my room and eased me into bed. The surgeon visited me in the afternoon and said he felt the operation was a success. He gave me a small bottle with the part of the disc they had removed inside; lovely.

119

"He came the next day and asked me to allow him to lift my leg. I was dubious. Before the operation I could only lift my left leg about nine inches off the bed. He lifted it about two feet and there was no pain. By Sunday I was walking around, and I was discharged on Wednesday.

"The cost? Each physiotherapy session combined with a doctor consultation cost around 2,000 baht. I had about eight of these. The MRI cost 10,080 baht. The X-ray and consultation cost 4,400 baht. The pre-op tests 2,800 baht. The actual operation, room fees, nursing costs, medicine: 155,353 baht. So I make that around 188,633 baht ($4,700).

"So far it's been a complete success. I can only recommend the hospital and the doctors. If anyone out there is suffering like I was, I hope you are as fortunate as I have been."

John Copeland, Las Vegas, Nevada, 2005

"I thought I would share my experiences of medical and dental care in Thailand. I am one of the millions of self-employed, uninsured Americans. I have been having problems with my hip and lower back, and thought that I had a heart attack a few months ago. After spending thousands of dollars on tests with local doctors, a friend who lives in Thailand suggested I go there for a complete examination. I had seen a '60 Minutes' show on Bumrungrad Hospital in Bangkok and decided to go there for additional opinions on my problems.

"It was very impressive. The doctors there were wonderful. The facilities are state-of-the-art, and all for a fraction of the medical and dental cost here. I had the comprehensive check-up and a full orthopedic exam. I also had eye and hearing tests, some skin growths removed and tested.

"I found that for my age (58) I am in pretty good shape. The main cause of my problems was being 20 percent overweight and not getting enough exercise, and my tall frame that puts

120

added stress on my back. They discovered a gallstone during the abdominal ultrasound, and they recommended changing my blood-pressure medicine, which turned out to be a very good change.

"I was so impressed with the fact that I was told I did not need any of the more radical treatments I had considered. I was not pushed into any kind of treatment, which was something I thought might happen. I had been thinking of surgery and angiogram. The doctors instead suggested diet and lifestyle changes.

"After considering my options I elected to have my gall bladder removed there, rather than risk an emergency in the States that would send me to the poor house. I was in for only 48 hours and then back out sightseeing and shopping and walking like nothing had ever happened. It cost $3,400 total, including a beautiful private room with all the amenities. My sister said her laproscopic gall bladder surgery bill to her insurance in Los Angeles was around $30,000 and she ended up having complications. My surgery was problem free.

"I was treated like a VIP. All the various doctors had studied or interned in the States and spoke very good English. They spent so much time with me going over all my tests, I felt they really cared. The technicians all seemed well trained and the nurses and administrators were a different breed from my experiences in the US.

"Dental work is just as good. My teeth have been an embarrassment since I was young. I have had many bottom molars removed over the years. My friend recommended a clinic in Bangkok and I had my teeth fixed while I was there, as well. They did four veneers, four crowns, a root canal, and a full lower partial. The clinic was not only beautiful but had state-of-the-art equipment and was staffed by some of the most considerate, gentle, and caring personnel. My dentist went to school at New York University, spoke perfect English, and really went out of the way for me. All the work came to $2,600 and my teeth now look and feel great.

"I spent around $10,000 for all the medical and dental work, my airfare, three weeks' hotel, great food, entertainment, and lots of shopping. I had a fantastic time. My experiences at Bumrungrad and the dental clinic were everything I could possibly have hoped for. I was very satisfied."

Harry DePietro, Ohio, 2006

"In September 2005, I came to Thailand for the first time because I was dying. I was 50 years old. For several years my memory, strength, and ability to focus on tasks deteriorated insidiously. Eventually, I was awakened in the middle of the night with enough fluid in my lungs to make sleeping and breathing difficult. A trip to the emergency room turned into a stay in hospital which included a cardiac catheterization. That's when I learned the left ventricle of my heart was so weak that my cardiac output was low enough to recommend a heart transplant.

"I didn't want to have a heart transplant. Tests showed that the structure of my heart was in pretty good shape overall. The bad thing was that the muscle of my left ventricle was very weak. Cardiac output is measured in terms of 'ejection fraction.' The left ventricle never pumps out all of its blood. Some blood always remains, and that which is pumped out is represented by the EF. A normal EF is between 50 and 70 percent. At 30 percent, a heart transplant is necessary. Without a transplant, the heart will eventually just fail. According to which test you looked at, my EF was between 15 and 25 percent.

"I have a degree in medico-legal science, and was a paramedic a long time ago. I was acutely aware of the seriousness of my situation. I could barely do anything anymore. I would get out of breath when talking on the telephone for five minutes. I could hardly take my three dogs outside for their breaks. I used to live in Florida, but I got so weak I could no longer function, and returned to Mom's house because I couldn't work.

"When I was so sick that I could no longer even keep up the pretense of working, I applied for public assistance from the Social Security Administration. When I thought about the heart transplant, all I could think about was the statistical length of survival time for transplant recipients, and the increased susceptibility to infection secondary to the lifetime of anti-rejection drugs which would be necessary to survive. At 50, I just didn't think a heart transplant presented me with much of a chance to have a real life.

"While at the Cleveland Clinic, I was put on the 'transplant floor.' A nurse mentioned to me that a doctor at the University of Pittsburgh Medical Center was doing stem cell research and that I might be a good candidate for his research. I found the doctor through the Internet and learned that he had developed an innovative technique to inject stem cells directly into heart muscle while it was beating. No open-heart surgery, since I didn't need any bypasses. That meant a faster recovery.

"I learned that the doctor taught his new technique to the esteemed Kitipan Visudharom, MD, cardiothoracic surgeon and medical director of the Bangkok Heart Hospital at Bangkok General Hospital. I learned that the name of the stem cell company in Bangkok was Theravitae.

"Theravitae developed the process by which stem cells are harvested from the patient's own blood, multiplied in Theravitae's lab, and delivered to the surgeon minutes before the patient's surgery (seven days after the blood was drawn). I was sold on the idea.

123

"I made the trip to Bangkok and arrived late out of Tokyo to meet some wonderfully kind, bleary eyed ladies from Theravitae. They had arranged for my hotel, and took me there and let me know that I would be picked up by a Theravitae driver about four hours later to be transported to the hospital.

"At the hospital, I met another Theravitae staffer who made sure I was comfortable while blood tests were done, my records were reviewed by the surgeons, and we waited until the evening when some of my blood would be drawn for shipment to the Theravitae lab in Israel for processing. Israel! Yes, but very soon, Theravitae will have a new lab in Bangkok.

"The transport of my blood sample, harvesting and multiplying of my own stem cells, and delivery of the stem cell 'product' (now called Vescell, not stem cells) took seven days.

"The stem cells harvested from my blood were transported from the airport while my surgeon waited. I was already prepped and on the operating room. The surgery started at 9 p.m., 19 September 2005. At 9 a.m. the next morning, I was walking the halls of Bangkok Heart Hospital's CCU. I visited another patient who'd had the same surgery the night before. Two days after the surgery, I was transferred to the international ward. The day after that, I was 'good to go' and returned to my hotel.

"The first evening, I walked with Pat (whom I first met online at a Thai dating site, and then met in person during the week I waited for my surgery) about three kilometers down Ratchada Road to a restaurant and back. I had to stop twice because of shortness of breath. The next evening, I stayed in my hotel room and rested. But the evening after that, I went to dinner with both Pat and Aoy (the lovely nurse who originally drew the blood from which my life-saving stem cells were harvested).

"During the next two and a half weeks, I enjoyed the company of Aoy and Pat, and moved out of the hotel and into an apartment. I loved being away from the hotel and in a neighborhood where everything around me was Thai.

"Unfortunately, stem cells do not grow into viable, functioning heart muscle immediately. Six weeks after my surgery, I had an incident in Ohio. A blood clot formed (probably due to the still turbulent blood flow between the two chambers in the left side of my heart) which traveled to my left retinal artery. Consequently I am 90 percent blind in my left eye. Only a little peripheral vision remains.

"Following that episode, echocardiograms were done, which showed that six weeks was too soon to see any improvement in my cardiac output. My EF was still only 25 percent. It would take until the end of December (14 weeks after surgery) to actually see some improvement. According to a cardiac MRI done at the University of Pittsburgh Medical Center at the end of December 2005, my EF went up to 31 percent.

"While the numerical improvement is not staggering and the number is still below the normal range, I feel unbelievably better. I can talk on the phone without getting winded. I can take my dogs out. I've been back to Thailand twice. I can walk whenever and wherever I want, and can out-walk the young CCU nurse who has agreed to marry me next year. I couldn't be happier.

"The stem cell surgery and Theravitae's fantastic technology has given me a new life. Before the surgery, I used to wonder if I would live another week. Now I'm in the midst of wedding arrangements—and future plans include children!

"Will my condition kill me? Maybe. I am not cured of it, nor has the insidious damage done to the various other

125

organs and body tissues during the years of inadequate blood supply been undone. But I'm alive!

"Back in Ohio, I go to a cardiac rehab aerobic exercise program, yoga classes, and I'm learning t'ai chi. I feel stronger and I'm no longer depressed all the time. I believe part of that is because Thailand's medical community and government believes in the ethical use of a patient's own cells to attempt to cure the patient. I think also, that a big part of my recovery is because of Aoy, who loves me and believes in me. Because of her, I plan on being in Bangkok most of the time in the not-too-distant future.

"Do I have hopes and dreams for a future that never existed before I was lucky enough to go to Thailand and get treated in a way that not only could I never have afforded in the United States, but which the laws there will not even permit? You bet. Thank you Thailand!"

Dental Services

Dental services in Thailand in my experience are comparable, or superior, to the USA, at a fraction of the costs (see below for comparison table). I have had bad dental work from America fixed in Thailand. My dentist on Koh Samui was fast, inexpensive, professional, spoke good English, and used modern equipment.

In America, it is quite common to wait weeks for an appointment. Even when the dentist is working on you, he may be working on several other patients at the same time. In Thailand, in my experience, waiting time is usually only a few minutes with an appointment, and maybe 30 minutes without one. The dentist only works on you, so the procedure is fast. Also, the dentist will often perform advanced procedures, such as gum recession, himself rather than send you to a specialist, which is usual in the West.

126

Bangkok, Pattaya, and Phuket boast world-class dental hospitals. Visitors from all over the world come for top-quality care. Cosmetic dental prices are much lower than in most Western countries.

Comparison of dental treatment costs[1]

	Check-Up, X-Ray, Cleaning	Filling	Crown	Implant (Including Crown)
Thailand	400 baht ($10)	800 baht ($20)	8,000 baht ($200)	55,000 baht ($1,375)
USA	$78	$97	$677	$1,250 to $3,000
UK NHS (private, add 70 percent)	$52 ($92)	£50 ($90)	£224 ($400)	£628 ($1,120)

1- prices shown may not be the best available, and this information does not constitute a recommendation

We regularly use the services of the **Dental Hospital** in Sukhumvit Soi 49. This hospital is solely dedicated to dental services. It is located just a few hundred meters before Samitivej Hospital (which might be better known by taxi drivers). Here, you will get a general dental check-up on your first visit. Prices are not low, though certainly cheaper than in the West. Dental cleaning is priced at about 1,200 baht. There is an abundance of various dental specialists, and you could get any necessary dental work done here. Another facility with good services we know about is at the basement of Glasshouse, at the entrance of Sukhumvit Soi 25. The dental departments of the hospitals mentioned also offer good dental services.

Ophthalmic, Optometrists, and Eye Glasses

If you need any eye treatment, we can recommend **Rutnin Eye Hospital,** on Soi Asoke (Sukhumvit 21). It is located on the right side (when you enter Asoke from Sukhumvit) close to Petchaburi Road. A general check-up is not expensive at about 600-700 baht, and includes eyesight measurements, eyeball pressure measurements (necessary on a regular basis after 40 years of age), and examination by an ophthalmologist.

You can have your eyes checked, if you just need new glasses, on almost every street corner in Bangkok. Some optical shops are run by individuals, others are chains such as Top Charoen Optical and Beautiful Optical. In most chains, the personnel—usually attractive young women—will be uniformed. It is always difficult to be sure about the quality of service provided. Staff in the chains are more inclined to sell you their product, but might not always be capable of performing repairs on the spot, since your eyewear will have to be sent to the repair facility and then be sent back. Minor changes, such as changing nosepads, however, are usually done instantly.

Some family shops have been in business for a long time, have good knowledge and experience, and provide good services at very reasonable prices.

You should certainly bargain on the frames. Usually prices can be bargained down by 20-50 percent. Lens prices are more fixed. Nowadays, one only has to wait a few days to get the finished product. Hoya lenses seem to be widely available and are good quality.

Most shops have equipment to measure your eyesight and have lenses made accordingly. However, we prefer to have this done at the Rutnin Eye Hospital, where you get additional examinations and are seen by an ophthalmologist. Our experience is that proper eyesight examination takes some time, and the procedure seems to be done rather quickly in most shops. You can use your prescriptions for glasses from a hospital at any shop, and have your eyewear made accordingly.

You can have laser surgery done at a number of places in Bangkok. There are regular advertisements for this in the newspapers. Personally, we do not really recommend such treatment, since there is always a risk involved, however much this is talked down by both the practitioners and the recipients. Strictly speaking it is seldom medically necessary (that is, it is mostly done for cosmetic reasons and the comfort of not having to wear glasses). We are sure prices are competitive in Thailand. We read on one website that you are advised to moisturize your eyes every 15-30 minutes if you go back home on a plane soon after the surgery due to cabin conditions.

Laser vision correction is one of the most popular reasons medical tourists visit Thailand. Bangkok, Pattaya, and Phuket are home to literally hundreds of Lasik clinics, and most major private hospitals (including Bumrungrad, Bangkok Hospital, and Samitivej) provide Lasik eye surgery.

The cost of Lasik eye surgery is about 35,000 baht ($875) per eye in Thailand versus about $1,800 per eye in the US and £850 ($1,517) in the UK.

Other Medical Services

Chiropractic
There are several chiropractic clinics in Bangkok, mostly staffed by Western doctors (chiropracticthailand.com, clark-chiropractic.com). At Clark Chiropractic, an initial

visit costs 1,800 baht, and a return visit 1,000 baht. This is not a licensed profession in Thailand.

Cosmetic Surgery And Treatments

Thailand is one of the leading world centers for cosmetic surgery. The availability and quality of treatment in Thailand is considered excellent and the prices are reasonable—a big factor, since no insurance policy will cover cosmetic treatments.

Sample price comparison of cosmetic procedures[1]

	Hair Transplant (Per Graft)	Facelift	Eyelid Surgery	Botox
Thailand	100 baht ($2.50)	120,000 baht ($3000)	12,000 baht ($300)	8,000 baht ($200)
USA	$5	$7,300	$4,700	$400
UK	N/A	£5,000 ($9,000)	£3000 ($5,400)	£250 ($450)

1- Prices shown may not be the best available, and this information does not constitute a recommendation.)

Prescription Drugs

People aged 65 and older consume more prescription and over-the-counter medicines than any other age group, according to the US National Institute on Aging. Older people tend to have more long-term, chronic illnesses such as arthritis, diabetes, high blood pressure, and heart disease than do younger people.

Many drugs that are available only by prescription in the West are commonly available in Thailand without prescrip-

130

tion. For harder-to-find prescriptions, you may have to see a specialist doctor in your area, or a hospital pharmacy.

Some drugs are imported into Thailand under license and some manufactured locally. Locally manufactured drugs will be significantly cheaper than imports, but are often not of the same quality.

All pharmacies are required by law to have a licensed pharmacist on staff. However, they may not necessarily be working when you visit, so it pays to ask when the pharmacist will be in. Once you have settled in Thailand, ask the locals for a pharmacist recommendation. There are significant differences between the cost of drugs and quality of service between pharmacies.

Often, the same drugs will have different names, depending upon the suppliers. It is useful to know the generic name of the drug. Most pharmacies and all doctors will have a cross-reference guide, but beware of self medication. If in doubt, consult a doctor.

If you have a prescription-drug plan in your home country, it would be advisable to stock up prior to your trip to Thailand. Please note that importation of medications is prohibited into Thailand—although I assume that those in your personal possession are acceptable. Drugs such as tranquilizers and sedatives are only available in hospital pharmacies.

Medications may be significantly more expensive in a hospital pharmacy than a pharmacy, but the availability of higher quality imported and hard-to-find drugs will likely be better.

If you feel you are paying too much for imported drugs, ask your doctor or the hospital pharmacist if an equivalent Thai version is available. They may simply assume that because you are a foreigner you want the imported drug, when a local one may be just as good.

Doctors in Thailand often have a propensity to over-prescribe medications. The US Food and Drug Administration website includes the following warning:

"When prescribed and taken appropriately, drugs have many benefits: they treat diseases and infections, help manage symptoms of chronic conditions, and can contribute to an improved quality of life. But medicines can also cause problems, and the medical and physical needs of older people can sometimes make being aware of potential problems especially important.

"Of all the problems older people face in taking medication, drug interactions are possibly the most dangerous. When two or more drugs are mixed in the body, they may interact with each other and produce uncomfortable or even dangerous side effects. This is especially a problem for older people because they are much more likely to take more than one drug. The average older person is taking more than four prescription medications at once, plus two OTC medications."

This problem can easily become more severe in Thailand where drugs, normally available only with prescription, are freely available at most pharmacies.

Storage And Expiration Dates

Carefully check expiration dates on drugs, especially if you live in a rural area where stock turnover is low. Also, check the storage requirements. Some drugs should not be stored in warm temperatures; it may be necessary to keep them in a refrigerator. If storage temperature is an issue, you should also check how the pharmacy stores them.

Staying Healthy In Thailand

Thailand is a tropical country, and as such has a few unique medical and environmental issues you should be aware of.

132

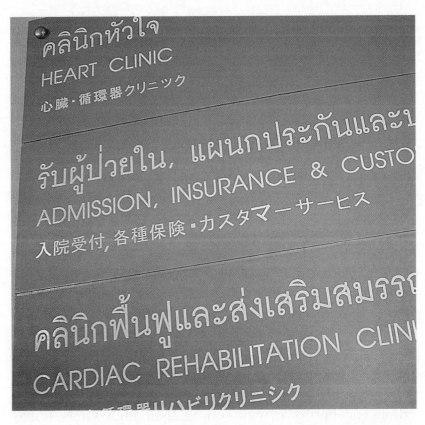

Multi-lingual signs at a major Bangkok hospital

According to Dr. Narong Budhraja, director of Bangkok Hospital, Samui, many foreigners, especially those from cold countries, benefit significantly while living in Thailand. Cold weather aggravates joint and muscle problems. Many patients feel a significant reduction in joint pain and back pain living in a warm climate and swimming in warm water. Hydrotherapy is also very beneficial.

Personally, I am almost never ill since moving to Thailand. Gone are the routine winter colds and seasonal allergies. Also, the air quality where I live is far better than my previous home in the San Francisco Bay Area. I have found it's

133

best to avoid closed, air-conditioned places. I also drink far more water and eat much more fruit than before.

On the two occasions I have had stomach problems in Thailand, I am sure it was from drinking the water from the plastic jug on the table in a small restaurant. I have never had a problem when drinking from a sealed plastic bottle. Never drink tap water in Thailand; use only bottled water.

Accidents (Including Motorcycles)

In many parts of Thailand, motorcycle accidents are the single biggest cause of serious injury. About 25 percent of all patients visiting Bangkok Hospital Samui have been involved in a motorcycle accident. Tourists tend to make up the majority of the victims because they are unfamiliar with Thai roads and driving habits, inexperienced at motorcycle riding, and often drunk. Expats are not immune to accidents, of course. The best defense is to wear a helmet, drive slowly (especially on corners), and always assume everyone else on the road is out to kill you.

In some places, especially tourist resorts, be careful of falling coconuts or mangos, especially in high winds. It may sound like a stupid warning, but a coconut landing on your head from forty feet above can kill you.

Immunizations

The following immunizations may be recommended for adults living in Southeast Asia: immune globulin, tetanus, diphtheria, rabies, influenza, oral typhoid, hepatitis A and B, cholera, meningitis, polio, and Japanese encephalitis. Remember that no vaccine is 100 percent safe or effective.

Blood Transfusions

Blood banks in Thailand screen for hepatitis B and C, syphilis, and HIV. Interestingly, only about 0.3 percent of Thai people have rhesus negative blood, compared to 15 percent of westerners. Contact the Thai Red Cross Society in Bangkok at 02 524-106-9.

Making Your Medical Intentions Known

It is wise to discuss with a relative, friend, or lawyer—or even write down your preferences with regard to medical treatment— what should happen to you in the event of permanent incapacitation. For example, you may not want to be kept alive in the event of brain death or coma, or resuscitated in the event of cardiac arrest. If you are permanently unconscious and a hospital does not have clear instructions on how you wish to be treated, they will contact your embassy who, in turn, will attempt to contract relatives in your home country.

Organ Donations

There is a chronic shortage of transplant organs in Thailand because many Thais believe that if their body is missing a certain part, that same part will be missing in the next life. My wife is adamant she will not donate her organs for this reason.

If you wish to donate your organs upon death, you should carry an organ donor card. It is important to carry the card at all times, since organ harvesting must be done in a timely manner.

Organ donor cards are available at the Organs Donation Center, Thai Red Cross, Henry Dunant Road, Pathumwan, Bangkok 10330.

Comparison Of Healthcare Costs In Thailand And The West[1]

	Basic Check-Up[2]	Diagnostic Coronary Angiogram[3]	Herniorrhaphy[4]	Hip Replacement[5]
Thailand (private hospital)	2,500 baht ($62)	45,000 baht ($1,125)	60,000 baht ($1,500)	400,000 baht ($10,000)
USA	—	$3,000-$5,000	$4,000-$5,500	$35,000
UK (private hospital)	—	£1,000 to £3,160 ($1,785-$5,642) BUPA hospitals	£1,400 to £2,700 ($2,500 - $4,800)	£7,000-£8,900 ($12,500-$15,892) BUPA hospitals

1- Sample medical procedure costs in Thailand, the USA, and the UK. (Note: prices shown may not be the best available and the services may not be equivalent. This information does not constitute a recommendation.)
2- Vitals, X-Ray, Labs
3- Room Charges, Labs, X-Ray, EKG, Medications, Cardiologist Fees
4- One Side
5- Room Charges (5-6 Days), Operating Room And Equipment, Doctors' Fees, Medications, Rehabilitation And Physical Therapy

Besides the obviously lower cost of medical treatments in Thailand, it is interesting that many Thai hospitals publish their prices for popular procedures on the Internet, making it easier for consumers to shop around.

Government hospitals in Thailand typically charge from 20 percent to 50 percent of the private hospital charges listed in the table opposite.

Why Are Medical Costs In Thailand So Low?

Most doctors, nurses, and service staff are paid far less in Thailand than the West, and buildings and facilities are cheaper to construct and maintain. But besides these obvious cost savings, Thailand has other advantage for keeping costs low.

Medical malpractice lawsuits are almost unheard of in Thailand, probably because Thais are less lawsuit-happy than Americans, and Thais do not question their doctor's decisions. I doubt Thai doctors make fewer mistakes.

Facilities and equipment are often used very economically. At Bumrungrad Hospital, consulting rooms are used 16 hours a day, and CT scanners 20 hours a day. Many modern Thai hospitals boast an entirely paperless process through admission, diagnostics, treatment, to billing. Doctors and medical staff can call up test results such as X-rays as soon as they are taken, and the patient's entire history is available on computer.

"Half the patients I treat with artificial disc replacement come from overseas, and especially from North America," said Dr. Wicharn Yingsakmongol, orthopedic surgeon at BNH. "In the US, the disc implant costs about $11,000, and in Europe at least €5,000 (US$6,158), not counting hospital fees and other associated costs. Here it's about $4,000,"

Home Nursing Care

Home nursing is available in Thailand through your local hospital, clinic, or pharmacy. For a registered nurse visit, expect to pay 500 baht or more depending on the type of care required, location, and travel distance. For a nurse aid to stay in your home, expect to pay 8,000 baht per month or more depending on your needs and location. (The average hourly rate for home health aid in the USA is $19 per hour, and in the UK £10 to £25 per hour.)

Nursing Homes

Thailand does not appear to have nursing homes in the sense of Western-style residential homes for older people with on-

137

site nursing care. In Thailand, people stay with their families until they die.

Some developers are considering building retirement resorts, presumably with nursing staff, spas, and golf courses. As older people move to Thailand, this is a natural development, but in all probability will not be cheap.

Some private hospitals may offer long-stay at a reasonable price, but private home care may be a better option for older people who need constant medical and general assistance.

Health Insurance

There are basically four choices for health insurance in Thailand: continue health insurance from your home country; travel insurance; buy health insurance in Thailand; or pay-as-you-go (i.e. no insurance at all).

If you plan to continue health insurance from your home country, check its validity to see whether it's covered after you permanently move to Thailand. Also, check the cost versus a new policy in Thailand. You may find a new policy in Thailand will be cheaper than the existing one in a Western country, particularly America. However, if you want the option of returning home for medical services, a policy in Thailand may not cover it.

Travel insurance may be cheaper for younger people, but may be harder to renew as you get older. Some travel insurance may cover some percentage of treatment costs for pre-existing conditions.

If your insurance company is based outside of Thailand, you will almost certainly have to pay for medical treatment first and get it reimbursed by the company later. This could be a problem if you do not have a large sum of money in Thailand.

There are three main health-insurance companies operating in Thailand: BUPA, AIA, and Thai Health Insurance.

138

Many expats in Thailand self insure; they just pay as they go. If you rarely get sick, this is the lowest cost option, but it leaves you very exposed to major problems if you get seriously ill or are in an accident. Also, some insurance will cover you past 65 or 70 years of age, but only if you have been with them for several years already.

There does not appear to be any family health insurance options in Thailand. Each person in your family will need their own policy. However, some companies will offer a discount if purchasing several policies at the same time.

Health Insurance Companies Operating In Thailand

BUPA

BUPA is an internationally known health insurance provider, operating in Thailand for over 25 years. BUPA offers two packages for individuals and families: *Platinum Care* and *Personal Care.*

Platinum Care covers the cost of inpatient treatment up to 5 million baht per disability. There is no overall annual maximum limit. Personal accident and emergency medical assistance come as standard.

You have three choices of optional outpatient cover up to a maximum of 50,000 baht per year. Maternity care is also optional.

Cover is worldwide except in the USA, where cover is restricted to treatment for injuries resulting from an accident.

Members may join up to and including the age of 65 years only. Renewal is guaranteed up to and including the age of 70 years. However, if you join before the age of 60 years and are continuously insured, renewal is guaranteed for life.

There are three levels of coverage with overall maximums of 1,000,000, 2,000,000, and 5,000,000 baht per disability

Comparison Of Health Insurance Cost In Thailand, the USA, And UK[1]

Country	Plan	Coverage Amount	Annual Cost	Worldwide Coverage
Thailand	BUPA Platinum with outpatient	5,000,000 baht ($125,000) per illness	55,849 baht ($1,400)	Yes, except accident coverage only in USA
Thailand	BUPA Personal Sapphire with outpatient	300,000 baht ($7,500) per illness	10,074 baht ($260)	Yes, except accident coverage only in USA
USA[2]	Healthnet SimpleChoice 4,000 HAS PPO	$6,000,000 lifetime maximum	$2,028	Yes, but may only cover 50 percent for none preferred providers
USA[3]	Blue Cross Individual Select HMO	Unlimited	$4,908	No, only Blue Cross providers
UK	BUPA Select 3 Healthcare Plan	No excess (deductible)	£5,969	
Travel insurance (USA)	MultiNational Underwriters, Inc. Atlas International plan	$100,000	$1,626 (US citizen)	Asia
Travel insurance (UK)[4]	travel-insurance-online.com - AXA insurance UK	£1,000,000	£225 ($401) UK address only	Excludes USA

1- For a 50-year-old male, non smoker, no pre-exiting conditions. Coverage amounts are different because healthcare costs differ from country to country. Where possible the examples attempt to include a similar level of coverage such as inpatient and outpatient coverage and tests such as MRI or CT

2- This plan has a $4,000 deductible, meaning the first $4,000 of medical expense per year is not covered.

3- This plan is a HMO, meaning you are limited to using medical providers in their network only but it has no deductible or co-insurance.

4- The premium is the same up to 65 years old.

(illness). The cost is from 21,005, 22,192, and 25,747 baht per year for a 31-year-old to 46,629, 49,262, and 57,159 baht per year for a 65-year-old for hospitalization coverage only. With outpatient benefits, the cost is about 40 percent higher. Outpatient benefits are from 25,000 to 50,000 baht per year.

Personal Care offers four levels of cover: *Sapphire, Ruby, Emerald*, and *Diamond*.

All plans cover the cost of inpatient treatment and include personal accident. Outpatient and maternity cover is optional. Emergency medical assistance comes as standard with the *Emerald* and *Diamond* plans. Cover is worldwide except in the USA, where cover is restricted to treatment for injuries resulting from an accident.

For the four levels, the overall maximum inpatient benefits are 300,000, 400,000, 500,000, and 600,000 baht per disability. The cost is from 4,423, 7,336, 10,685, and 16,256 baht per year for a 31-year-old to 9,817, 16,284, 23,718, and 35,910 baht per year for a 65-year-old. With outpatient benefits, the cost is about 40 percent higher.

Outpatient benefits are from 400 to 2,500 baht per visit. Expensive tests like MRI and CT are covered by outpatient benefit, so this coverage amount may not be enough.

BUPA will exclude personal accident coverage resulting from bacteria infections, and 50 percent of motorcycle accidents. However, treatment of injuries resulting from these is fully covered up to the limit of the emergency coverage amount.

Several people have reported BUPA's willingness to refuse payment because of what they consider pre-existing conditions. BUPA will consider many conditions that take a long time to develop a pre-existing condition, regardless if it has been diagnosed or not.

'Sojourner' writes: "I would stay away from BUPA. My Thai wife contracted a rather rare affliction called achalasia that comes on very slowly and is hard to diagnose in the early stages.

"We bought BUPA health insurance for ourselves while planning a trip to Italy, as she needed insurance coverage for the trip and my Cobra (US health insurance) was finished anyway.

"About nine months later, the disease took hold and wouldn't allow her to swallow food or water. After the doctor gave her a barium swallow test, she was diagnosed with achalasia.

"When the doctor recommended surgery, we contacted BUPA to let them know she was going under the knife. They kicked it out and refused to cover it because it was a 'pre-existing condition'; their reason being that it takes years for achalasia to become critical and she must have had it before we bought the insurance."

Please contact BUPA for more information.

AIA Thailand
AIA offers three plans: *Plan A*, *Plan B*, and *VIP Plan*. For the three, the total maximum payment per injury or illness is 335,500, 398,750, and 509,750 baht. The premiums for a 47-year-old male are 11,877, 13,667, and 19,788 baht per year; and for a 37-year-old male 13,877, 16,677, and 24,888 baht per year. These plans also cover death benefits up to 375,000, 475,000, and 1,700,000 baht.

AIA differs from most other insurers in that they include life insurance and other benefits as part of the package.

Please contact AIA for more information.

Thai Health Insurance Co. Ltd.
Thai Health Insurance offers 2 plans for individuals: *Simply Healthy* and *Wealthy Healthy*.

Simply Healthy provides inpatient coverage from 100,500 to 335,000 baht per disability, accident benefit of 14,000 to 50,000 baht per incident (50 percent coverage for motorcycle accident), and outpatient benefits of 400 to 1,000 baht per day. The age of the applicant is not over 65, renewable to 70 years. There is no coverage after 70. Coverage is worldwide.

Wealthy Healthy inpatient coverage is from 100,000 to 750,000 baht per disability, accident benefit of 20,000 to 150,000 baht per incident (50 percent coverage for motorcycle accident), and optional outpatient benefits of 400 to 2,000 baht per visit and 4,000 to 20,000 for lab tests.

The age of the applicant is not over 65, with guaranteed renewal to 99 years for coverage over at least ten years. Coverage is worldwide.

Thai Health Insurance Co. Ltd.
123 Ratchadaphisek Road, Bangkok
Tel. (02) 246-9680-2; Fax. (02) 246-9806
http://www.thaihealth.co.th

There are many more plans, and differences between plans. Please review each insurer's information carefully before deciding which plan is right for you. The above is intended only to provide a brief overview of the major features and costs of a few sample plans.

Review Of Health Insurance In Thailand From Thaiwebsites.com
"Before reviewing the health insurance possibilities in Thailand, we need to mention that we come from one of the

smaller European countries, where basically healthcare is socialized. As a result, we are somewhat accustomed to the best healthcare in the world (for the average person) at a low price. Health insurance is obligatory and not for profit, and covers basically the whole lot.

"When moving abroad, this is one of the benefits one loses. Even when keeping the same insurance company as before, the rules change for expatriates. Things become more expensive and complicated, even when you move to a country where health services are cheaper (as in Thailand).

"Recently we were advised about another rather steep increase in our health insurance premium, so we started looking around for coverage in Thailand. Now, of course, health insurance in Thailand is for profit. Furthermore, there are not really a lot of insurance companies catering to the needs of expatriates, so competition between companies is hardly present. The important thing, however, is what they cover. Their prices may be considered high, but still less than what we would pay for our present health insurance.

"We evaluated both BUPA (Thailand) and AIG Insurance (Thailand). The latter was until recently known as Royal and Sun Alliance Insurance (Thailand). BUPA and AIG do not actually directly compete with each other, since their premiums are quite different.

"BUPA's offices are centrally located at Convent Road (off Silom Road).

'As an example, we quote their *Platinum* plan that covers up to 2 million baht per disability for hospitalizations and outpatient benefits up to 50,000 baht total per year. The premium for this coverage is 50,202 baht in the age band of 41 to 45 years of age. If you want coverage for hospitalization only, the premium is much lower at 28,111 baht per year. There are different rates for hospitalization coverage per disability of 1 million and 5 million baht respectively.

"Important remarks and exclusions:

- Coverage is worldwide, but in the United States BUPA will only cover medical expenses which are the result of an accident.
- Annual check-up (one visit per year) covered up to 700 baht; emergency medical assistance fully covered.
- Overall maximum coverage of 2 million baht applies (per disability).
- Pre-existing conditions are *not* covered.
- Not covered (this is not a complete list)—birth control, treatment for infertility, hormone replacement therapy, congenital abnormalities, mental illness and stress-related conditions, dental treatment, sexually transmitted diseases, alcoholism, drug abuse, transplant surgery, renal dialysis, treatment for injuries resulting from dangerous sports (interestingly, not more than 200,000 baht will be paid for injuries occurred while driving a motorcycle or riding pillion).

"Bacterial infections are also not covered according to their leaflets, although we must think this is a mistake in printing or translation from the Thai language.

"AIG's offices are located on New Petchaburi Road. As an example, we take their *Comprehensive* insurance package in the age band of 40 to 44 years. The premium is 59,589 baht per year. With increasing age, rates go up rather steeply (much more than at BUPA). For example between the age of 60 and 64, you would pay 135,897 baht per year.

"This package has a standard excess per medical condition applicable to outpatient claims of 1,800 baht. You have to pay this yourself before coverage starts.

145

"Important remarks and exclusions:
- Overall maximum of coverage is 80 million baht.
- Outpatient treatment is covered up to 340,000 baht (in excess as stated of 1,800 baht per condition).
- Dental treatment covered up to 34,000 baht (but the insured has to pay 25 percent of the costs incurred per claim).
- Medical check-up covered up to 10,200 baht.
- Chronic medical conditions covered up to 34,000 baht per year.
- Organ transplants covered up to 13,600,000 baht.
- Nursing at home covered up to 170,000 baht.
- Emergency evacuation and repatriation covered in full.
- Emergency medical treatment outside covered up to 2,040,000 baht.
- Exclusions (this is not a complete list)—pre-existing medical conditions (after two years of continuous insurance, some pre-existing conditions may become eligible again), chronic medical conditions, hormone replacement therapy, congenital abnormalities, kidney dialysis, injuries due to professional sports, sleep apnea, sexually transmitted diseases (including HIV/AIDS).

"What to think of all this? It is clear that neither of the insurance companies mentioned offers complete comprehensive coverage. Admittedly, both follow accepted insurance industry standards. Rather dubious is the exclusion of some diseases by both companies. Striking is the non-coverage of kidney dialysis and sexually transmitted diseases.

146

"The most important issue in practice is the non-coverage of pre-existing medical conditions. If the insured is young, he may be covered for most events that occur afterwards. However, most middle-aged and older people will have a variety of minor and major chronic pre-existing conditions. In other words, their weak body parts have been revealed already.

"Now, before we say anything more, we have to point out that both insurance companies ask you to fill out a form, and will afterwards give you a personalized list of things covered or not-covered. So, to know exactly what will be insured in your particular case, you will have to wait for this evaluation first.

"As an example of a pre-existing condition, we may point out hypertension (high blood pressure). At age 45, about 30-35 percent of people will have developed hypertension (statistics apply to US citizens). If you duly fill out this on your forms, you are surely not covered for treatment of this condition and possibly all related diseases. Now, about 50 percent of all serious life-threatening diseases are somehow related to high blood pressure (like heart diseases, strokes). So, bad luck for you.

"To make this even more striking, neither insurance company asks for a medical check-up prior to admission to their insurance programs. About 30 percent of people that have high blood pressure are not aware of it, and thus are actually covered. Bad luck if you have been looking after your health and are aware of your problems! (Smoking, which is probably as lethal as high blood pressure, does not result in higher premiums or exclusion from insurance at all!)

"The message is clear. If you are young and have no important pre-existing conditions, these insurance companies may consider you. Their premiums and coverage for hospitalization expenses are quite different, so make a choice depending on your financial status and personal preference. Both companies have some variations on the insurance described above available. However, if you have pre-existing conditions, check carefully what they are able to provide to you as health insurance for anything resulting from these conditions.

"If you already have health insurance, you may be better off, for peace of mind, to stick with it as long as you are financially able to do so. Most insurance companies will continue covering you for conditions that arise while you are in their health insurance program.

"Most Europeans do not realize how lucky they are to be able to benefit from not-for-profit health insurance in their countries.

"We certainly do not want to put the insurance companies mentioned into a bad light. The information provided, by necessity, is not complete. If you are looking for health insurance, we strongly advise you to contact the above-mentioned companies yourself, and evaluate their health insurance benefits independently.

Be Prepared For The Worst
The following is quoted from ajarn.com, a website for English teachers in Thailand.

" I've held a Thai health insurance card for around eight years. For seven of those years it remained in some dark compartment of my wallet. I often felt the 8,000-baht annual expense of renewing the card was something I just didn't need to pay, especially when you consider that the policy didn't cover me for outpatient visits (which most hospital visits tend to be) and I was in good health. In fact, other than an eye infection and a minor operation to remove a tiny growth from the back of my neck, I can't think of any other time when I took advantage of

Thailand's medical services. Then I reached my fortieth birthday in April 2004 and it all seemed to go horribly wrong.

"Just four days after I'd blown out the candles, I went to bed before midnight with a strange pain in my side. It was nothing too alarming, but rather like a stitch. I managed to fall asleep. Then at about four in the morning I woke up in agony. The pain from my lower abdomen was excruciating. I paced around the bedroom, willing it to go away. I was about as scared as I've ever been. I had to get to a hospital.

"I threw on some clothes and stumbled the quarter kilometer to Rama 9 Road (pausing several times to throw up on the way). The taxi driver who picked me up realized the gravity of the situation and got me to Samitivej Hospital in Sukhumvit 49 within minutes. Upon reaching the hospital doors, the pain got worse and I literally sprinted up to the duty receptionist, screaming for help. For those who don't know this hospital, it fits easily into the five-star category (in my blind panic it had been the nearest hospital I could think of). The night staff brought a wheelchair and pumped me full of painkillers.

"I was admitted for three days, underwent an emergency operation to remove a kidney stone, and at the end of the ordeal was presented with a bill for 107,000 baht. The insurance company thankfully coughed up almost 95 percent of it. If I had been unsure up to that point that health insurance was all a waste of time, then I had just been given one hell of a wake-up call.

"Health insurance is something you cannot afford to be without! And yet most of the teachers I meet have no cover whatsoever. No pun intended, but without adequate health insurance, you're an accident waiting to happen.

"One name that often crops up in health insurance circles, and the company that many Thai people use, is AIA (American Insurance Association). However, this company

149

specializes in health insurance/life assurance/sick pay/saving plans all rolled into one convenient bundle. As you would expect, the premiums can be a little more costly than your run-of-the-mill health insurance cover.

"My wife has a package with AIA that costs about 40,000 baht a year. That's a fair chunk of change for a teacher earning 25,000-30,000 baht a month. As part of the package, my wife receives about 1,000 baht a day for every day she cannot work through illness, and she gets some kind of financial return every three years and a sizeable return after twenty years.

"There are two miscellaneous points I need to cover before moving on to the topic of why you should choose a more expensive hospital for your treatment. Firstly, a great advantage of the health card is that it works like a credit card. When you check out of a hospital, you simply present your card to the billing department and you leave the hospital to fight the insurance company over the claim. There's none of that fannying around paying the bill from your own pocket and then having the rigmarole of trying to get your money back. The hospital should give you a fully itemized bill that shows what you have to pay and what the insurance company will pay. It's also worth mentioning that checking out of a hospital/settling with the insurance company can take up to a couple of hours. You can sometimes find out that if you feel well enough to leave a hospital after five in the evening, and the insurance company office is closed, you may need to stay an extra night so the claim can be settled during office hours.

"Hospitals do want to know that you have the necessary funds or insurance cover. At Samitivej, when I was writhing in agony on a trolley with three nurses trying to hold me down, one nurse still had the task of gently inquiring if I had a passport (the first step to finding out if I had any money).

"The second important point is the difference between an insurance policy that covers outpatient treatment and a policy that doesn't. You will find with all insurance companies that the premium doubles if you want outpatient cover. And that generally you are covered for something like 20 outpatient visits per year. (If you need to go to hospital twenty times or more a year, then you should seriously think about going home anyway.)

"I've always opted for a card that excludes outpatient treatment (simply because it's half the price). The piddly outpatient visits I can take care of as and when they arise.

"The definition of being 'admitted' to hospital may very from hospital to hospital. Thai Health Insurance (the company I use) considers anything over six hours as 'patient being admitted.' Contrary to misguided belief, you do not need to stay in hospital overnight to be classed as an inpatient.

"There's a school of thought that outpatient treatment in Thailand is ludicrously cheap, but I'm starting to change my opinion on this, certainly as regards the better hospitals like Samitivej. I didn't know until very recently that doctors in private hospitals are allowed to charge patients whatever they like. Talking to admin staff at Samitivej (where I sometimes conduct customer-care training sessions), one of the biggest complaints is the inconsistency of the pricing structure. One week a patient might see Dr Somchai, who charges 300 baht a consultation, whereas next week he pays 500 baht to see Dr. Banharn. The reasoning behind this is simply that Dr. Banharn is older, more experienced, and feels he's probably worth more. Try explaining that in a second language to a customer banging his fist on the desk.

"Private hospitals also make a small fortune on the prescribed medication, sometimes charging patients twenty times more than in a pharmacy. With the doctor's fee and the 'rip-off' prescriptions, at a good private hospital you can expect to pay 1,000 baht for a five-minute chat with the doc and a bag of pills.

"So what about the hospitals themselves? There are five-star private hospitals and there are private hospitals barely a step above a Thai government clinic. I've had treatment in both kinds and I would opt for the five-star every time. Why? The key word is dignity. Cheaper private hospitals are cheap for a reason. They will still make you better, but they have fewer staff and less equipment. These shortcomings are often ruthlessly exposed on your path to wellness. Going for an X-ray in a lower-class establishment could involve waddling gingerly to the X-ray room in front of dozens of sniggering Thai outpatients. If they're lucky, they might get a flash of bare buttock from under your ill-fitting hospital gown. Dignity. That's what it's all about.

"A final point worth mentioning is pre-existing conditions. Insurance companies will always ask you to fill in an application form that includes a section on pre-existing or past health problems. Obviously there is a temptation to be 'economical' with the truth, but this is something you should not do. Hospitals and insurance companies sometimes find these things out, and when they do, they will terminate your policy in a heartbeat. Generally, it pays to stick with the same hospital for all your treatment. I was told that in the case of my kidney problem, the insurance company wouldn't hesitate to pay for further treatment of kidney stones provided that three months had elapsed between the hospitalization.

"So, to summarize, health insurance is certainly a very wise idea. If peace of mind is the only thing you are buying, then it has to be well worth it."

Shortcomings Of
The Healthcare System In Thailand
The following is quoted with permission from http://www. thaiwebsites.com/healthcare.asp.

There Is No Established Primary Healthcare System
Doctors in Thailand are mostly specialists. So you will not find a good, reliable, all-round physician at the corner of your street for your minor ailments. As a foreigner, you will have to visit a general hospital, where you most likely will be examined by a doctor specialized in one field or another. Since we usually have different medical problems that might interact, this is not always easy for a specialist to handle. For example, it is better to see a gastroenterologist rather than ask your cardiac surgeon about stomach aches.

The best way to go if your ailment is not quite clear, is to ask a general medicine (internist) for an evaluation, and take it from there.

Most Thai Doctors Working
In Hospitals Do Not Do So Full-Time
Physicians and surgeons have working schedules in different hospitals all over Bangkok and go from one place to another to do their clinics and perform medical procedures (like surgery). Besides working in hospitals, they are also likely to have a private clinic somewhere. They work long hours, often in the evening, and spend time traveling by car, we can presume.

One can imagine the complications this can create. Suppose you had some surgery done in hospital A, and some problem turns up after surgery. Well, your surgeon might be working in another hospital, or stuck in traffic, trying to solve your problem on the mobile phone, communicating with the nursing staff.

Another result is that you will not see your doctor that often while you stay in the hospital, and he or she will turn up at unusual hours, after doing his clinics (at various other places).

There Are No Adequate Emergency Transport Facilities
Very few hospitals run a good emergency service. You will have to get to the emergency room by yourself. If you have a heart attack, well, good luck. If it happens during the day time, you will spend a lot of time in traffic. Thai drivers do not give way to ambulances. There is certainly no established emergency transportation system in Bangkok, where the ambulance will bring you to the nearest suitable hospital.
For some ailments, urgent treatment is essential for long-term benefits. In a heart attack, treatment given within minutes or the first hour may save your life, or allow you to lead a normal life afterwards, as compared to death and disability. Those at risk of medical emergency should try to live close to a suitable hospital.

Paying The Bill
Most Westerners will have medical insurance, or will be assumed to have insurance. Still, you'd better have cash or a credit card ready. In case of admission to hospital, you will be asked to pay up front for your treatment. We have read stories in Thai newspapers of injured and sick Thais being turned down upon arriving at a private hospital because they cannot show the money—only to get into trouble on their way to a government hospital. This is a major ethical flaw in the healthcare system in Thailand. Although admission and general treatment in the hospitals is otherwise quite pleasant, asking for money up front is inappropriate and impolite to say the least.

154

Language Issues

While some of the well-known hospitals have a policy of catering to foreigners, and Thailand is promoting itself as a place to go for reasonably priced medical treatment, language remains an important issue. Although in the cities most nurses have good to excellent English, many provincial and village nurses have only a basic English ability. Even communicating with doctors can be a drag. They are busy and do not often take a lot of time to have a chat with their patients—even in Thai. If you go to hospital for a problem that does not require a lot of explanation, it doesn't matter that much, but if you need medical support during a prolonged stay, being unable to express yourself—and be understood—is a significant problem.

Pitfalls Of Being Assertive

There are some pitfalls in being assertive and expressing your opinions and disagreements with doctors and nursing staff at Thai hospitals. Thais are not assertive and will defer to almost anything a doctor says. As a foreigner, Thai hospital staff may defer to you in much the same way; they may take your objections and opinions too much into account. (I doubt Thai doctors behave the same way with Thai patients.) If you do not want a certain medicine for whatever reason, well, they will not give it to you. You can almost bargain the whole time how you want to be treated. But this attitude is not always beneficial to the patient. What it means is that staff at Thai hospitals just give in to your wishes, just because you are a foreigner, and they apparently want to please you this way. Medically speaking, this is not always optimal.

You may not see the doctor as often as in Europe or the US, but the nursing staff give you ample attention, so much so that it might be difficult to get a good sleep because they seem to turn up around the clock to check on your condition.

155

Buying And Leasing Land And Building A House

There are several options available for accommodation depending on the area of the country.

Condominiums And Apartments

In Bangkok, Pattaya, Phuket, and other places with large foreign populations, you will find many condominiums and apartments for sale, lease, and rent. Condominiums and apartments usually offer the convenience of a modern building in close proximity to shopping and services, often with a swimming pool and maintained grounds. Maid services may be provided.

Condos in Bangkok, Jomtien Beach, Pattaya, or Phuket typically rent for about 10 to 40,000 baht per month, or about 300 to 600 baht per square meter.

Houses

If you want more private space, or you live outside a city, you can buy or lease a house. Costs vary dramatically based on size, condition, and location. A simple one-bedroom house, up to about 500 square meters with basic Thai-style bathroom and kitchen would typically start at about 4,000 baht per month in an upcountry village or small town.

A larger house, up to about 100 square meters with simple Western bathroom and kitchen, starts at about 10,000 baht per month.

For a larger, nicely appointed modern house with three bedrooms and bathrooms, expect to pay 16,000 baht per month or as much as 40,000-60,000 baht per month in popular locations and big cities such as Bangkok, Pattaya, or Phuket.

หนังสือสัญญาเช่าบ้าน, เช่าตึกแถว

เขียนที่...
          เมื่อวันที่................เดือน.................................พ.ศ................

       โดยหนังสือฉบับนี้ ข้าพเจ้า...อายุ...........ปี
อยู่บ้านเลขที่...........หมู่ที่..........ถนน.................ตรอก/ซอย.............ตำบล...........
อำเภอ.................จังหวัด.............ซึ่งต่อไปในสัญญานี้เรียกว่า "ผู้ให้เช่า" ฝ่ายหนึ่ง
กับข้าพเจ้า..อายุ...........ปี
อยู่บ้านเลขที่...........หมู่ที่..........ถนน.................ตรอก/ซอย.............ตำบล...........
อำเภอ.................จังหวัด.............ถือบัตรประชาชนเลขที่.................................
ออกให้โดยที่ว่าการอำเภอ..............เมื่อวันที่............เดือน.................พ.ศ.............
ซึ่งต่อไปในสัญญานี้เรียกว่า "ผู้เช่า" อีกฝ่ายหนึ่ง ทั้งสองฝ่ายตกลงทำสัญญากันมีข้อความต่อไปนี้คือ

    ข้อ 1. ผู้ให้เช่าตกลงให้เช่าและผู้เช่าตกลงเช่าบ้าน,ตึกแถวเลขที่...............หมู่ที่..............
ถนน.................ตำบล...............อำเภอ.................จังหวัด..............
มีกำหนดเวลาเช่า...........ปี เริ่มตั้งแต่วันที่..............เดือน...................พ.ศ.............
ครบกำหนดเช่าวันที่..........เดือน..................พ.ศ.............

    ข้อ 2. ผู้เช่าตกลงให้ค่าเช่าเป็นรายเดือน ๆ ละ.................บาท (..................)
มีกำหนดชำระเงินค่าเช่าทุกวันที่............ของทุก ๆ เดือน หากผู้เช่าไม่ชำระตามกำหนดยอมให้ผู้ให้
เช่ายึดทรัพย์สินและใส่กุญแจห้องของผู้เช่าได้

    ข้อ 3. ค่าภาษีโรงเรือนและที่ดิน ทั้งสองฝ่ายตกลงให้.......................เป็นผู้เสีย

    ข้อ 4. ผู้เช่าได้ตรวจดูบ้าน,ตึกแถวที่เช่าแล้ว เห็นว่าทุกสิ่งอยู่ในสภาพเรียบร้อยใช้การได้
อย่างสมบูรณ์จะดูแลมีให้ชำรุดทรุดโทรม และจะบำรุงรักษาให้อยู่ในสภาพดี พร้อมที่จะส่งมอบคืน
ตามสภาพเดิมทุกประการ และตกลงยอมให้ผู้ให้เช่าหรือตัวแทน เข้าตรวจดูบ้าน,ตึกแถวที่เช่าได้ทุกเวลา
ภายหลังที่ได้แจ้งความประสงค์ให้ผู้เช่าทราบแล้ว ถ้าผู้เช่าต้องออกไปจากบ้าน,ตึกแถวที่เช่าไม่ว่ากรณีใด ๆ
ผู้เช่าจะเรียกร้องค่าเสียหายและ/หรือค่าขนย้ายจากผู้ให้เช่ามิได้

    ข้อ 5. ผู้เช่าไม่มีสิทธินำบ้าน,ตึกแถวที่ออกให้ผู้อื่นเช่าช่วง หรือทำนิติกรรมใด ๆ กับผู้อื่น
ในอันที่จะเป็นผลก่อให้เกิดความผูกพันในบ้าน,ตึกแถวที่เช่า ไม่ว่าโดยตรงหรือโดยปริยาย และจะไม่ทำ
การดัดแปลงหรือต่อเติมบ้าน,ตึกแถวที่เช่าไม่ว่าทั้งหมดหรือบางส่วน เว้นแต่จะได้รับความยินยอมเป็นหนังสือ
จากผู้ให้เช่า และหากผู้เช่าได้ทำการดัดแปลงหรือต่อเติมสิ่งใดตามที่ได้รับความยินยอมเมื่อใดแล้ว ผู้เช่า
ยอมยกกรรมสิทธิ์ในทรัพย์สินสิ่งนั้นให้ตกเป็นของผู้ให้เช่านับแต่เมื่อนั้นด้วยทั้งสิ้น

    ข้อ 6. ถ้าเกิดอัคคีภัยขึ้นไม่ว่ากรณีใด ๆ ให้สัญญานี้เป็นอันสิ้นสุดลง

    ข้อ 7. ถ้าผู้ให้เช่าตกลงจะขายบ้าน,ตึกแถวที่เช่าให้แก่ผู้ใดก่อนครบกำหนดการเช่าตามสัญญานี้
ผู้ให้เช่าจะต้องแจ้งให้ผู้เช่าทราบล่วงหน้า เพื่อให้ผู้เช่าเตรียมตัวออกจากบ้าน,ตึกแถวที่เช่าเป็นเวลาไม่
น้อยกว่าสองเดือน และผู้ให้เช่าจะต้องแจ้งให้ผู้เช่าทราบด้วยว่า จะตกลงขายให้แก่ผู้ใด เป็นเงินเท่าใด
เพื่อผู้เช่าได้มีโอกาสตกลงซื้อได้ก่อน ในเมื่อเห็นว่าราคาสมควร

    ข้อ 8. เมื่อผู้เช่ากระทำผิดสัญญาข้อหนึ่งข้อใด ผู้ให้เช่ามีสิทธิบอกเลิกสัญญาได้ทันที และ
ผู้เช่ายอมให้ผู้ให้เช่าทรงไว้ซึ่งสิทธิที่จะเข้ายึดครอบครองสถานที่และสิ่งที่เช่าได้โดยพลัน

    คู่สัญญาได้อ่านและเข้าใจข้อความดีแล้ว จึงลงลายมือชื่อไว้เป็นสำคัญต่อหน้าพยาน

Boilerplate Thai lease form (detail)

157

Buying A Condo Or Villa

Villas close to Jomtien Beach in Pattaya sell for 6 to 20 million baht, or about 15,000-20,000 baht per square meter. Condos in Bangkok, Jomtien Beach, Pattaya, or Phuket typically sell for 1 to 10 million baht, or about 30,000-80,000 baht per square meter.

Be *extremely* careful about buying into places still under construction. In Thailand, building projects are almost never completed on time, if at all, and countless people have lost deposits and more.

Buying Land And Building A House

Should you decide to make Thailand your home for the rest of your life, you may want to purchase land and buy or build a house. The ultimate resource for information about land and housing issues in Thailand is *How To Buy Land And Build A House In Thailand* by Philip Bryce. Here are some highlights of the main points.

Can Foreigners Own Land In Thailand?

This is the first question everyone asks when thinking about building a house in Thailand. The direct answer, unfortunately, is no. But there are ways to legally secure the right to use land and build a house.

Thirty-Year Lease With Option To Extend

The simplest way to 'own' land in Thailand is to buy the land in the name of a Thai citizen and lease it back from them for 30 years with the option to renew. By 'simplest,' I mean cheapest and quickest. The Thai citizen has their name on the title deed for the land, which means *they own the land, not you.* However, at the time of the purchase, you enter into a separate agreement with the new landowner to

158

lease back the land for 30 years with an option to extend for another 30.

Many real-estate companies will attempt to convince you that land can be leased with up to three continuous 30-year leases, for a guaranteed total lease of 90 years. Warning: there is *no* provision in the Civil and Commercial Code for continuous leases.

The least must be renewed after each 30-year period. Section 540 of the Civil and Commercial Code states: "The duration of a hire of immovable property cannot exceed thirty years. If it is made for a longer period, such period shall be reduced to thirty years. The aforesaid period may be renewed, but it must not exceed thirty years from the time of renewal."

Any lease over three years must be registered at the *amphur* and there will be a 1.5 percent fee for registration and stamp duty. Also, the lease value will be considered taxable income of the Thai owner.

The lease agreement can specify any terms you want, such as the lease amount; what happens in the event of your death or the death of the real owner; what happens if you want to sell the property. Your lawyer should also add that, if the laws change to allow foreign ownership of land, the land title will be transferred to you.

If your relationship with the landowner (often a spouse) becomes uncooperative, you may have problems with the lease extension. Thai courts have found lease extensions to be a legally binding, contractual matter between the parties involved, but you may have to go to court to enforce the contract—and Thai courts are not known for their sympathy towards foreigners. The conditions of the lease extension, such as price, taxes, and registration fees, should be specified in the lease contract, but the option to extend the lease cannot be registered at the land office.

The lease will survives the death of the landowner and transfer to their heirs, or transfer of the land ownership to another party, but you may find the new owners uncooperative and unwilling to extend the lease.

Your lease should allow for sub-leasing. If in future, you want to sell, and you don't have the support of the landowner, you can sell a sub-lease on the land, plus the house. However, you will probably not get the same price as if it was freehold land and house.

If your Thai wife is buying the land, you have to sign a document stating that the money did not come from abroad and that the property is the separate property of your wife and that you acknowledge that you have absolutely no rights or interest in the property. This is significant in case of divorce.

Create A Majority-Thai-Owned Company

Another popular way for foreigners to "own" land in the past, was by setting up a majority owned Thai company (usually using nominee shareholders) and buying land in the name of the company. However, in May 2006, the government made it almost impossible for would be home owners to use this method by requiring that all Thai shareholders provide proof of investment and investment experience. Some creative lawyers have found ways to work around the laws and I'm sure if you look hard enough you will find someone to take your money. But beware, most of these schemes are on the gray areas of the law and you could risk losing your land, being fined or even jailed if caught purchasing land illegally

160

Other Land Ownership And Right Of Use Methods

Sit Thi Jap Gin Ta Lord Chiwit

There is a legal mechanism that may allow a foreigner to secure guaranteed access to and use of a piece of land for his or her lifetime.

The Thai legal term '*Sit thi jap gin ta lord chiwit*' is a translation from Roman Law of the term '*Usufruct*' (the right to use and enjoy the profits and advantages of something belonging to another as long as the property is not damaged or altered in any way). It is similar to a lifetime lease. However, some *usufruct* agreements have been appealed by the landowner and, in some cases, the period of the *usufruct* has been reduced to 30 years in line with French Law.

The *usufruct* or *sit thi jap gin ta lord chiwit* is a notation that is added to the land title document together with your name. It costs 75 baht to add this to the land deed or title and must be done at the time of purchase and title transfer. I believe there is a limit of one rai on the size of the land this can apply to, and there may be other restrictions.

This method has the advantage over a lease because it is not limited to 30 years. However, unlike a lease, it cannot be willed or transferred to another party; the benefit dies with you.

Very few people, including Thai lawyers and real-estate professionals, have ever heard of *sit thi jap gin ta lord chiwit*. I suspect that lawyers don't want to know about it because there is no way for them to make money out of it. Check with your lawyer, and if he hasn't heard of it, ask him to research it. It may be a very useful way to secure a lifetime lease without the limits and expense of a lease agreement. This method may have advantages over a lease if you plan to live in Thailand longer than 30 years, plan to keep the land

161

until you die, and are happy to leave everything to your Thai partner and their heirs when you die.

I have heard that not all land offices will register a *sit thi jap gin ta lord chiwit*. You should check with your local land office before you purchase the land.

Long-Term Lease From Current Owner

Many properties are offered on a long-term or 'never ending' lease by the current owner. You would agree upon a price, payable at one-, three- or five-year intervals, or for the duration of the contract, or any other interval. The terms and conditions of the lease are generally open to negotiation with the owner. If you are not paying the full lease amount up front, the contract should specify the periodic payment schedule and amount. If the amount is allowed to change, there should be a formula describing how the change is calculated (i.e. inflation rate plus 2 percent per year, for example).

This method has the advantage that you may not have to commit a large amount of money up front. Also, the transaction is relatively simple. However, any lease over three years must be registered with the *Or-Bor-Tor's* office and tax must be paid on the lease amount. For your protection, you should register the lease with the land office. The land must have a title that allows leasing (i.e. *Nor Sor 3* or *Chanot*).

This may be a good method if you do not want to spend too much money in advance or if you prefer a lease to the company method but you do not want to buy the land in the name of your Thai spouse. But be careful: building a house can cost two or three times the cost of buying land, so do your homework before you commit. Also, you may never be able to liquidate (sell) your investment. You should have the option to sub-lease written into the contract, so if you do want to move on, you can sub-lease the land and sell the house, or rent the land/house as described above.

If you lease land through a broker or real-estate company, they may already have a standard lease contract. You should have your own lawyer check the contract to be sure your rights are protected.

Talk to your lawyer about what would happen if you die, or the landowner dies, and any other risks associated with this method, and write a will coupled with the lease.

Can My Thai Spouse Own Land?

Yes, there was a law prohibiting Thai women married to foreigners from owning land, but that law was revoked in 1999; now any Thai spouse can own land.

If you are already married to a Thai national, and you wish to buy land in the name of your Thai spouse, there is one small detail you should be aware of. Since assets acquired while married are considered the community property of the couple, and since foreigners are not allowed to own land, then technically speaking, the married couple cannot own land in Thailand because it would be partly foreign owned.

However, if you sign a document stating that the money to pay for the land came from your Thai spouse exclusively, and you make no claim on the land, then the Thai spouse can legally own the land. However, this does mean that, in the event of a divorce, you will have no claim to the value of the land when determining community assets.

Taxes And Fees

When transferring land, there will be a 2 percent transfer fee, 1 percent withholding tax and 0.5 percent stamp duty. If the land is being sold by a company or an individual that has owned it for less than five years, there will be business tax of 3.3 percent. Also, company income tax or capital gains tax for individuals must be paid on the profit.

Taxable value for calculating transfer fees is based on the higher of the purchase price or the government valuation. The government valuation can often be significantly higher than the purchase price—and be quite a surprise to the seller and buyer.

You should negotiate with the seller to pay some or all of the costs. If there is back tax owed on the land, it will have to be paid before transfer.

Real-Estate Agents And Fees

In parts of Thailand with a well developed infrastructure for foreigners (Bangkok, Chiang Mai, Pattaya, Koh Samui, Phuket, and other places), you should have no problem finding English-speaking real-estate agents offering land, houses, and legal and building services.

Like in America, the seller usually pays the agents' commission, so the buyer should not be asked to pay agent fees. The usual agent commission is 5 percent, although sellers may have room to negotiate if there is a lot of realtor competition in your area.

Many Thai landowners selling land through an agent for the first time may not fully understand the 5 percent commission idea until they have a buyer. When the agent tells the seller how much the agent fee is, the seller may want to increase the price to cover the 5 percent or try to do a deal with you directly, outside the agent. I would advise against going around the agent, since they have more experience buying and selling land in your corner of the world than you do, and may provide you with valuable protection. It's up to you if you want to accept the price increase, of course, but you may want to offer to cover some of the seller's cost as a gesture of goodwill.

In off-the-beaten-track places, you may find that the lady selling hammocks in the corner shop, who speaks a little

English, knows some people selling land, or some such thing. Be extremely careful in these situations. Have your lawyer check everything before you give any deposits or commit to anything.

There are a number of good Internet resources for classified advertisements for land and houses for sale such as bahtsold.com and cragslist.org. Since there is a very small commission (or none at all) on classified ads, you may be able to get a better deal than through an agent.

However, the best way to find a good deal on land is to ask around, get to know the locals and look for "for sale" notices (usually in Thai) nailed to a tree.

Land Types And Titles

Thai law recognizes two types of land holding. The first is the right of possession (possessory right) which says that land can be used by an individual for its benefit (such as agricultural use) under the Civil and Commercial Code. The second is the right of ownership, where an individual or company holds title deeds and ownership documentation to a piece of land.

Land Sizes And Costs

All land documents refer to lot sizes in *rai*, *ngaan*, and *dtaa-raang waa* and the numbers will be written in Thai.

- A *waa* is 2 meters, a square *waa* (*dtaa-raang waa*) is 4 square meters.
- A *ngaan* is 100 *dtaa-raang waa* or 400 square meters.
- A *rai* is 1,600 square meters. (1 acre is 2.53 rai and 1 hectare is 6.25 *rai*.)

Prices for *Nor Sor 3* and *Chanot* land can range from as low as 20,000 baht per *rai* in remote villages with difficult

165

access to 10,000,000 baht per *rai* and above for beachfront lots in Phuket and Koh Samui. The typical land price in a reasonably popular location with good access is about 1,000,000-2,000,000 baht per *rai*. Lesser land titles would be cheaper, but since they cannot legally be sold, it is somewhat irrelevant.

Designing a house and estimating The Cost Of Building

Before talking to an architect, it is a good idea to firm up your ideas about a house design as much as possible. Look at houses in your area for style ideas and look in home plan books (there are many of them in most Thai bookshops) for layout ideas. Sketch your own design ideas on paper or better yet, pick up a home 3D software designer from Pantip plaza. Don't go with something complicated like Autocad at first unless you are an expert. Use a simple package designed for the home owner. Remember to design for the building site if you already have land. You will need to take slopes, big rocks and other natural features into account.

When designing a house, remember to dimension the rooms and compare them to what you are familiar with to check that the size is comfortable but not crazy big. Once you have a floor plan, you can quickly estimate the cost of the house.

A very rough estimate for total building cost (materials and labor) for 2007 is:

- Very basic (bungalow): concrete on grade or raised wood floor; single-sided cheap wood walls; lightweight grass or asbestos (yes they still use asbestos here) roof—5,000 baht per square meter or less.
- Mid-level (house): concrete floors and walls; nice tile or wood floor covering; hardwood window frames and doors; heavy concrete roof tile; good

166

quality fixtures—10-15,000 baht per square meter or less.

- High-end (luxury villa): quality construction and fixtures; marble, granite, or hardwood floors; glazed roof tile; all the bells and whistles—probably more than 20,000 baht per square meter.
- Swimming pool, about 15-20,000 bath/m2.

These estimated can vary greatly depending on your part of the country and access to your site. If your site is only accessable by 4 wheel drive pickup, you could easily pay 20% more for a house than one with good access.

Builders

When you have the plans ready, you should ask several builders for quotes. If the quote seems reasonable, you will want to do due diligence. Look at other houses he has built, or better yet, is currently building, and if possible find out about the houses he doesn't want you to see.

You should also find out how many projects the guy has on the go, how many people at his disposal, and how often he plans to show up at your site. If he has several ongoing projects, it's likely he will only visit your site for an hour or so per day, so you will be heavily dependent on the quality of the site foreman. It's unlikely you will get to check out the foreman ahead of time, since your builder may not even know who he will use, so you basically have to trust your builder's judgment and team.

Ask if the same foreman is going to stay with your house until it is finished. Depending on your part of the country, the laborers may be migrant workers. Often, when they have enough money, they simply vanish back to the farm for planting or harvest season. Funerals, holidays and other societal events may take days with hangovers following.

If you have a foreman or a key worker you are happy with and you are well into the job, check that he will stay to the end. Maybe offer him a little bonus to stay if necessary. It is quite frustrating to spend a lot of time helping the foreman understand how you want things done, only to find he is leaving and the new guy has no idea what is happening.

If your builder is managing several simultaneous building jobs, that is not necessarily a bad thing. It probably means he has access to a bigger pool of specialists. So you may get one team for foundation and concrete, and another for woodwork. Each team may be more skilled in their own field than the jack-of-all-trades that a smaller operation may have access to. I had different teams for foundation and concrete, walls, wood floor, roof, plumbing, electrical, and finishing work.

You should estimate the labor and materials cost for your house independently of the builder, so you can check and compare the different quotes. You may want to change a few things based on the estimate and/or the quotes. It's always best to change before you start building.

When I was shopping for a builder, I was offered three totally different arrangements, as described below. There may be more. (I use the word 'arrangements' rather than contracts because a contract implies something more concrete than what I was actually offered.)

Deposits

I am personally convinced that many Thai landowners and builders make a good living from collecting deposits from unsuspecting foreigners, or making a quick baht by buying and selling cheap land.

Because much of the land for sale in Thailand is in large lots that require sub-dividing, or because there are right-of-access issues, or for a host of other reasons, you will often find that you cannot simply buy plots of land in Thailand without having to wait a significant amount of time for something to happen.

Usually the landowner will ask you for a deposit before splitting the land, securing access rights, or whatever. This can range from 20,000 baht to 50 percent of the value of the property, or more. You must decide how much you are comfortable giving, based largely on how likely it is you will get that money back if something goes wrong with the deal, and how likely it is the seller may find someone willing to pay more than you.

When paying a deposit, you can be almost 100 percent certain that you will never see that money again. Even if you have an iron-clad contract and are successful in wining a judgment against the deposit holder for breach of contract, there is virtually no chance you will ever get a refund. Where possible, you should get some kind of security for your deposit money.

Pay As You Go

With 'pay as you go,' you pay the wage bill for each worker that works that day, plus the wage for the boss. Typically the men get 130-300 baht per day, the women 120-200 baht, and the boss 300-500 baht or more depending on how experienced he is and how much you think he is worth. In the North and North East rates may be even lower.

You are usually responsible for ordering the materials and paying for them when they arrive. If your materials arrive late and the workers are idle, you still pay the wage bill.

There are some disadvantages to this arrangement. The biggest is that you have no idea how much your house is going to cost until it's finished. The other major problems are that you have to monitor how many people show up every day, or you will likely be paying for no shows, and every time

169

they take another two-hour lunch break you wonder where your money is going.

However, if you have building experience and the time to be involved 8 hours a day, 7 days a week, building like this probably is the only way you will get the house you want at a reasonable price. It's also a great, through often frustrating experience and will definitely be a great way to get to know Thailand and Thai people.

Pay For Labor, Buy Your Own Materials
In this type of arrangement, the builder will usually quote you a labor price for the whole job, which is typically based on the number of square meters and adjusted for the complexity of the design. His price should be fixed, but don't be too surprised if he needs to raise it to finish the job because of some change you made or some unforeseen circumstance. It would be safe to allow a 30 percent margin on top of the quote for what the final labor cost will be.

Often the builder will not include things like electrical, tile, wood finishing, kitchen cabinets, or painting. Everything required to get the house completely finished should be discussed and documented as to whether it's included in the price or not. There is a checklist at the end of this book for the things to ask about.

In this arrangement, as in 'pay as you go,' you are responsible for buying the materials. However, your builder may order some basic materials such as concrete, steel, brick, structural wood, concrete-form wood or plumbing fixtures. You will typically order doors and windows, tile, bathroom and kitchen fixtures, wood floors, and paint. You should determine with your builder who orders what before you start, to avoid confusion and over buying.

In my opinion, this is the best way to build your house. You can make a reasonable estimate as to the cost at the start of the project. If you change your mind during the build

170

and say, change the size, you can easily agree on a new price based on the square meter rate. Also, since you are responsible for buying the materials, you can choose the quality and supplier to suit your own taste. If the builder is buying, as in the next case, you can be sure he will buy the cheapest regardless of quality.

In this arrangement, you may be asked to pay by the week or month, or when a milestone is reached, such as foundation complete, or floor complete. Clearly the milestone method is better for you because if the builder suddenly disappears and never comes back (it happens), at least you have got something for your money.

My builder built about one third of the whole house before he asked me for a single baht. You will probably need to pay something to get started and make frequent progress payments. Be clear about what the payment schedule is. It will probably be written in Thai, so you will want to translate and re-write it in English so that you can rference it easily.

A good rule of thumb is: 25 percent—footings, posts and slab/floor complete; 25 percent—walls and roof complete; 25 percent—doors, windows, floor/wall, stairs, plumbing, electrical complete; 25 percent—house complete and outside cleaned up. You may want to offer a 10-20 percent bonus to finish on time with satisfactory quality.

Builder Does Everything

With this arrangement, the builder will provide labor and materials and will hand over a finished house. You will have to negotiate how 'finished' the house actually is. Things like kitchen fixtures, electrical, and plumbing fixtures, may be extra. You will need to be sure exactly what is included and what is excluded from the contract.

Also, you will need to be specific about the quality and type of material, especially for things like floor tiles and bathroom and kitchen fixtures. You will probably want to

171

select these items yourself, even though the builder will be buying them, so you should work out how much is budgeted for those items in the contract. Your builder may say 'everything grade A, no problem'—but your idea of grade A and his will likely be very different.

This may be your preferred way to build the house if you do not plan to be heavily involved in the process, or if the house is from a standard plan and you can see a similar example already built.

This method has the advantage that you should know exactly how much it's going to cost at the start of the project—but jacking the price up is common.

Contracts And Payments

Your builder may have a building contract that can be modified to fit your situation, or your lawyer can write a contract for you. Many builders prefer not to have any contract at all. You will likely get a better price quote without a contract.

A building contract should specify exactly what is and is not covered by the contract, material quality, approximate time schedule, payment schedule including bonuses or penalties, and guarantees. If the builder provides a contract, have your lawyer check it to make sure your rights are protected.

Check there is a provision for early termination of the contract. In the event that you are not satisfied with the quality or the work, you will want a way out of the contact without having to pay the full amount.

Be very careful about how much money you give before any work is done and materials arrive. Ideally, you will not pay anything until a significant milestone is reached, and the amount you pay is consistent with the value of the work and materials you have acquired.

My builder quit before the house was finished (actually, it was by mutual agreement since I was not satisfied with the quality of the finish). However, I feel I got a fair amount of work for what I paid, which was considerably less than the price had he finished the house.

Builders quitting in the middle of a job is quite common, especially during times where there is a high demand for builders. Many builders, especially in busy housing markets, will demand a large deposit before any work begins. Often, the builders will not start building your house for a long time, maybe never; they will just sit on your deposit.

Your building contract should specify the start and completion date of the project, so if your builder misses the start date, in theory you can get your deposit back. You may have to go to court in such a case, and you would incur legal bills. Even if you win the case, it does not mean the builder will simply pay up. You will likely have to go to the police to seize the builder's assets. The police will charge 10-15 percent for this service. The builder will then probably plead hardship: 'Oh, you can't take my truck, I need that for work. You can't take my house, I need somewhere to live.'

The bottom line is, it may be cheaper to walk away from your deposit and hope for better luck next time!

Do not pay for materials and services until you have received them, and keep contact information of other builders in case you end up needing them to finish your house. Also, remember to get written receipts from the builder to prove you have paid.

The contract should include a warrantee. Often, problems will not become obvious until you have lived in the house for a while. Check that the length of the warrantee covers at least one rainy season, as problems like doors and windows not fitting, and roof leaks will become far more noticeable in wet weather.

Pimai Historical Park, Nakorn Rachasima Province

PART 3
TIPS ON HOW TO LIVE
A SUCCESSFUL RETIRED
LIFE IN THAILAND

Do as much research as possible. There is a lot of information on the Internet. Talk to people who are knowledgeable
about Thailand or retirees who have lived in the country for
a while. The more you know, the better you will be prepared
for the various situations you will encounter. Make sure that
retiring in Thailand is something you want to do and that
you will be happy there before committing to a permanent
move.

General Tips
- Try an extended stay first. Thailand is a charming
  place, but don't fall in love with the country too
  quickly. You should visit as many areas of Thailand as you can and investigate all the important
  areas that concern you. We suggest you rent a
  place at first. Don't rush to buy a home until you
  are satisfied that all your criteria can be met. Your

175

initial impression may change after a trial period. Go for a test drive, kick the tires; see if it's right for you.

- Learn the Thai language and aim for everyday conversational ability. This will provide you with a deeper understanding of Thai life. Outside the cities and tourist areas (even in parts of Bangkok) people only speak Thai. The Thais will appreciate your effort in trying to speak their language. Even though you may not be proficient, they will enjoy hearing you try. It's likely you will hear people complementing you on how well you speak Thai just from the ten phrases you know. Many expats just hang out with their expat friends. They don't cultivate any Thai friends. They don't know how to speak Thai. If your spouse is Thai and doesn't speak your language, you will have to learn his or hers.

- Communicating with your Thai spouse is very important. In order to discuss any issues in depth, you will have to be familiar with their language. Learning Thai can remove a lot of barriers and make your needs more easily understood. It is also the key to making good friends. You will have a more rewarding experience if you can converse with the local people in their language.

- Make friends with Thai people. It's common for retirees to stick together and only associate with their expat friends. But this reduces the chance of experiencing a fuller life with the people around you. At first it may be hard to integrate into Thai society. You will need to understand the language and culture to be comfortable in your surroundings. Having local people as friends will help you a great deal. Good Thai friends can help keep an eye on your property, find a plumber for you when you need one, or help you read documents in Thai.

- You will probably want to make friends with other retirees. If you live in an area where there are many tourists and expats, you shouldn't have any problem. If you have a particular interest, join an expat club or even start one of your own. This will allow you to extend your network of friends and keep up with current events. Retirees who have been in Thailand for a while are usually well informed about ongoing activities and events. They can provide you with suggestions and referrals on many subjects.
- Keep busy and healthy. Thailand is a place we call paradise, where you can participate in many lively leisurely activities such as walking, reading, playing bridge, dancing, taking a cookery course, working out in the gym, or doing volunteer work. Avoid passive leisure activities such as hanging out in bars, watching TV, or gambling.
- Take advantage of Thailand's convenient location as a base for travel to neighboring Laos, Burma, Cambodia, and Vietnam (and other countries in the region).
- Keep in touch with your friends and family back home. If your friends don't know Thailand well, they may be worried about how you live there. It may seem to them that you are too far away and out of touch. While e-mailing is a great way to communicate, calling once in a while makes a big difference. Long-distance and international phone calls are more economical than they used to be.

The Internet now provides much cheaper (even free) telephone options. Invite family and friends to visit you in your new-found home.

- Watch your finances. This is very important. You want to retire happily in the Land of Smiles—but don't squander your money. Although living in Thailand is a bargain for many people, it's quite easy to get carried away by indulging in pleasures that you actually can't afford. There are lots of temptations. If you overspend, you'll soon find out that living in Thailand is just as costly (or even more expensive) than back home.

- Try to be happy in your decision. Work out your purpose or goal and know what your passions are. Try to enjoy what you do. Find things that make you content and have fun doing them. Learn to meditate, dance, involve music in your life, have a relationship, and look for trusted friends. The Thais are an easy-going people and want everyone else to feel the same way; and in the case of retirees, to enjoy being retired in this wonderful country.

Cultural Tips

Knowing the basics of Thai culture is a must for foreigners living in Thailand. Here are just a few tips for you to know to keep you from experiencing an embarrassing situation.

- Train yourself to smile a lot. Don't forget that you are in the Land of Smiles. Thais smile for many reasons. They smile either for amusement, to cover embarrassment, or to say thank you without using words. Knowing when and how to smile gives you a big advantage in Thailand. When you wear a smile, it's easy to make friends. Thais love it—especially a big smile from a foreigner.

- Don't get angry or upset in public. Learn how to control yourself in frustrating situations. In your country, it may be acceptable to yell or express yourself openly. But public displays of anger and

Thailand has thousands of wat *or temple complexes*

shouting in public will not help you get what you want; in fact, the opposite will happen. This kind of behavior is considered extremely impolite. Thais will probably not say anything to you, but they will think you crazy or uncivilized. They will be reluctant to help you, and you will not get your problem solved quickly. *Jai yen*, as the Thais say. 'Keep your cool' and try to deal with things calmly.

179

- Don't look down on the Thais or things Thai. The people are proud of their country, culture, and all Thai things—especially the monarchy. For better or worse, they have been taught that the Thai culture is the best in the world. Many Thais think Thai food is the best and will only eat their own food. They believe in the supernatural and life after death. Don't argue. Just go with the flow, even though you disagree or don't like some aspects of the culture.
- Avoid personal criticism, especially in public or even in a small group of people. Learn about 'saving face.' This is an important issue that you have to get used to. Thai people don't take criticism very well. Even constructive criticism may not be appreciated if it is made directly or in an insensitive manner. You will have to learn how to say things to please the ear of the Thai people. You may have to beat around the bush to convince them to change what they think. You may have to say ten nice things to make a Thai happy before you can even start to give advice.
- Understand these basic Thai values: *karma* (the Buddhist belief that good and bad things happen as a consequence of actions in this life and past lives); *jai yen* (keeping one's cool under stress, being calm for inner peace, and avoiding conflict); *kreng jai* (respect for the feelings of others, having reservation in your own actions so as to not bother other people, not imposing on others); *mai pen rai* (the national catchphrase, which can be translated as 'no problem,' 'never mind,' 'it doesn't matter,' or 'forget it'); *nam jai* (generosity, a desire to give one's time and attention to others).

- These are the important concepts you have to understand. Adapt to them, use them, and your daily encounters with the local people will be happy and harmonious.
- Learn something about Buddhism and what to do and not to do when in a Buddhist temple. More than 90 percent of Thais are Theravada Buddhists. It has a tremendous influence on the Thai way of thinking. Monks are highly respected and you should be respectful (but not necessarily *pay* respect) to them just as everyone else is. Women are not permitted to touch monks or even their robes, and are not permitted to sit next to them on public transport. (We recall an occasion when a female tourist sat next to a monk on a bus. Not realizing her mistake, she sat there oblivious as the other passengers tried to hide their embarrassment; it was the monk who had to get up and move to another seat.) No one is allowed to mistreat or show disrespect to a Buddha image. You should not wear shorts or other skimpy outfits in temples. Avoid sitting cross-legged in front of a monk or Buddha image, or mishandling objects when you make an offering. As a foreigner, you will be excused for not knowing exactly what to do. However, you can avoid any *faux pas'* by observing what the Thais do and imitate them. When in doubt, ask whether it's all right to do certain things. Thais appreciate it when you show that you care by asking first.
- Be careful when you talk to a Thai about politics or the royal family. These are extremely delicate subjects. Unless you have something good to say, *don't* say anything. Some educated Thais may

181

value your opinions or suggestions, but most ordinary Thais won't. They will think 'why is this foreigner telling us what to do' or 'what does he know about Thailand.' Even if you know much more about Thailand than your Thai friends (actually a very common occurrence), just let them be the experts. Don't argue. If you must comment, do it with your expat friends.

- Learn some Thai etiquette. This will come in handy and can get you out of trouble when you are in public. When eating at a restaurant or eating with a Thai family, use a fork and spoon rather than a fork and knife. Thai people cut their

Everyone's favorite: Pad Thai

food with the edge of the spoon rather than with a knife. Watch how Thais eat and copy what you see. Use the fork to put a small amount of food onto your spoon and use the spoon to put it in your mouth. Thais eat family style,' with communal dishes in the middle of the table, each with a serving spoon. Everyone gets their own plate or bowl of rice. When serving yourself from the bowls, put a small amount on your plate at a time. Try to learn to use chopsticks if you don't

182

already know. This will come in handy when you eat in restaurants in Southeast Asia. Never touch a Thai on the head (unless a young child or your close friend or your lover). Do not use your feet to point; and definitely do not put your feet up on desks, on books, rice sacks, or sacred objects. Don't use your fingers to point at people (especially their face). Don't wave your hands about when trying to make yourself understood. These are just the basics. Thai etiquette is different from that in the West, but it's not such a big thing to get used to. Good manners and politeness are, after all, universal qualities.

- Be ready to be part of your Thai family. If you have a Thai loved one and are in a long-term relationship, whether you are married or not, you will have to deal with his or her family. You will go through good and bad experiences with their family—just as you have done with your own. For those who have a Thai lover, we suggest that you read *Thailand Fever*. This book explains the differences between Western and Thai cultures in detail—in both English and Thai. It clearly explains Eastern and Western values, and will help you understand each other. It covers all the important issues regarding Thai-Western relationships like money and trust. Its observations are informative even if you are not in a relationship with a Thai person.

- Thailand is an extremely hierarchical society. As a foreigner (and especially as a Caucasian), you will be accorded special social status. The workings of Thailand's class society are very subtle, but soon enough you will understand how the Thais treat

183

each other according to their rank. Social stature is determined by family (royal, high, famous, or common), wealth (the main criteria now), education (the higher, the more respect, even with lower income), age (the older you are, the higher the status, even for dumb old dudes), and career (a poor civil servant has a more prestigious occupation than a wealthy restaurant owner). Monks are automatically accorded high social status. In Thai society, people with higher social status are expected to do certain things, such as paying the bill in the restaurant. Foreigners are assumed to have money because they can afford to travel to Thailand. Thais will simply assume you are rich. Thus, *farang* equals 'you will have to pay for everything.' This is not a belief held by educated Thais or those who have traveled outside of Thailand.

- Finally, you will have to accept the fact that you will always be regarded as a foreigner for the rest of your life in Thailand—even if you have lived half your life there and you can speak Thai fluently (and more eloquently than some Thais).

Cautionary Tips And Things To Be Aware Of

- *Drugs*: You want to enjoy your retired life in Thailand, so the last thing you want to do is use illegal drugs. Marijuana, heroin, and methamphetamine (yaa baa or 'crazy medicine') are easy to obtain. Penalties for the possession of, use of, or trafficking in illegal drugs in Thailand are severe. If you are prosecuted, you will have to go through the Thai criminal system—which is not fun. Rights that you may take for granted in your country

184

may not exist, or be accorded to you, in Thailand. You get no special rights or privileges as a foreign national. You will struggle to find out what is going on in your case. If you are lucky, officials or interpreters (who don't speak much English), might be able to explain something to you, but don't expect much help. Being in a Thai jail just isn't worth it. Convicted offenders can expect long sentences under harsh conditions (and often a heavy fine). Thailand has the death penalty for serious drug offenses, and has executed convicted traffickers. We strongly advise you against having anything to do with drugs.

- *Drinking*: Alcohol is available everywhere in Thailand and very affordable. The temptation to drink (to excess) is increased by the sheer number of bars and other entertainment venues. Drinking is part of Thai culture—as it is in many countries. If you come from a country that accepts drinking as part of the culture, then Thailand will easily accommodate your habit. Every year, the deaths of several foreigners are reportedly attributed to premature heart attacks after drinking alcohol or using drugs. Try to find healthier pastimes to enjoy yourself while in Thailand.

- *Child Pornography And Sex With Under-Age Children*: Southeast Asian countries are popular destinations for child-sex predators. Recently, the Thai government has enforced laws on this issue and has vigorously prosecuted offenders. Punishment is severe. Those who lure children into prostitution in Thailand now face up to 15 years

185

in jail (previously, they were only fined). Engaging in sexual activities with children or possessing or disseminating child pornography in Thailand is a crime. Convicted offenders will be deported at best. Many Western countries now prosecute their own nationals for sex crimes committed abroad. Don't even think about it!

• *Prostitution*: Along with all the good things Thailand is known for, it is also, unfortunately, famous for sex and prostitution. Prostitution is officially illegal, but the laws are rarely enforced and prostitution is widely tolerated even among older traditional Thais. The number of prostitutes in Thailand, male and female, varies depending on who does the research. However, we can tell you that the number is quite high. Sex is for sale around the clock, and it takes a number of forms. Brothels, massage parlors, karaoke bars, gentlemen's clubs, and hostess bars mainly cater to Thai and Asian customers—at all levels of the economic spectrum. For Western expats and tourists there are beer bars, go-go bars, and gay bars. 'Freelancers' can be found in bars, discos, hotel lobbies, on particular streets, and in some parks. Although the chance is remote indeed, you may be arrested or fined for having sex with a prostitute. Being fined hurts your wallet and cavorting with prostitutes can be dangerous to your health.

• *Health And Disease*: Make sure that you have reliable medical insurance, either in Thailand or your own country. If your medical insurance company is located in your home country, consult with

186

them before your relocation to verify that your policy is valid in Thailand and whether it covers emergency expenses such as surgery or medical evacuation. Even though treatment in Thailand is very affordable, we strongly recommend that you have some kind of medical insurance. HIV, AIDS, and STDs are common among prostitutes of both sexes. Be sure to protect yourself when having sex with anyone. Malaria and food related diseases are also common. Talk to your doctor and check government heath recommendations to find out which vaccinations and other current health precautions you should take. Research food and water safety for the particular area you would like to move to.

- *Love And Infatuation:* We personally know many people that came to Thailand once and went home having found a boyfriend or girlfriend while in the Land of Smiles. A lot of these 'friends' were actually in the sex business. Some of these tourists wanted to move to Thailand right away. Some even sent money to their boyfriend or girlfriend whom they barely knew. Some of them won and some of them lost. We are glad if you realize that Thailand is a wonderful place to live. But we want to warn you not to make a decision on impulse because if you do, you may eventually regret it. Below is instructive advice from an anonymous wise person about love and infatuation to give you a little guidance and help you make a decision.

Infatuation*	Love
Infatuation is instant desire. It is one set of glands calling to another.	Love is a friendship that has caught fire. It takes root and grows, one day at a time.
Infatuation is marked by a feeling of insecurity. You are excited and eager, but not genuinely happy. There are nagging doubts, unanswered questions, little bits and pieces about your beloved that you would just as soon not examine too closely. It might spoil the dream.	Love is real. It gives you strength and grows beyond you. You are warmed by your beloved's presence even when he/she is away. Miles do not separate you. You want him/her nearer, but near or far, you know he/she is yours and you can wait.
Infatuation makes you impatient of the imperfection of the other.	Love is the understanding and mature acceptance of imperfection.
Infatuation says, 'We must get married right away! I can't risk losing you!'	Love says, 'Be patient. Do not rush. Plan your future with confidence.'
Infatuation has an element of sexual excitement. If you are honest, you can admit it is difficult to be in one another's company unless you are sure it will end in intimacy.	Love is the maturation of friendship. You must be friends before you can be lovers.
Infatuation lacks confidence. It brings feelings of jealousy and distrust. When he/she is away, you wonder if he/she is cheating. Sometimes you check.	Love means trust. You are calm, secure, and not threatened. Your beloved feels that also, and that makes them even more trustworthy.

Infatuation might lead you to do things you will regret later, but love never will.	Love is an 'upper.' It makes you look up. It makes you think up. It makes you a better person.
Infatuation stimulates and you are thrilled, but not really happy. It is an instant fire which fades away with time.	Love has a balanced interest in other areas of life besides the relationship. It means a feeling of long-term commitment to the other.

*Permitted for reproduction by http://jmm.aaa.net.au/articles/5223.htm

- *Crime*: Violent crimes against foreigners in Thailand are relatively low. However, less serious crimes such as pick pocketing, purse-snatching, and burglary can be common. Don't carry a lot of cash. Watch your wallet and purse when walking in crowded markets, tourist sites, on buses or at train stations. Thieves can cut into purses or bags with a razor and remove items. Taxis and *tuk-tuks* (three wheeled motored taxis) are pretty safe. Don't get dropped off in a remote or dark area especially when it's late at night. Try to be with somebody when you go to an unfamiliar place. Having a Thai friend with you in the vehicle may ensure additional safety. In Thailand, taxis don't pick up additional passengers, so never take a taxi that already has someone in it. If you are a victim of crime, immediately report it to both the local police and the Tourist Police (who may understand English much better than the regular police) and then contact your nearest consulate or embassy. You can be assisted in finding medical care by the Tourist Police, and in contacting your family and friends by your consulate or embassy staff.

189

- *Tourist Traps*: Thousands of tourists have reported that they have been cheated on purchases of expensive items such as jewelry or antiques. Beware of taxi drivers or overly friendly strangers who offer to take you to a gem store, a hotel or a particular place that has a special deal that day. These people receive commissions from the often inflated sale prices in such venues. Credit card theft is increasing. So only use your credit card at well established businesses.

- *Gambling*: Thais love to gamble. There is legal and illegal gambling everywhere. The government-run lottery is held twice a month. Horse racing is also legal in a number of cities. However, there are many more illegal gambling opportunities all over the country. Thais use any event as an opportunity to bet: the underground lottery, the closing numbers of the New York Stock Exchange or the Thai stock market, football matches (a billion-baht business now), boxing matches, cockfights, fish fights, insect fights, the Olympics, and card games. There are casinos just over the Cambodian and Burmese borders that cater almost exclusively to Thais. Many Thais are victims of gambling. They carry the addiction with them when they move to a different country and end up bankrupt just as they did in Thailand. If your Thai spouse loves to gamble, it's a bad sign for your relationship. You should try to break their habit as soon as possible. Otherwise, you would be better off finding a new mate. Gambling is a bad investment anywhere, and no matter what country you are in, the house always wins. Use your money for more rewarding activities in Thailand.

- **Investments:** If you want to invest in Thailand, do as much research as possible. There are many books and websites that can provide you with information regarding investing in Thailand. The advice we offer is to be very wary of giving money to your Thai friend or spouse to invest. Don't let them talk you into doing something they think will make lots of money without investigating and doing your own homework, and making your own decision. Consider whether they have any experience running the type of business they suggest, and whether the business makes sense, or if the enterprise will make a reasonable profit or not. Your friend/spouse may work very hard to make it and have good intentions, but may not be good at making an actual profit. The money you give to them is free money. It's easy for them to just blow it. This is a common mistake some foreigners make when trying to run a small business with their Thai partner. However, we know of success stories as well. A Canadian friend of ours gave his wife's family just enough money to grow papayas, coconuts, and vegetables. He taught them what to do and oversaw the process. Now the family is generating 30,000 baht (over $700) a month. He doesn't have to keep giving his wife money for her family anymore. In general however, we hear of more financial failures than successes. So don't put your hard-earned retirement money into some hare-brained risky investment. Don't give your money away. Be very careful.

- *Noise Pollution*: In Thailand, if the volume control goes from 1 to 10, most Thais will try to set it at 11 or higher. Thais love making loud noise and don't seem to mind when others do it. Before you rent or buy property, check out the neighborhood. Make sure the place is quiet enough for you to sleep without using earplugs or sleeping pills. Choose a quiet location, unless you don't mind noise. Some of the things that will ruin the peace are: dogs that sleep all day and bark all night; mosquitoes that sing right into your ears (besides leaving red calling cards all over your body); the loudspeakers from mobile vendors' pick-up trucks; meaningless loudspeaker announcements from temples; the *muezzin's* 4 a.m. wake-up calls in Muslim neighborhoods; the loud music from a karaoke bar; or the high-school kids next door. In the city, of course (especially near markets), there's the continual din of traffic and construction sites. Bangkok is one of the—if not *the*—noisiest cities on earth.

- *Customs*: When you bring your belongings into Thailand, you will need to comply with Thai Customs regulations. Items such as firearms, explosives, drugs, radio equipment, books, or other printed material and video or audio recordings which might be considered a threat to national security, or are obscene, or in any way harmful to the public interest could result in a hefty fine and possibly jail time. Please contact the Thai embassy or consulate near you for specific information regarding Customs regulations. If you want to bring a gun into the country you must already have a gun license and you must receive permission beforehand from the Customs Department. Bringing a lot of cash into the country without declaring it may lead to the seizure of that money should you later try to take it out of Thailand.

- *Driving And Road Safety*: Traffic moves on the left in Thailand. Although sometimes you may think that not all Thais are aware of that fact! The road system and traffic safety has improved a great deal in recent years, but the carnage on the roads still takes an appalling toll each year. You will quickly notice that the way people use the road and the road conditions differ significantly from well-ordered Western countries. You often see bicycles, motorcycles, or motorized carts that illegally travel against the traffic flow. Thais routinely risk their lives when they cross a busy street. Thai drivers are almost totally ignorant of pedestrians—who have no rights whatsoever. Many Thais ride their motorcycles on the sidewalk. Many don't bother wearing a helmet, or just put it on loosely so as not to be fined by the traffic police (on the rare occasions when the helmet law is enforced). In this regard you shouldn't do like the Thais. Look carefully before crossing streets. If there is a pedestrian bridge or an underground walkway, always use it instead of playing with the traffic. Motorcycle accidents are all too common in Thailand, and many are deadly. We don't recommend using motorcycles, or motorcycle taxis. The latter are a cheap and fast way to get around, but it's not worth risking your life. Drunk driving is common, especially during

193

major festivals. Death tolls during Songkran (the traditional Thai new year in April) and New Year are a bonanza for funeral parlors. Be on guard during the festivals, whether you're a driver or pedestrian. Many traffic accidents occur at night. On two-lane roads, reckless overtaking of slow-moving trucks causes numerous accidents. Most of the truck drivers are wired on amphetamines. It is a requirement that vehicles are covered by third-party liability insurance for death or injury. But there is no mandatory coverage for property damage. There are thousands of vehicles that are not properly registered, without insurance, and in poor condition. The number of hit-and-run accidents is high. "The driver fled the scene" is a phrase you are guaranteed to read in any newspaper traffic accident report.

- *Traveling In Remote Areas*: You don't have to risk your life to see the beauty of the countryside. Traveling in remote areas should be done with extra caution and preferably only with an experienced local Thai guide. The Burma and Malaysian borders are sites of armed conflicts and robbers, pirates, drug traffickers and smugglers operate along these areas of Thailand's borders.

- *Water Hazards:* During the rainy season, it can be extremely dangerous to swim or surf. Strong currents and mud slides can occur from heavy rains and a tsunami can happen at anytime. Try to avoid going where you won't be aware of a warning or where help is hard to reach. When traveling to an island or on a river, avoid overcrowded boats

194

or ferries and ensure proper safety equipment is available for your use before boarding.

- *Illegal Stay*: You want to retire in Thailand as a legal citizen. We recommend you do not overstay your visa or remain in the country illegally. You should know when your authorized stay expires. Check the conditions of your permit or visa to determine what you have to do to maintain your legal status. Any foreigner who violates the terms and conditions of their visa or work permit and stays in Thailand without having received an official modification or extension will be liable to an immediate cash fine when departing Thailand. If found by the police to be of illegal status (for example, during an Immigration check at a guesthouse, or caught in a criminal act), the offender will be jailed at his or her own expense, fined, and then deported—again, at his or her own expense. The offender may also be barred from re-entering Thailand. Do not use the services of private agencies for visa extension—even those advertising in major newspapers or located close to Immigration offices or police stations. They are illegal. You could be arrested at border crossings when the visas and entry stamps obtained through these services are discovered to be counterfeit.

Young Lisu women at a festival

PART 4
RETIREMENT LOCATIONS

Now let's take a look at some locations in Thailand that might appeal to you. The places listed in this section are more popular among retirees than most other parts of the country. However, there are many other areas in different provinces of Thailand that may be more attractive to you. Your spouse might live in a smaller town and may want you to move there. Well, you should go check it out yourself. You may actually like it more than the places we mention here.

There are some areas in Thailand not discussed here that are home to quite a few retirees. These include: Pai, a unique district in Mae Hong Son province; Nakhon Ratchasima (also known as Korat), which is one of the largest cities in the northeast; Krabi, a beautiful coastal province near Phuket; and many others.

It is our goal to update this book at least every other year. The material in this part of the book will provide you with a guideline only. Please keep in mind that information listed for each location could change, and you need to do your own research as well.

The retirees that we spoke to have been kind enough to provide information on their chosen homes, and their quotes are their own opinions and not necessarily the position of the authors.

Reading what they have to say, you will get a feel for how retirees are experiencing their lives in various areas of the kingdom.

Bangkok

The history of Bangkok, the capital and biggest city in Thailand, dates back to 1782. Today it is a steaming Asian metropolis of over 10 million inhabitants. The city is bisected by the Chao Phraya River. It is the political, administrative, commercial, and cultural capital. It boasts a lively nightlife, fantastic international cuisine, hundreds of clubs and organizations to belong to, and some of the best shopping in the world, with the most incredible malls and markets.

If you can't find what you're looking for in Bangkok, you're unlikely to find it anywhere else in the region.

It's best to pick up a map of the city and explore neighborhood by neighborhood to see which area takes your fancy for living and entertainment.

Why Bangkok?

Pros

- Bangkok is the city that never sleeps; it's where all the action is.
- The cultural Mecca of Thailand; notable events include the Annual International Dance and

198

Music Festival, the International Jazz Festival, two international film festivals, and concerts by big-name international performers.

- With two international airports and one domestic terminal, Bangkok is an important hub for travel throughout Southeast Asia. Here you can find cheap flights to all major cities in Thailand and Asia.
- Numerous transport options link Bangkok with almost every other town and city in the country.
- Exotic Buddhist temples.
- Lush green parks (Lumpini, Sanam Luang, Benjasiri).
- Exciting nightlife, Thai and international cuisine; unlimited options for night owls or the more culturally inclined.
- Unlimited accommodation options from the very basic to the unimaginably luxurious. Whatever living style suits your pocket, Bangkok provides.

Cons
- The city is congested and it's impossible to walk in a straight line anywhere. Broken pavements and street vendors blocking the sidewalk quickly become a real source of irritation.
- Long queues and massive crowds at popular cultural events and during festivals.
- Noise pollution, especially in malls and on the streets, is mind-boggling.
- Air pollution can leave your shirt collar black at the end of a day. The heat and humidity of the hot season can be unbearable.
- Rush-hour traffic can be appalling. In some areas, it's virtually impossible to get a taxi on the

199

last Friday (or the closest day to payday) of the month.
- During cyclical building booms, the city resembles a giant construction site.
- Flooding during the rainy season.

Leisure Activities And Things To Do
- Bangkok hosts international tennis tournaments, the Grand Masters Golf tournament, the Royal Orchid Masters for snooker, and badminton and takraw championships.
- Scores of golf driving ranges within the city, and dozens of courses within an hours' drive.
- Hundreds of clubs, organizations, and social societies for all kinds of interests ranging from chess to racquetball, from the Hash House Harriers to the British Council, Alliance Française and Goethe Institute.
- Archery, shooting, ice-skating, ice hockey, go-karting, and many other 'minority' sports can easily be found. Whatever your sporting interest, you'll probably find it in Bangkok.
- Temples, churches, mosques, and synagogues for spiritual health.
- Endless choices for excellent international dining. You'll find almost every national cuisine under the sun, and unlimited Thai food options from street stalls to very stylish restaurants.
- Music bars and venues for rock, blues, jazz, reggae, folk and country music, and much more.
- Classical music concerts, ballet, and opera,
- Classical Thai theater and dance.
- Numerous art galleries and shops.

- Pulsating nightlife including girlie bars, beer bars, pubs, gay bars, cocktail lounges, hostess clubs, discos, karaoke lounges, dance clubs, and coffee shops.
- Visit the backpacker haven around the Khao San Road area of Banglamphu for cheap travel tickets, CDs, and DVDs.
- Dozens of cinema multiplexes for the latest Hollywood and international films. Smaller cinemas and the British Council, Alliance Française, and Goethe Institut occasionally show art movies (sometimes with waiters serving food and drinks).
- English-language bookstores (both new and used) are found all over Bangkok (Kinokuniya, Bookazine, B2S, Asia Books and others); prices are reasonable and the selection improves all the time. The larger stores also offer international magazines on almost every topic from sailing to computers, from real-estate to car racing.
- Sightseeing at the Grand Palace, Buddhist temples, Jim Thompson's House, Dusit Zoo, Chinatown and Little India. The options in the capital are without limit.
- Trips to the ancient ruins of the old capital, Ayuthaya (an hour from Bangkok), the floating markets, the crocodile farm, or a tour of Bangkok's canals by longtail boat; once again, the number of attractions just outside the city are unlimited.
- Sunset dinner cruises on the Chao Phraya River, or dining at one of the many riverside establishments.

201

- Thailand has two English-language national news-papers—The Nation and the Bangkok Post. There are also a host of monthly listings and features magazines like Metro that provide full details of events in Bangkok, directories of entertainment, real estate, and classified sections.
- Thousands more ideas besides the list above.

Shopping

- Some of the most modern shopping malls in the world are found in Bangkok: Siam Paragon, Siam Center, the World Trade Center, Emporium, Central (various locations), The Mall, MBK, Tokyu, Sogo, and countless others. These huge, air-conditioned complexes are found all over the city. All have fancy department stores, most have cinema complexes, and some offer a host of other activities including amusement parks and even aquariums.

One of the numerous modern shopping malls in Bangkok

- Specialty supermarkets catering to expat tastes include outlets of Villa, Foodland, Tops, Big C, Carrefour, and Tesco Lotus. All over the city there are dozens of giant superstores (Big C, Tesco Lotus, and Carrefour are the three biggest chains).
- All kinds of markets (day and night) cater to locals and specialty needs.
- The weekend Chatuchak Market, near the Mor Chit 'skytrain' station, is the biggest market in the country. It is impossible to see everything in this gargantuan place in one day. The market is vast and fascinating, and is surrounded by 'satellite' market areas. Clothing, crafts, domestic goods, and food, are the main items on offer, but these are only the tip of the gigantic ice-berg. It is hot and crowded (95 percent of visitors are Thais) but an absolutely unforgettable experience. Take your time and visit over a period of weekends to get the full picture. Buy a copy of Nancy Chandler's map, which covers the entire market.
- A host of smaller malls, department stores, and specialty stores for food, electronics, jewelry, clothing, handicrafts, and just about everything else.

Transport

- The Suvarnabhumi International Airport and Don Muang Airport are served by airlines from most world and all domestic destinations.
- All national routes lead to Bangkok. Trains and buses will get you almost anywhere in the country. The central rail terminus is Hualamphong Station. There are three main bus stations: East

(at Ekamai, Sukhumvit); North and Northeast (at Mor Chit); and Southern (on the Thonburi side of the river near Pinklao [this also serves some western provinces like Kanchanaburi]).

- Buses, *tuk-tuks*, metered taxis, motorcycle taxis, the 'skytrain' and the subway system, ferry boats, canal boats, and minivans will transport you from one end of the city to the other cheaply (and usually quickly). River taxis on the Chao Phaya River are not only cheap but offer views of Wat Arun (The Temple of Dawn) that are unsurpassed.
- The closet visa and border runs are to the east at Poipet on the Cambodian border, a full day's ride, there and back, from the city.

Work Opportunities

- Teaching English to Thai students is a popular activity for many retirees in the city. There are hundreds of schools and institutes in desperate need of qualified English teachers.
- Helping out on charity projects, at orphanages, in slum development work, animal welfare projects, or getting involved with local non-profit organizations makes for a rewarding way to enjoy your retirement days.

Healthcare

- As we have seen, Bangkok offers state-of-the-art medical services at scores of private and government hospitals. There are numerous clinics, dental surgeries, cosmetic centers, beauty salons, spa and fitness centers, massage parlors (and animal hospitals) to take care of all your health needs—at cheaper prices than back home. (See earlier sections for full details.)

Property

- Foreigners are only allowed to buy condominiums or apartments in Thailand. Once you decide that Bangkok is the place for you, there are many real-estate agencies that can point you in the right direction.
- Remember: do not rush into anything. Wait until you've identified the best location at the best price with the facilities to suit to your needs.

Bangkok Retiree Profiles And Interviews

Jeff Harper is a 63-year-old British national born in South Africa. He lived in Spain for ten years and Krabi, southern Thailand, for one year, but prefers Bangkok now. He rents a condo for 10,000 baht a month (which includes a swimming pool). He lives with Aet, 38.

"In Bangkok, living location is very important for getting around to places you like to go.

"This is a good place if you want to be left alone. I avoid places where young people and booze are put together. I prefer the peace and quiet of my own place, my woman, and socializing with select friends.

"I am content living here. I spend my free time reading books, watching TV, and swimming. At night, I enjoy drinking with friends. Keep physically fit, or you'll become impotent!

"Language is a problem, so Aet becomes my translator. She protects me from getting ripped off. It helps that she's a strong character.

"Being with Aet makes it easier to have Thai friends. I can drink with them despite the language barrier.

"Thailand is not a reality, it's a fantasy. Don't try to make it into a reality. Get to know the rules of the game before you invest here, even if it takes time. Thais don't go to lawyers to solve problems like back home. They solve them the Thai way. You learn that as you go along.

"I should have read more books on Thai life before I came. Learn by observing others and do as they do.

"The *mai pen rai* attitude to everything still frustrates me. Not releasing frustrations or not getting upset takes getting used to. Smiling doesn't mean trust here. Smiling can get you broke, too!"

Alan and Margie Needleman are a retired American couple from Connecticut. Alan is a former IBM worker. They live in the Pinklao area of Bangkok near the Central shopping mall. After looking around, they have a long term lease on a three-bedroom condo with good security, gym, and a view of the Chao Phraya River. They have easy access to boat transport on the river.

"Our place is much like a hotel atmosphere. Time is the most valuable commodity in Bangkok. You have plenty of it. A typical day here involves working out at the gym downstairs for 40 minutes every morning, 25 laps in the pool, shopping for house items, and dining at restaurants at night.

"To keep myself busy, I read books, the *New York Times*, the London *Times*, and some Dutch newspapers online. The Foreign Correspondents' Club is a great place to make friends, eat good food, and listen to good speakers. The American Women's Club has a very good support network for Margie. Her circle of friends has coffee afternoons every month. They have fun doing day tours and helping out at orphanages.

"We haven't had any crime or safety problems here. The pride of Bangkokians, even in the slum areas, is quite refreshing.

"My family loves visiting Thailand.

"Driving is not a good idea. Public transport is cheaper and safer. A good trick I learned to avoid getting lost and overcharged by taxi drivers is to take my cellphone and have the driver talk to the place I want to go.

"Bumrungrad Hospital provides excellent health and dental services.

"Properties are much cheaper and certainly more spacious here. But avoid realtors. They won't let go. Study location maps and do Internet research before you buy a place. Pick a spot and go there to check it. Bangkok neighborhoods differ in price and quality of life.

"I find the weather is too hot here. Avoid daytime chores during humid heat."

Richard Rubacher, the author from New York City, has lived in Bangkok since 2000. He explored Pattaya as a living option but preferred Bangkok. He rents his condo off Sukhumvit Road for 15,000 baht a month. He is 70, single, and has a retirement visa.

"Bangkok is a magical place. Tonic for the soul. This place makes you become more soft-spoken and polite. It's contagious. Sell the home. Divorce the wife. Move here!

"I am a big city boy from NYC. I can play the numbers here in perfect anonymity. Last week I danced with two beautiful women from Kazakhstan. This week I danced with a Muslim woman for the first time in my life here in Bangkok.

"Teeth implants are a steal here. I had two eye cataracts taken out. Now I can drive a car. I have a good case of 'Thailand Fever.'

"Busy you ask? In between writing books and articles about Bangkok life, Latin dancing at La Rueda club, seeing my girlfriend twice a week, watching tennis and basketball championships on cable TV, frequenting massage parlors and hanging out with expats for coffee, I am lucky if I have time for myself.

"Don't jump off the Golden Gate Bridge yet. Thailand is waiting for you!"

Chiang Mai

Chiang Mai, the largest city in the North of Thailand, has a population of about 300,000. It sits in a lush tropical valley surrounded by mountains that have historically protected the city from outside influences. Despite recent urbanization, this cool getaway, the Rose of the North, retains many aspects of its ancient Lanna culture with its wooden temples and unique crafts of lacquer ware, umbrella making, and wood carving.

The older part of the city, surrounded by moats and ancient walls (actually rebuilt not so long ago), has a thriving tourist trade that includes guesthouses, restaurants, and an exotic night bazaar. The soothing Ping River winds its way north for some 350 miles.

The climate between July and March is quite pleasant, when the air is cool and the hills are green. The hot season usually lasts from April through June and can be more extreme than in other parts of the country. The winter months of November through February bring on a thrilling autumn chill at night. Visitors from Thailand and abroad come here to escape from the humidity of the rest of the country. The Thais bundle up in sweaters, scarves, and big jackets, while the tourists wander round in shorts and T-shirts. It's perfect weather.

More and more foreigners are living here in Chiang Mai, and for good reasons. Chiang Mai has been rated among the top ten most livable cities in Asia because of its laid-back atmosphere, mild climate most the year, and, above all, very affordable lifestyle. During the last ten years, the foreign presence has become more significant. Some retire here; others come and go at their own leisure, while an increasing number enjoy making it their home for a few years. The Thais are very agreeable people and don't mind sharing their wonderful city with you—particularly if it helps the local economy.

Chiang Mai has a well-established network of services aimed specifically at foreigners, and the burgeoning expat community creates a comfortable 'safety cushion' to help newcomers to adjust. For starters there is the Chiang Mai Expat Club that boasts a membership of over 200 in the city. It meets twice a month on Sundays at the Orchid Hotel, which is centrally located and offers a scrumptious buffet breakfast for a mere three dollars. The club invites speakers to provide relevant information for long-timers and address issues of concern that come up from time to time. There are special interest groups for reading, retirement, volunteers, and English teachers.

Why Chiang Mai?
Pros
- Slower pace of life, but still offers most city amenities.
- The rich Lanna culture.

- Volunteer work with hilltribes gives meaning to day-to-day life.
- Old houses, ancient temples, local markets; the overall homey atmosphere of the city.
- Groups like the Expat Club and the Northern Thai Alliance make it easy to find a support network.
- Beautiful surrounding countryside.
- Pleasant weather; a generally cooler year-round climate.
- Good atmosphere for writing or other constructive, creative activities.
- Friendly and honest people (compared to other places in Thailand).
- Opportunity to gain a wide circle of friends, both Thai and expat. There are intellectual types, wannabe writers, NGO workers, the party crowd, English teachers, gourmets, backpackers and trekkers, antique collectors, outdoor sports enthusiasts.
- Houses with lots of space and big gardens available at very reasonable rates.
- Opportunities to find a Thai partner (often without the need for intellectual or even linguistic compatibility).
- Delicious Thai and northern cuisine; lots of flavors and good vegetarian choices.
- Very few beggars and few homeless people.
- 'Family values' are important here; children look after their parents.
- Communications, phones, and Internet are good.
- Many choose Chiang Mai because it is far more livable than Bangkok and not yet completely overwhelmed by tourists.

Cons
- The Thai Language can be difficult to learn for some, especially the northern dialect.
- Visa runs to the border (Mae Sai is a four-hour bus ride) can be an ongoing inconvenience.
- Rush-hour traffic can be as frustrating as Bangkok; it's not too bad during the day, except during special events like college graduation, the annual Flower Festival, Songkran, and Loy Kratong.
- The indirect communication habits—having to read between the lines most of the time—makes integration and friendships with locals a little harder.
- The over-emphasis on politeness here can come across as not genuine after a while.
- Free hand-out syndrome among the hilltribes takes getting used to.
- Abuse of police authority (though not as bad as other places) is a concern, especially for the Thais.
- Increasing noise pollution, especially in the shopping malls.

Leisure Activities And Things To Do
- A host of clubs and organizations for expats.
- Community support groups.
- Numerous churches, temples, and mosques for your spiritual needs.
- Seven golf courses around the city with reasonable green fees.
- Cooking schools that offer a wide variety of classes on how to master the delicious art of Thai cuisine.

211

- Four accredited institutes and a range of massage parlors that offer courses on Thai massage.
- Yoga and mediation classes for the spiritually inclined.
- Thai language schools to help you master the Thai language.
- Muay Thai (Thai kick-boxing) courses available at the Lanna Muay Thai Camp.
- Informal courses in t'ai chi, chi gong, jewelry-making, photography, and painting.
- Trekking into the lush mountainous interior of northern Thailand to visit the intriguing hilltribe villages is one of the most popular activities for both tourists and long-term residents; there are plenty of trekking companies to choose from in the city.
- Sightseeing trips to the mountains; nearby famous temples; handicraft centers at San Kamphaeng, Borsang and Baan Tawai; the Chiang Mai Night Safari; elephant farms; and local villages.
- Shopping at the famous night bazaar or one of the eight malls in the city; many great deals to be had.
- Western and Asian movies at four cinema complexes.
- Cable television channels (in English, Thai, and a few other languages) for couch potatoes.
- Gyms, cycling and trekking clubs, badminton and tennis courts, bowling alleys, swimming pools, snooker halls, all over the city.
- Chiang Mai nightlife offers a whole host of Thai and international restaurants, plenty of bars and pubs, plus venues for live music.

Shopping

- The night bazaar in the center of the city is a very popular attraction, with hundreds of handicraft and souvenir stores.
- Plenty of exotic markets.
- Supermarkets, two big shopping malls (Central and Airport Plaza).
- Post offices, Internet cafés, fax and photocopying shops, and telephone services.

Shopping for unique hill tribe crafts is fun in northern Thailand

Transport

- Six airlines serve Chiang Mai International Airport.
- Chiang Mai has very few metered taxis; most people prefer to buy their own vehicle or motorcycle for getting around the city.

- *Tuk-tuks, songtaews,* motorcycle taxis, and a limited bus system provide cheap public transport.
- Buses and a very efficient rail service link Chiang Mai to many other places in the country.
- Visa runs back and forth to the Burmese border at Mae Sai can be completed within eight hours.

Work Opportunities
- Teaching English is a popular activity for many retirees in the city.
- Helping out on charity projects or with NGOs or hilltribe foundations.
- Volunteering at the Expat Club, with the Tourist Police of Chiang Mai, or just helping out a student with English homework provides its small pleasures.

Healthcare
- Chiang Mai has around 17 hospitals, plus numerous dental clinics, optometrists, and other clinics and pharmacies.

Property
- Once you've made up your mind that Chiang Mai is the place for you, talk to one of the dozens of real-estate companies (or chat with expats who have already made purchases) on how to go about buying your own house, apartment, or condominium.

Chiang Mai Retiree Profiles And Interviews

Roshan Dhunjibuoy is a retired widow, aged 75. A German citizen of Indian origin, and a world traveler, she works on projects to help abandoned dogs in Chiang Mai.

"With the money I have at my disposal, I would lead a very cramped life in Europe, but here I can live comfortably very easily.

"Define your late-age passions and then life becomes more meaningful, allowing you to integrate more into local communities.

"If you want to be happy here, give back some of what you're getting to the Thai people. I do, and I am happy.

"Buddhism is not a religion but a way of life that provides explanations I can accept.

"Home is where my dogs are. I may be dog-tired some nights from caring for them, but never tired of my dogs.

"But language is the most difficult obstacle for me, though I speak a few other languages. It has been my Waterloo.

"Chiang Mai is not a 'cultural hotbed.' If you're a 'culture vulture,' this may not be the best place for you."

Roy Askey is 66 years old. He's divorced and has five children in the UK. His former profession was stone mason. He has lived in Chiang Mai for six years.

"Do I miss home? Not at all. My pounds go much further here than in the UK. My travels to Phuket, Pattaya, and Bangkok confirm that Chiang Mai is the best place for me. I like the slower pace. Chiang Mai suits me down to the ground. I am content with my lot here. Nothing gets over me much. Neither do I envy others.

215

"Keeping busy occupies the mind and helps deal with the retirement blow once the sightseeing is over.

"Many Thai women like older foreign men. We are less demanding, have better income, and are not 'butterflies' (promiscuous).

"People with many expectations and not so open a mind will find it more difficult to adjust here."

Otome Klein, an anthropologist, is 75. She's a Dutch national of Japanese and Indonesian origin. She's lived in Chiang Mai for 13 years.

"I like the exotic. The tribal history and ancestry of the north continue to fascinate me after years of living here. For people that live on the fringe, like I do, this is the place to be. This is a *sanuk*-oriented community."

Pattaya

Pattaya, in Chonburi province, is about 150 kilometers southeast of Bangkok. It is probably the most popular destination in Thailand for both tourists and retirees alike. The resort city and its three beaches— Pattaya, Jomtien, and Naklua—grew rapidly during and after the Vietnam War, when the Americans built a naval base and American GIs invaded the town for R 'n' R.

Today Pattaya boasts dozens of five-star hotels, luxurious resorts, and a vibrant nightlife with hundreds of bars, nightclubs, and restaurants.

The resort is only two hours by road from Bangkok, and about an hour and a half from the new Suvarnabhumi International Airport.

Pattaya has a large expat community, with Americans and Brits topping the list. There's a sizeable population of as-

216

Beaches in developed areas have many tourist amenities

sorted Europeans and Australians, as well. Two Expat Clubs organize a host of activities for the foreign retirees. There's a myriad of activities going on in the city every day. There are two daily English-language newspapers—the *Pattaya Mail* and *Pattaya Today*—and one free bi-weekly magazine called *EXPAT.*

Why Pattaya?
Pros
- Two Expat Clubs that meet every Sunday: one at Henry J. Bean's restaurant and the other at the Grand Sole Hotel. They provide an extensive support network. Each club has a host of special interest groups. One of them provides cheap health insurance for expats.
- Easy access to Bangkok and all its attractions.

- Three beaches offer a host of water sports for the active resident.
- The city is one of the entertainment capitals of Thailand, with hundreds of beer bars and go-go bars that are open to the small hours.
- A haven for gay residents for both locals and foreigners.
- Amazing array of restaurants, especially for seafood and international cuisine; five-star hotels for comfortable dining and night entertainment.
- Some of the best sailing and yachting in the country; also a big-game fisherman's paradise.
- Well over 20 golf courses in the Pattaya area.
- Lots of clubs to join: five Rotary Clubs, a Lions Club, a Sportsman's Club, and two prominent yacht clubs.
- Many business centers to take care of financial and property needs.
- A radio station with daily English broadcasts.

Cons
- Up to a million tourists during the November-March peak season.
- Overcrowding of beaches during the tourist seasons.
- Inflated prices for foreigners, especially tourists.
- Pattaya residents often get mistaken for tourists until the locals get to know you better and see you frequently.
- Rush-hour traffic can be as bad as Bangkok, especially during holidays and festivals.
- Although much improved, the beaches are still polluted with sewage and garbage at times.

- Booming tourism has caused much environmental degradation of the area.
- Crime is on the rise.
- Pattaya continues to have the image of being a city of sin and sex.

Leisure Activities And Things To Do

- Water sports include jet-skiing, parasailing, scuba diving, snorkeling, wind surfing, fishing, and swimming.
- Go-karting at the Pattaya Kart Speedway, snooker, archery, tennis, target shooting, horse riding, bowling, bungee jumping, and many other pursuits.
- Golf courses and driving ranges galore, many with very reasonable green fees.
- Yachting and sailing at the Ocean Marina and Varuna yacht clubs. Some expats share costs to buy their own yacht.
- A host of gyms, spas, and massage parlors for the health conscious.
- Latin dance studios.
- The Pattaya Bridge Club for the more leisurely.
- Wandering along Walking Street and its many beer bars, girlie bars, music venues, cabarets, and restaurants.
- Day trips to the Tiger Zoo, alligator and elephant farms, sapphire mines, orchid gardens, and culture villages at Mini Siam and Nong Nooch Village; countless other places of interest in the Pattaya area.
- Latest Hollywood movies at the Big C and Royal Garden shopping centers; or purchase DVDs at bargain prices from street vendors.

- If you're creative, build a studio to write, paint, or invent things or join a writers group and write about your travels.
- Attend an international convention at one of the big hotels.
- Numerous places of religious worship: temples, churches, and mosques.

Shopping

- Royal Garden Plaza on Beach Road has many retail outlets, particularly for clothing and souvenirs.
- Big C and other large retailers like Tesco Lotus (on the main Sukhumvit Road highway) cater to all your domestic requirements.
- A dozen or so air-conditioned shopping plazas, and hordes of street vendors and tailors along Beach Road and Pattaya 2 Road.
- Post offices, Internet cafés, fax and photocopying places, and telephone services.

Transport

- Buses to and from Bangkok (Ekamai Eastern Bus Station) every half hour from the Pattaya Bus Station. Other bus links to the northeast. There's also a train from Bangkok, but most people prefer the bus, as it's faster.
- The main forms of public transport are the dark-blue *songtaews* (known as 'baht buses'), motorbike taxis, and a few taxis and *tuks-tuks*.
- Cars, jeeps, and motorcycles are available for rent at many places around town.

Work Opportunities
- Teaching English, especially to those in the tourist trade.
- Getting involved in your area of interest with the two Expat Clubs.
- Owning or running a bar, restaurant, hotel, or guesthouse.
- The tourist trade if you have an area of expertise.
- Volunteering with charity organizations.

Healthcare
- There are two big hospitals and many smaller clinics, as well as a variety of dental surgeries, one eye clinic, and numerous beauty clinics and pharmacies.

Property
- Pattaya and neighboring Jomtien offer condominiums with sea views and many other options for potential home buyers. The city is full of real-estate agents who are only too willing to help you make a decision.
- Don't rush. Chat with expats who have already made purchases; they'll be very happy to give you good advice. If you are married to a Thai, then building your own house is also an option.

Pattaya Retiree Interviews And Profiles

Roger Cox is an American from Connecticut. He's 66 and has been retired in Pattaya for four years. He is a veteran of the war in Vietnam. He is gay and has been with his Thai boyfriend for almost three years.

"This is a marvelous culture, even if we are paying to be here. We pay a lot less than at home, and yet they treat us like kings. Pattaya gives you a sense of revitalization (even if it is with Viagra).

"Be courteous and thankful. We may have the money, but we don't have the right to be otherwise.

"Dogs are out of control in this town. Pollution may overtake us one day, but the beach water won't kill you. The traffic is tolerable, even for bikers."

❧

Paul Back first came to Pattaya 39 years ago and has never left. He worked in nearby Sattahip building microwave systems during the Vietnam War. He has worked in Saudi Arabia and Bangkok, but now builds yachts for export. He is 67, is semi retired, and has Thai residency.

"Don't be afraid to get laughed at. Thais laugh with you, not at you. Keep a sense of humor and a smile on your face.

"Get a hobby. Write a book. Build things. Go sailing or scuba diving. Don't sit at home. Don't leave your brains and common sense at the airport. Watch out for the alcoholic syndrome and living your life on a bar stool.

"Nothing is up front here, and the young girls love you for a reason. Due diligence pays off, but being overcharged as a *farang* is 'SOP.' Get used to it."

Richard E. Smith, aged 75, is from Pittsburgh, Pennsylvania. He has been president of one of the Expat Clubs for four years. He is married to a Trinidadian wife who lives in Hong Kong. They bought properties there, but Richard prefers Pattaya. He bought his own three-bedroom condo with a spectacular sea view for 5 million baht (now worth 15 million). He retired in 1993.

"For guys wanting younger partners to take care of them, no place is as welcoming as Pattaya. Many Thai girls are supportive and dependable.

"The Thai festivals are fantastic. There's always something to do here.

"Medical care is unbelievably better than the US. Medical equipment here is state of the art and comparable to anything in the West.

"Growth and expansion is booming. It's an asset not a liability. But it's hard to fathom the government here. Expat relations with officials are getting better, but still need improvement.

"Being a couple makes it easier to get things done, but it hampers learning the language as fast.

"I'm the white ghost whenever I go out with my dark-skinned attractive wife. Going to Walking Street once a week is a must. The show is on the road."

Donald Maclahan came to Pattaya in 1967 and has been married to his Thai wife for 29 years. He is 66 and originally from Boston. An ex-navy man, he worked in communications; then owned a small hotel on Pattaya's lively Walking Street. He built a four-bedroom house 15 years ago. And draws social security payments on his ATM card.

223

"Thailand lets me live in the moment. Pattaya is the Disneyland of the East.

"I'm a Christian Buddhist who believes in *tamboon dai boon* ('make merit, get merit').

"This place offers lots of ways to keep working while retired. Teaching is a valued profession here, and a good hobby to get into.

"Knowing the right people means everything. Relationships open doors."

"Be on site and watch the development of your house. Watch the watcher. Don't expect it to happen on its own. Drink and eat with the workers and you'll get everywhere. But be aware of how much everything costs and how to account for it.

"My wife is the diplomat for us; much easier to have a buffer."

Hua Hin

About four hours by car or train south of Bangkok on the Gulf coast, Hua Hin was once a sleepy fishing village until King Prajadhipok (1925-1935) built a palace called Klai Klangwon ('Far From Worries') as a summer home.

Hua Hin boasts five kilometers of beaches, and it soon gained attention as a resort. The railway station and the exquisite Railway Hotel are now its best-known landmarks. Today it has a population of more than 125,000—and lots of upmarket hotels, restaurants, and high-rise condominiums.

The town attracts expats who prefer a more sedate life of leisure and sports, away from the hustle and bustle of Bangkok or Pattaya. Perhaps because of its royal connections (the current king still visits from time to time) the town retains a more genteel atmosphere. There is no brash nightlife scene—but if you want that, you're only five hours by road or rail from the capital.

Hua Hin has some of the best golf courses in the country. An international expat group based in the town enjoys year-round tournaments and golf trips around the country. They are managed by the Hua Hin Golf Society at Bernie's Inn, centrally located in the heart of the town. British and Scandinavians make up the two biggest groups among the expat community living here.

Why Hua Hin?
Pros
- Reasonable travel time to Bangkok.
- Long stretches of beach within walking distance of town; some water sports available.
- Royal connection means very good security and a very low crime rate.
- For the same reason as above, a very sedate and laid-back atmosphere. The town retains some of its old-world charm.
- New property development offering more options for accommodation.
- Great location for golfers.
- Good international hotels and restaurants to choose from.
- Annual Jazz Festival with many well-known international musicians.
- Spectacular views of the ocean from the hillside Wat Khao Lao temple.

Cons
- Lack of an international-standard hospital for serious medical cases. Ambulance service is not the best.
- Difficult to get golf tee times during the high tourist season.
- Rising property prices.

- Food and public transport costs are higher than some other places.

Leisure Activities And Things To Do

- Water sports on the beach include swimming, jet-skiing, parasailing, kite surfing, and fishing.
- Day trips to nearby Cha Am, fishing villages, and scenic Prachuap Kiri Khan province.
- Weekend trips to Khao Sam Roi National Park, known for its teeming bird life and a variety of unusual mammals (awarded UNESCO World Heritage status in August 2005).
- Dining at the night market, the fishing wharf, big hotels, or one of the many fine restaurants in town.

A unique dining experience at a restaurant over water

226

- Pool and darts leagues at bars and restaurants in town.
- Hua Hin Bridge Club for rainy days.
- Hua Hin Sixes cricket tournament.
- Hua Hin Hash House Harriers.
- Go-karting.
- Fantastic free music during the three-day Annual Jazz Festival, every June.
- Women's Group meets once a month.

Shopping
- Tesco Lotus (at the Hua Hin Market Village).
- Local specialty shops should provide you with all your domestic needs.
- Many tailor shops, souvenir shops, a central market area, and street vendors.
- Stores for electrical appliances, kitchen and bathroom fixtures, furniture, and air conditioners.

Transport
- Trains leave Hualamphong Station in Bangkok for Hua Hin five times a day. Travel time is about five hours. Seats are comfortable and are available in first, second, and third classes at very affordable prices. The route continues south as far as the Thai-Malaysia border.
- Air-con buses from Bangkok's Southern bus station leave for Hua Hin every hour and cost 300 to 500 baht depending on the level of 'luxury' desired.
- Minivans are also available from Bangkok's Victory Monument for as little as 200 baht and sometimes get there faster—though not necessarily safer.

- Private taxis are expensive to and from Bangkok (at about 2,500 baht one way); Bangkok-Hua Hin is a good asphalt road.
- Motorcycles and cars can be rented in town.
- Visa and border runs from Hua Hin are typically to Penang, Malaysia. Some visas can be extended at the Hua Hin Immigration office.

Work Opportunities
- Resorts, bars, restaurants, tourist services.
- Freelance from home via the Internet.
- English teaching.

Healthcare
- Sao Paolo and Hua Hin hospitals.
- Many local health and dental clinics.
- A variety of massage parlors and spa resorts.

Property
- Hua Hin is going through a housing construction boom, and real-estate agents can be found all over the town.
- A two-bedroom house can range from 1.5 million baht up to 7 million baht depending on size, location, beachfront access, and the standard of décor.
- Condominium prices range from 1.5 million baht up to 4 million baht based on the same variables.

Hua Hin Retiree Profiles And Interviews

Robert Kennedy is a 73-year-old American from the Washington, D.C. area. His brother, who lives in Thailand for six months of the year, introduced him to Hua Hin. Robert came over a few times, rented a townhouse with two bedrooms and two baths for 72,000 baht a year, and then finally made the permanent move nine years ago. He bought a house eight years ago in his Thai partner Nook's name, and built a four-bedroom house with four bathrooms.

"I love living here. I like golfing on weekdays and spending weekends in Bangkok. Since I'm not much of a beach person, I do a lot of reading.

"I did my stint with teenybopper girls. They are too much hassle. Nook, my wife, is 60, loves gardening like I do, and takes good care of me.

"Language is a problem. But since more and more English is spoken in Hua Hin now, it makes it much easier. They should have an annual food festival here just like the jazz festival.

"My wife took care of the whole building process after we hired a builder. Too frustrating for me to understand the Thai way of doing things, but it all came out right in the end. It took nine months to build and cost me $70,000. Prices are much higher now."

Chris Davidson, 47, is from Sheffield, England. He worked in telecommunications in Bangkok but was laid off during the 1997 economic crisis. He moved to Hua Hin and married a Thai with whom he has two children. He considers Hua Hin his permanent home.

"I play golf at least twice a week. There's always a club tournament going on. They organize golf trips to other places each year. During the low season, a round costs 2,500 baht and it can get as cheap as 800 baht for the whole month.

"Between getting the kids to school and golf and eating out at least twice a week, I keep myself well occupied. My seven- and eight-year-old kids go to a good bi-lingual school that has both Thai and British teachers.

"The Hua Hin expat community is more European than American. The biggest group is probably the Brits, followed by the Scandinavians.

"The street of international restaurants is one the best in Asia. There are too many tourists during the high season. But low season means less traffic and it's much easier to get tee time on the golf courses.

"Renewal of visas can be difficult, but at least it can be done here in Hua Hin. Knowing the right people helps, especially in Customs when you're shipping in personal goods.

"Land prices have gone haywire from what they used to be. It's still possible to get a decent house at 15,000 baht per square meter. Just depends on how lavish you want it to be.

"English-speaking property lawyers who are actually qualified as lawyers are hard to come by in Hua Hin. You may have to go to Bangkok. Lawyers here say the land office is one of the worst in Thailand."

❧

John McAllister is originally from Edinburgh, Scotland, but he emigrated to Sydney, Australia in 1974 and is now an Australian citizen. An accountant by profession, John, now 53, first came to work in Thailand in 1998. When he took an early retirement package, he moved with his Thai wife, Porn, and their six-year-old son to Hua Hin. They bought two houses at Orchid Villa estate, three kilometers outside the town, and have lived there ever since.

"We entertain a lot here. Food is cheap and fantastic. We have a growing group of friends with the same interests. Beware of too many bar-stool friends, though.

"The safety and security situation is hard to surpass. I never feel threatened. Hua Hin is also much cleaner than many places in Thailand.

"Don't jump at every fast deal that pops up. Buy an established house instead of building one, especially if you're not based here to oversee the construction. The stress level isn't worth it.

"Don't use the builder's lawyers. Find a good reputable lawyer on your own. Make sure the building specs and cash flow are fair to both parties.

"If you get into trouble, keep your cool and find a good lawyer. Embrace the fact that Thailand is a world apart. Be open and flexible. Taking the attitude 'Thais are there to rip off the foreigner' won't get you anywhere.

"Lay out the food and drinks for the workers, and things will go faster. Don't trust them too much, though.

"This house with four bedrooms, the huge patio for barbecues, and my swimming pool cost 3.2 million baht."

Phuket

Phuket, the Pearl of the South, is Thailand's largest island. It is one of the wealthiest and most beautiful provinces in the country. With the completion of the Sarasin Bridge connecting the island to the mainland, the province and Phuket town grew rapidly. The island is now one of the most sought after holiday and honeymoon destinations in Asia. The superb

231

beaches of Patong, Rawai, Kata, Kamala, and the picture-postcard islands make Phuket a retiree's paradise.

With a multicultural mix of inhabitants including Malays, Chinese, Muslims, Thai Buddhists and *chao lae* (fishermen), the island has a cosmopolitan flavor. As well as tourism, the island also has a thriving rubber and tin mining industry.

The yachting crowd and athletic types tend to live and congregate around Chalong Bay; the yuppies and property developers around Bang Tao and Surin beaches; the bar owners around Patong Beach—each forming little expat circles of their own. The Phuket Hash House Harriers and the British Bar Association (a social network) are perhaps the only two clubs that bring many of these groups together.

Why Phuket?

Pros

- Lots of beaches with all the corresponding activities that go with them.
- Gorgeous undulating hills, and well-preserved secluded islands with limestone cliffs in the turquoise Andaman Sea.
- Historic architecture of Phuket town dates back to the Portuguese and Macau styles; many old temples.
- Dozens of scenic spots including the romantic Promontory Point, national parks, offshore islands, limestone caves, and waterfalls.
- Superb snorkeling and diving.
- Some of the best sailing, yachting, and fishing in Southeast Asia.
- Gourmet seafood at bargain prices.

Cons

- One of the most popular travel destinations in Asia; more than a million tourists a month during the high season.
- Two-tiered price system for locals and tourists for some goods and services.
- Residents often get mistaken for tourists because of the large number of visitors.
- Booming property market means constantly rising prices.

Leisure Activities And Things To Do

- Day trips to blue-water beaches at Chalong, Rawai, Nai Harn, Kata, Karon, Kamala, Bang Tao, and Nai Thon.
- Water sports include jet-skiing, sailing, yachting, snorkeling, diving, and deep-sea fishing.
- Some of the best ocean views and coral reefs in Asia.

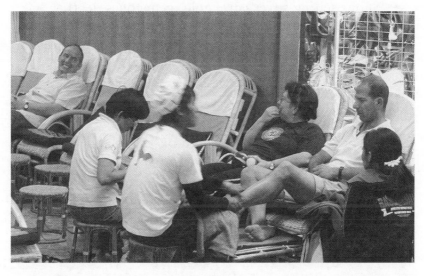

Thailand is famous for traditional massage; foot massage is also very popular

- Island hopping and cruises to world famous Phi Phi Island and the Similan and Surin islands.
- Rainforest national parks in Phang Nga province.
- Fine seaside dining at restaurants, resorts, five-star hotels, and many romantic settings.
- Nightly cabaret shows at Simon's and Fantasea.
- Lots of clubs and societies to belong to.

Shopping

- Big C supermarket, Tesco Lotus, and Robinson department store; Ocean Plaza in Phuket Town.
- A host of tailor shops at most beaches and in Phuket town.
- Great deals at the two markets in Phuket town and Chatuchak Phuket, an offshoot of the famous weekend market in Bangkok.
- Numerous shops for home appliances and domestic items.
- Shops selling silverware, gold, gemstones, leather, and batik.

Transport

- Phuket International Airport, an hour by road from Phuket town, is served by many international carriers from Europe and Asia.
- Airport limos run anywhere on the island from 600 to 1,000 baht per one-way trip. Cheaper airport bus goes to Phuket town and nearby beaches, but takes longer as it makes frequent stops along the way.
- The routes from Bangkok to southern Thailand don't go to Phuket, but you can get as far as Hat

234

Yai city and take overland transport from there to Phuket if you prefer the train and bus.

- Air-conditioned buses leave every hour, day and overnight, from the Southern Bus Station in Bangkok. The journey takes about 12 hours, but you can break it up by stopping at one of the many smaller towns along the way.
- *Tuk-tuks*, *songtaews*, private taxis, motorcycle taxis, and minivans will get you anywhere on the island, although they tend to charge inflated prices, especially during the rainy season.
- In Phuket town and many of the beaches, you can easily rent your own car for as little as 1,000 baht per day, or a motorcycle for about 200 baht.
- Visa renewals are usually done at Penang in Malaysia—a minimum three-day trip including visa processing. Border runs can be completed within a day if you don't mind long hours on the bus. Some visa services are provided at the Phuket Immigration office.

Work Opportunities

- English teaching is much needed, given the large number of locals (and many from other parts of Thailand) working in the tourist industry.
- Property and real-estate management is something that many long-term expats get involved with in local and international companies.
- Bars or restaurants, usually with a Thai partner.

Healthcare

- Phuket International Hospital and Bangkok Phuket Hospital offer modern medical equipment and good service for both outpatient and inpatient needs.

- Patong Hospital and Vachira Phuket Hospital provide more basic health services, as do many different health clinics, opticians, and dental centers.
- There are several plastic surgery clinics and hundreds of spa resorts and massage parlors at the beaches and in Phuket town; there are also two animal hospitals.

Property

- Phuket's real-estate market is booming, and the prices are going up faster in comparison to other parts of the country.
- The cost of building a house on beachfront property, depending on location and size, can range from 2 to 10 million baht. Also take into account the level of interior decoration.
- Condos, some with spectacular views of the Andaman Sea, start at 2 to 3 million baht and go much higher, depending on location and the number of bedrooms.

Phuket Retiree Profiles And Interviews

Glen Dunkley, 62, is from Calgary, Canada. He was a volunteer worker in Thailand in 1971, and has been married to a Phuket native for 30 years. He has lived in Phuket since 1992.

" A laid-back 'devil may care' attitude is why I live here. Between the weekly Hash runs, scuba diving, and maintaining my home, I keep myself pretty busy. Phuket

236

has lots of groups with special interests. You can find your own niche easily.

"Expats here form their own cliques, since the beaches are spread all over the island; they don't all come together in one place or belong to one club.

"Even though the retirement process is much easier and quicker in Malaysia, people tend to prefer to live in Thailand because of the more open, friendly society.

"Mentally prepare yourself that paradise is a different country from home.

"Traffic is out of control during high season, but never as bad as Bangkok or Chiang Mai. If you have an accident here, you'll have to pay, whether it's your fault or not—so don't have one.

"Public services haven't kept up with the very fast growth of Phuket.

"Don't buy a pre-built house unless you know how it was constructed. Labor shortages and shoddy construction are a way of life here. I built my own house in my wife's name. Beachfront locations go for as much as 20,000 baht per square meter nowadays.

"Hire an on-site supervisor. Expat developers for top-notch construction and supervision are readily available.

♨

Keith Norris, an American from Maine, age 45, has been coming to Phuket regularly since 1996. He is semi-retired at 45 and spends half of each year in Phuket. He works in investment portfolios for a London Stock Exchange company from his Phuket home.

"I came here with an Adidas bag for the Hash House Harriers run. Now I have two houses, two cars, and I can go golfing any morning. Phuket is like living in 'La

La Land.' You forget what day it is—every day. My only calendar here is the social calendar.

"I hang out with friends at trivia quiz nights on different beaches. The rugby tournaments every year are a lot of fun. Wine and cheese tasting at expat hangouts are a blast.

"My partner got so tired of me having my friends sleeping over on the sofa, so I got into the apartment-selling business. Condos are the best value for money, but choose carefully, since many can be overpriced. I take at least a year to build a house here, from top to bottom, before occupation."

Rod Palmer is from Banbury, Western Australia. After a mining accident in Australia, he needed three years to recover. With the compensation money he received, he moved to Phuket five years ago and bought two properties and a yacht. He now does sailing trips for clients. Rod is semi-retired at 45. His wife, Yara, is from Surat Thani and they have an 18-month-old son.

"Being on holiday all the time can be contagious. It's all here, so why go anywhere else?

"Germans hang out around the Nai Harn area, the Brits around Baan Thao and Kamala, and the business crowd and yachters around Chalong Bay. Hooking up with annual returnees always makes for good parties every year.

"Get to know the driving rules, Thai style, quickly though. Motorcycle accidents and swimming during rip tides cause a few deaths every year.

"I paid 180,000 Australian dollars for my four-bedroom house with an ocean view. The big garden on the one *rai* of land keeps me and Yara busy and happy."

Alan Cooke, 64, first came to Phuket in 1986 to construct the port at Ao Makham. He returned in 1994 to retire. Now he runs a furniture company with his Thai partner, and is the British Honorary Consul in Phuket. He's a founder member of the Hash House Harriers Phuket chapter, and he received an MBE from Queen Elizabeth for his efforts in the post Tsunami recovery of Phuket.

"Except for chocolate biscuits and Marmite, I can get everything else here. My shopping list is the same as in England. You can get by here without having to master the language.

"Do I rent or buy? This is the question that faces many who come here. Depends on your circumstances and whether you have someone you would like to leave it to.

"An independent on-site supervisor—one who knows Thai business and the language is a must.

"Having a cricket field near my house is something I always wanted. I am planning to build cricket, rugby, and football pitches on 20 *rai* of land near my place."

Northeast Thailand (Isaan): Khon Kaen, Udon Thani, Nong Khai

For those who'd prefer a quieter and more sedate retirement, away from the hustle and bustle of popular tourist destinations and city life, the northeast of Thailand (Isaan) offers quite a few options.

Khon Kaen, the capital of the northeast and the geographical and cultural center of the region, is located 449 kilometers from Bangkok. The city's surrounding areas are full of ancient artifacts from the Lao and Khmer cultures, and the region in general is well known for its dinosaur fossils.

Khon Kaen is a small city but it offers most modern conveniences and is easily accessible from Bangkok by rail, road, and air

About 110 kilometers north of Khon Kaen lies the city of Udon Thani, which was an American army base during the Vietnam War. Many American veterans and retirees stayed on and settled here after the war. It too, boasts many fine historic sites and temples.

Another 55 kilometers north of Udon is Nong Khai, on the banks of the mighty Mekong River. This slow provincial capital has charming restaurants with sunset views over the river to neighboring Laos.

Nong Khai attracts some retirees as well. Laos is just over the Thai-Lao Friendship Bridge. The capital Vientiane makes for nice excursions and is handy for visa runs.

These three cities make up the biggest communities of foreigners in the northeast, although there are many retirees living in small Isaan villages (dotted here and there, all over the region) with their Thai wives and adopted families.

Why Isaan?

Pros
- Quieter pace of life in the northeast.
- A strong Lao culture with genuinely friendly and welcoming people.
- Life is much cheaper than in other parts of Thailand.
- Easier to make expat and Thai friends, since the communities are small.

Cons
- No local English newspapers, bookstores, or expat clubs.
- No English-soundtrack movie theatres.

Rural Thailand outside the main cities

- Very hot during the four-month dry season.

Leisure Activities And Things To Do
- Day trips to numerous historic sites and temples.
- The Surin Elephant Festival and numerous other Isaan festivals.
- Scenic Ubonratana Dam.
- Khmer ruins at Phanom Rung Historical Park.
- Evening walks and aerobics at the Bueng Kaen Nakhon man-made lake in Khon Kaen.
- Hanging out with friends at expat bars—good places to socialize and find cheap Western food.
- International food at the five-star Kosa and Sofitel hotels in Khon Kaen.
- Micro-brewery pub and restaurant in Khon Kaen.
- Bars, live music, dance halls, and karaoke bars in all three places.
- Golf and bowling in all three places.

Shopping
- Tesco Lotus or Big C in all three cities.

- Oasis and Ferry Plaza and Macro Mall in Khon Kaen.
- Silk and cotton fabrics, silverware, and Isaan handicrafts at many outlets in all three cities.

Transport
- Good airport in Khon Kaen.
- There are cheap flights on two local airlines from Bangkok to Udon.
- Thai Airways has three flights (slightly more expensive) to Khon Kaen and Udon.
- Overnight rail services and air-conditioned buses stop at Khon Kaen and Udon on the way to Nong Khai and the Lao border.
- Bus services from Chiang Mai and other places in the north and northeast.
- In town, *tuk-tuks*, *songtaews*, and motorcycle taxis for public transport. Metered taxis do not exist.
- Motorcycle rentals are also an option.
- Buying your own car, new or second-hand, is the best option if you live out of town.
- For those on retirement visas that are annually renewable, as long you show finances of 800,000 baht in a Thai bank, you can report in every three months either at Udon or Nong Khai Immigration.
- Khon Kaen does not have an Immigration post. You can mail in your current address via the post instead of having to appear in person.
- Monthly tourist-visa renewal and border runs to Laos can be done in less than a day from all three places.

- Long-term visas for Laos and Vietnam are at the respective consulates in Khon Kaen which saves time and expense travelling to Bangkok.

Work Opportunities
- Teaching English or helping students with their homework at Khon Kaen University.
- Bars or restaurants.
- Internet-based freelance work.

Healthcare
- Khon Kaen Ram and Srinakarinvirot hospitals are the best private hospitals in the region, with good private rooms for inpatient care at affordable prices. Many of the doctors speak English there.
- The government hospitals, though cheaper, have reasonable facilities but longer waiting times.
- Clinics and opticians in all three places.

Isaan Retiree Profiles And Interviews

Duncan Williams, 48, is from Cheshire, England. He came to Khon Kaen three years ago and opened a bar called "Eric's Bar." It is now a very popular expat hang-out. He has a Thai wife, who he lived with in England for 18 months. They have two young kids.

"Loy Kratong, New Year, Songkran, and Chinese New Year celebrations here are sights to behold.

"Life in a village is not as good as it sounds despite the cheaper housing prices. Many expats who don't speak good Thai have no one to talk to and come to my bar to retain their sanity.

"Real-estate services are not the best in the northeast because it's so cheap to rent. Best to rent for the first year and then make your move.

"Don't pay a deposit on a home until all the paperwork is confirmed and signed off.

"Selling your house is difficult. Both Thais and foreigners prefer to buy a new house than a second-hand one, so be sure before you buy. Land is more important than the house here."

Swend Risum, from Copenhagen, is single. He worked for a tobacco company in Khon Kaen for six years and stayed on, taking early retirement. He is 38. He owned a bar for two years but gave that up and now lives a life of leisure. He bought a house of 400 square meters for 6 million baht.

"Wheels are needed to get around in Khon Kaen, especially if you live out of town.

"Strangers who want to relocate get good help here. We do have two websites: www.ericsbarkhonkaen.com and www.khonkaen.com to get you started. Internet access depends on your phone connection. ADSL can be slow here.

"The paperwork for the already built house I bought took three days. No need for lawyers here.

Casey, aged 39, is from Rotterdam, Holland. He lived in Phuket for five years but prefers Khon Kaen because of the business opportunities. He is married to a Thai wife, and they built a six-bedroom farmhouse in one of the villages nearby on 2.3 rai of land. The house cost 800,000 baht. He owns a motorcycle rental shop near Khon Kaen Airport.

244

"Get involved in projects to keep busy. Open a bar, get into business, teach, do charity work with the Round Table, or you'll drink your life away.

"Lots of English teaching opportunities here. Not great money, but you can make up to 40,000 baht a month, which pays the bills.

"Eric's bar is our local newspaper; we really don't need one.

"Between biking, fishing, drinking at Eric's, buffet dining, and taking care of the family and the farm, I usually have little time on my hands.

"I'm a foreigner in my own country. Too crowded back home. Here? Good food, nice people, nothing to complain about. It only gets better and better with business opportunities.

"I'm safer here than in Rotterdam. No ATM robberies here.

"Hospital surgery can be tricky unless you're willing to pay for it."

Barry Jennings from Reading, England, was a refrigeration engineer back home. When an early retirement opportunity came up, he explored Cyprus, Spain, and Nairobi as options before he decided on Thailand. He made the rounds in Phuket, Chiang Mai, and Samui before deciding on Khon Kaen after a few visits. He lives in Nam Phong Village where his Thai wife, 31, is from. He has a two-bedroom house which was built with his wife supervising while he was in England tying up loose ends before retirement. He is 58.

"Many expats move up here because their wives are from this area. The first year needs a lot of adjustments. I realize that I'm not on holiday anymore. Now, after six years, I'm one of the lucky ones with a happy

245

marriage and a life that my pension easily takes care of.

"I come into Khon Kaen three times a week from Nam Phong to go to the gym, get some Western company, and eat good food.

"I take care of my garden, my two dogs, and my wife and her family. UBC cable TV has good reception to pass the time at night. That's more than enough for me at this age.

"Thai ways are more ancient than ours. Respect them and you'll be happy. Get your head out of the English way of doing things.

"House and land prices here are cheaper than anywhere else in Thailand.

"I use BUPA individual insurance but take care of my optical needs by myself.

⚬

John Bowles, 53, is from Bristol, England. He has a Thai wife who he lived with in England for seven months before they moved back to Khon Kaen five years ago. His wife is from nearby Kalasin.

"No hordes of backpackers coming through. But don't come here if you're expecting a lot of intellectual contacts.

"You're less likely to get ripped off here. You get to know who you can work with and trust very quickly. Qualified engineers for building or repair are hard to come by. No Yellow Pages here. You rely on local repairmen and hope they have the right tools for the job. And you get used to the power cuts after a while.

"Many housing complexes in this area never get finished for whatever reasons. My already built house was purchased from the developer in six weeks. Took two years to get all the small things fixed.

246

"If you don't know someone at TOT, getting a phone line can take forever. It's a business here, selling phone lines.

"But if you ever need dental work, come and get it done here."

John Carter is from Ohio. Aged 60, he first came here in 1968 during the Vietnam War. He came back to Thailand in 1976 and taught English at Thammasat University in Bangkok, where he met his wife. They moved to Khon Kaen in 2003 to settle down. John bought a house in one of the villages nearby. He says there are some 450 foreign retirees in the Khon Kaen area.

"Come here knowing very well what you want out of retirement. If you're the kind of retiree who wants a quiet place with not that much to do that requires brain stimulus, this is a good place to be.

"Don't let the small stuff get to you. Lay back and enjoy life. Teaching English keeps me occupied. I clean the house, take care of my dogs, go for walks in the village, and do my shopping at the local market for fresh produce. The days go by fast.

"No need to buy medical insurance here. Services are cheap enough unless you need major surgery. But I'm apprehensive about emergency ambulance services—they are non-existent. Private clinics have good services but lack the modern equipment found in private hospitals. Srinakarinvirot has good equipment. Good bang for your buck."

Gulf of Thailand Islands:
Koh Samui, Koh Pha-Ngan, and Koh Tao

The beautiful tropical islands of Koh Samui, Koh Pha-Ngan, and Koh Tao lie in the Gulf of Thailand about 400 kilometers south of Bangkok. All three islands, part of Surat Thani province, are major tourist destinations and home to many foreign residents and business owners.

All three islands boast fine beaches, lush jungle, and crystal-clear topical seas. Yet each has its own unique identity.

Samui, the largest and most developed of the three—and the only Gulf island with an airport—offers good shopping, a host of activities, as well as hospitals, clinics, and a wide range of houses and condos to choose from (some in the millions of dollars range).

Koh Pha-Ngan is the quintessential chill-out island. The tourist population explodes during its famous full-moon parties—which may not appeal to many retirees.

Koh Tao is a diver's and sportsman's island. Definitely for the more adventurous, and those who want to get away from the crowds on the other islands.

Koh Pha-Ngan and Koh Tao have only basic shopping and healthcare options, but offer plenty of bars and restaurants. Residents of these islands inevitably find themselves making regular, time-consuming trips to Samui or the mainland for better shopping, healthcare, and administrative reasons.

Over the past ten years, all three islands have undergone significant changes. Samui now caters for upmarket visitors and residents. There are more luxury resorts, shopping centers, restaurants, and expensive homes. Pha-Ngan hasn't gone quite as upmarket as Samui, but has still experienced wide-scale development, mostly lower-end bungalows, resorts, and private houses.

Samui hosts a large expat community. Pha-Ngan is home to about 300 foreign residents, of which the majority works full- or part-time, either as employees or running their own business.

Spectacular views and picture book sunsets

Why The Islands?
Pros
- Tropical beaches, clear seas, mountains, jungle, waterfalls, and glorious nature.
- Easy to get away from it all, particularly on Pha-Ngan and Tao.
- Fresh, clean air.
- A laidback lifestyle.
- It's a paradise.

Cons
- An island is an island; getting there requires a flight or a boat trip.
- Boats are the only option for Koh Pha-Ngan and Koh Tao and take at least three hours from the mainland; this becomes quite tedious after a while.

249

- Things are usually more expensive than the mainland because of transportation costs and lack of competition (especially on Pha-Ngan and Tao).
- Shopping choices are limited on Pha-Ngan and Tao.
- Too much traffic (Samui).
- Too much development (Samui and now also on Pha-Ngan).
- Deforestation and environmental damage.
- Infrastructure not keeping up with the pace of development.
- Limited availability of high-speed Internet outside of main towns.
- Mediocre healthcare options on Ko Pha-Ngan and Ko Tao
- Seasonal flooding (especially Samui).
- Frequent power cuts (Pha-Ngan and Tao).
- Occasional water shortages in the dry season.
- Too many tourists.

Leisure Activities And Things To Do
- Lots of expats to socialize and make friends with (Samui has an expats club).
- Beaches and water sports.
- Diving (especially Koh Tao).
- Plenty of golf courses.
- Sea fishing.
- Jungle trekking, elephant rides, waterfalls.
- Good Thai and Western restaurants (especially Samui) and great seafood.
- Plenty of nightlife (especially Samui); European pubs (Samui); live music (mostly Samui and Tao).

- Movie theater (Samui, and a small one on Pha-Ngan); bowling (Samui); fitness clubs; library (Samui).

Shopping
- Good shopping on Samui: Tesco Lotus (Chaweng), Home-Pro, Home Mart; plus clothing, domestic ware, electronics, building supplies.
- Good supermarkets, Western foods, and electrical and electronic items in Nathon town, Samui.
- Tourist shopping centers at Chaweng and Lamai on Samui.
- Tops and Colibri supermarkets in Chaweng, Samui; good selection of fresh and imported produce.
- Good markets in Nathon, Samui.
- Some Western foods available in Limpipong and Big C supermarkets, Tongsala, Pha-Ngan.
- Market in Tongsala, Pha-Ngan.
- About four reasonably well stocked but expensive building supply outlets in Tongsala, Pha-Ngan.
- Good banking and legal services (mostly Samui).

Transport
- Samui Airport is owned by Bangkok Airways, which allows no competition, so flights are expensive compared to other local airports such as Surat Thani. Flights to Bangkok (one hour), Phuket, Pattaya, Singapore, and Hong Kong.
- Trains from Bangkok typically leave early evening and arrive at Surat Thani in the early morning. The trip takes about 12 hours and costs 550 to 750 baht depending on upper or lower berth, air conditioning or fan.

- From the train station, it is over an hour by bus to Don Sak ferry terminal (about 100 baht).
- A train to Malaysia leaves Surat Thani at 1 a.m., arriving in Penang around noon, and costs about 1,500 baht.
- Several private bus companies run 'VIP' buses from Bangkok to Surat Thani for about 500 baht. They are typically very uncomfortable. A 'luxury' government bus is available from Bangkok for about 800 to 1,000 baht including boat.
- For destinations other than Bangkok, buses are available from Surat Thani.
- Car ferries from Don Sak leave for Samui every hour, and for Pha-Ngan about four times a day. Cost is about 200 baht to Samui and 300 baht to Pha-Ngan. Crossing times are about 90 minutes to Samui and 150 minutes to Pha-Ngan. Songserm runs a smaller, slightly faster boat.
- Night boats to Samui and Pha-Ngan leave Surat Thani town at about 11 p.m. and arrive in the early morning. The night boats will accept goods packages and you can buy your ticket upon arrival at the port. This ferry is very useful when buying items in town.
- Between the islands themselves, three companies offer both fast and slow boats throughout the day. Samui to Pha-Ngan takes about one hour; Pha-Ngan to Koh Tao takes about 90 minutes.
- Most tourists rent motorcycles or jeeps on the is-lands. Private taxis are expensive and *songtaews* are very slow.
- Motorcycles and cars can be purchased on the islands, but better deals will be found on the mainland.

- Samui and Pha-Ngan have good ring roads, but accidents are very common; drive very carefully.
- Visa runs are typically to Penang, Malaysia; border runs are typically to the town of Ranong for a crossing into Burma. There is an Immigration office on Samui, where visas can be extended.

Work Opportunities
- Resorts, bars, restaurants, and tourist services.
- Some expats freelance from home (in various capacities) via the Internet.

Healthcare
- Good options on Samui only. Private hospitals include Bandon International, Bangkok Samui, Samui International, and Thai International Hospital.
- Government hospitals: Samui Hospital, and Koh Pha-Ngan.
- More than 50 clinics on Samui.
- About six clinics on Pha-Ngan and Koh Tao.
- More than 40 dentists, including cosmetic dentistry, on Samui.
- At least one dentist on Pha-Ngan.

Property
- *Nor Sor 3* and *Chanot* land on Samui ranges from about 700,000 baht per *rai* with poor access and limited views to 10 million baht per *rai* and above for beachfront or good views and good access.
- Houses on Samui start from about 2 million baht for two bedrooms with no view to 35 million baht and above for a four-bedroom luxury villa with beach, view, pool, and guesthouse.

- *Nor Sor 3* and *Chanot* land on Pha-Ngan ranges from about 500,000 baht per *rai* with poor access and limited views to 6 million baht per *rai* and above for beachfront or good views and access.
- Houses tend to be simpler and cheaper on Pha-Ngan and Koh Tao. Most people buy land and build.

PART 5
REFERENCES

Helpful Websites
www.thaivisa.com - The most comprehensive site for visa information

www.expatfocus.com
- For anyone moving or living abroad

http://en.wikipedia.org/wiki/Thailand
- Facts about Thailand

www.orientexpat.com - Information and online community for expatriates

English Language Newspapers Online
www.bangkokpost.net - Bangkok Post Newspaper online

www.nationmultimedia.com - The Nation newspaper online

www.pattayainfo.com - Pattaya info. Online version of Pattaya's local newspaper

www.phuketgazette.net - Online version of Phuket's local newspaper

www.chiangmai-mail.com - Chiang Mai mail newspaper

www.pattayamail.com – Pattaya mail and online newspaper

Tourist Information Sites
www.tourismthailand.org - Tourism Authority of Thailand

www.bangkoktourist.com - Bangkok Tourism Division

Thailand Government Sites
www.weather.go.th - Thai weather site

www.thaitrade.com - Department of Export Promotion

www.correct.go.th - Ministry of Justice

www.th.embassyinformation.com - Locate the Thailand Embassy in any country or any country's embassy address in Thailand.

Miscellaneous
www.salsabangkok.com - Guide to salsa and Latin dance in Bangkok

www.tangobangkok.com - For Tango dancers

www.dance-centre.com - For ballroom dancers

www.paiboonpublishing.com - Learning Thai and other Southeast Asian languages www.pattayabridge.com - Pattaya Bridge Club

www.ThaiLoveLinks.com - Online dating

www.amchamthailand.com - The American Chamber of Commerce in Thailand

www.bangkoksports.com - Everything about sports in Bangkok

www.fccthai.com - The Foreign Correspondent's Club of Thailand

www.siam-society.org - The Siam Society

www.stickmanbangkok.com - Stickman's popular guide to Bangkok

www.thaiticketmaster.com. - Check out current concerts and buy tickets online.

www.thaiwebsites.com – English language website about Thailand

http://finance.yahoo.com/currency - Currency converter site

Info for Expats in Thailand
The following is a list of the expat clubs and events we have found in Thailand. You may be able to locate others. All information listed here should be verified since everything is subject to change.

Chiang Mai Expats Club
They meet every 2nd and 4th Saturday of the month at 10.30am.
Website: www.chiangmaiexpatsclub.com
Contact: Jim info@chiangmaiexpatsclub.com

Pattaya City Expats Club
The Pattaya City Expats Club meets every Sunday morning.

Website: www.pattayaexpats.com
Contact: Richard rickksc@ksc.th.com or
Contact: Drew drewnoyes@yahoo.com

Pattaya Biz Club
The Pattaya Biz Club and support group hold monthly meetings.
Website: www.pattayabizclub.com
More info:
Dave info@pattayabizclub.com

Pattaya Expats Club
This club promotes Saturday lunch-time entertainment sessions.
Website: www.pattayaexpatsclub.com
Contact: Pete
webhits2000@yahoo.com
Contact: Niels:
dragone@loxinfo.co.th

Expats' Association of Northeast Thailand
Monthly meeting is held on the last Saturday of each month in central Khon Kaen city.
Email: Jim expatne@thai.com
Email: Peter pjreading@hotmail.com

Bangkok Expats Association
Meetings have been taking place on Sundays & Tuesdays.
Email: Bob or Kurt
bangkokexpatsassociation@thai.com

Samui Expats Club
Socials are held first Friday of most months at different venues.
Website: www.samuiexpats.com
Contact: Linda info@samuiexpats.com

Other Thailand Expat Websites
www.thaivisa.com
www.phuket-info.com
www.huahinafterdark.com
www.khonkaen.com
www.thailand.alloexpat.com

Note: The authors of this book do not endorse any of the expat clubs or websites listed here. We have provided contact information only.

Provinces of Thailand by Location

In this section we have grouped the 76 provinces of Thailand by location and also ranked then in size of population. The first number is the ranking of the province according to population size.

Central Thailand:
Because of the influence of the Chao Phraya River the central region is relatively flat and very fertile for growing rice crops. This area contains many historical sites and also Thailand's capital city Bangkok.

0	Bangkok Metropolitan Area . . .	8,600,000
1	Bangkok.	5,900,000
18	Samut Prakan	1,000,000
22	Nonthaburi	950,000
26	Suphanburi	860,000
27	Ratchaburi.	840,000
28	Kanchanaburi	830,000
29	Nakhon Pathom	820,000
31	Pathum Thani	780,000
32	Lop Buri.	770,000
34	Ayutthaya	760,000
37	Chachoengsao	650,000
39	Saraburi.	630,000
46	Sa Kaeo	540,000
58	Phetchaburi	460,000
59	Prachin Buri	450,000
60	Samut Sakhon	450,000
64	Chai Nat.	340,000
67	Ang Thong.	290,000
70	Nakhon Nayok	250,000
74	Sing Buri	220,000
75	Samut Songkhram	204,000

Eastern Thailand:
The four provinces of eastern Thailand extend along the Gulf of Thailand coast. This area of Thailand is famous for its beaches, gem trading, tropical fruits and rice noodles.

14	Chon Buri	1,200,000
44	Rayong	560,000
48	Chanthaburi	510,000
73	Trat	220,000

257

Northern Thailand:

Bordered by the countries of Laos and Burma this vicinity of the country is distinguished by forested mountains and luxuriant river valleys. The north encompasses working elephants, hill tribes, ancient cities, colorful celebrations, superb northern Thai and Burmese-style temples and the legendary Golden Triangle area.

5	Chiang Mai	1,650,000
13	Chiang Rai	1,230,000
16	Nakhon Sawan	1,130,000
19	Phetchabun	1,040,000
25	Phitsanulok	860,000
30	Lampang	790,000
33	Kamphaeng Phet	760,000
41	Sukhothai	620,000
43	Phichit	580,000
47	Tak	520,000
51	Phayao	490,000
54	Nan	482,000
55	Uttaradit	480,000
56	Phrae	479,000
61	Lamphun	410,000
66	Uthai Thani	330,000
71	Mae Hong Son	240,000

Northeastern Thailand:

The part of Thailand known as Issan comprises a large area which traditionally has been the poorest region of the country due to a thin layer of topsoil and being historically prone to droughts. Farming is the main occupation but the region contains some of the largest cities in the country. Bordered by the Mekong River and the countries of Laos and Cambodia this area receives the least amount of visiting tourists.

2	Nakhon Ratchasima	2,610,000
3	Ubon Ratchathani	1,800,000
4	Khon Kaen	1,770,000
6	Udon Thani	1,540,000
7	Buri Ram	1,550,000
9	Si Sa Ket	1,460,000
10	Surin	1,400,000
11	Roi Et	1,320,000

258

```
15 . . . . . Chaiyaphum . . . . . . . . . . 1,140,000
17 . . . . . Sakon Nakhon . . . . . . . . . 1,120,000
20 . . . . . Kalasin . . . . . . . . . . . .   997,000
23 . . . . . Maha Sarakham . . . . . . . .   946,000
24 . . . . . Nong Khai . . . . . . . . . . .   913,000
36 . . . . . Nakhon Phanom . . . . . . . .   702,000
40 . . . . . Loei . . . . . . . . . . . . . .   627,000
45 . . . . . Yasothon . . . . . . . . . . .   551,000
50 . . . . . Nong Bua Lam Phu . . . . . . .   500,000
63 . . . . . Amnat Charoen . . . . . . . . .   371,000
65 . . . . . Mukdahan . . . . . . . . . . .   338,000
```

Southern Thailand:
Consisting of hilly terrain, rain forests, lush tropical islands and rich mineral deposits the south receives the most annual rainfall of any place in Thailand. World famous islands of Phuket and Koh Samui attract hordes of tourists ready to enjoy the sea, sand and nighttime entertainment. The most southern provinces attract less western tourists and are not as affluent.

```
 8 . . . . . . Nakhon Si Thammarat . . . . . 1,530,000
12 . . . . . Songkhla . . . . . . . . . . . 1,300,000
21 . . . . . Surat Thani . . . . . . . . . .   950,000
35 . . . . . Narathiwat . . . . . . . . . . .   710,000
38 . . . . . Pattani . . . . . . . . . . . .   630,000
42 . . . . . Trang . . . . . . . . . . . . .   610,000
49 . . . . . Phattalung . . . . . . . . . . .   505,000
52 . . . . . Prachuap Khiri Khan . . . . . .   497,000
53 . . . . . Chumphon . . . . . . . . . . .   480,000
57 . . . . . Yala . . . . . . . . . . . . . .   470,000
62 . . . . . Krabi . . . . . . . . . . . . .   390,000
68 . . . . . Phuket . . . . . . . . . . . .   280,000
69 . . . . . Satun . . . . . . . . . . . . .   277,000
72 . . . . . Phang Nga . . . . . . . . . . .   240,000
76 . . . . . Ranong . . . . . . . . . . . .   179,000
```

Royal Thai Embassies and Consulate General by Country

Please verify the contact information listed here. Phone numbers and embassy locations may have changed since the printing of this book.

Argentina
Virrey del Pino 2458-6 Piso, 1426 Buenos Aires
Tel: +541 785 6504, 6521, 6532 Fax: +541 785 6548

Australia
111 Empire Circuit
Yarralumla, A.C.T. 2600, Canberra
Tel: +06 273 1149, 273 2937 Fax: +06 273 1518

Level 8 131 Macquarie Street, Sydney, NSW 2000
Tel (02) 9241-2542, 9241-2543 Fax (02) 9247-8312
Email: **thaicon-sydney@diplomats.com**

87 Annerley Road
South Brisbane Qld 4102
Tel (07) 3846-7771 Fax (07)3846-7772
Email:**consulofthailand@hotmail.com**

Level 1, 72 Flinders Street, Adelaide SA 5000
Tel (08) 8232-7474 Fax (08) 8232-7474
Suite 301 566 St Kilda Road Melbourne Victoria 3004
Tel (03) 9533-9100 Fax (03) 9533-9200

Austria
Weimarer Strasse 68, A-1180
Vienna
Tel: 310 3423, 310 1630, 310 8988
www.mfa.go.th/web/1277.php?depid=181

Arensbergstrasse 2, Salzburg
Tel: +0662 646 5660

Bangladesh

House No. NW(E) 12, Road No.59
Gulshan Model Town, Dhaka
Tel: +880 2 601 634, 601 475 Fax: +880 2 883 588

Belgium
Square du Val de la Cambre 2, 1050 Brussels
Tel: +322 640 6810, 640 1986 Fax: +322 648 3066
www.thaiembassy.be/portal

Brazil
Lote 10-Setor de Embaixadas Norte, Avenida das Nacoes Norte
P.O. Box 10-2460, 70.433 Brasilia, DF.
Tel: +061 224 6943, 224 7943, 223 5105
Fax: +061 321 2994, 223 7502

Brunei
No.1 Simpang 52-86-16, Kampong Mata-Mata
Gadong 3280 Bandar Seri Begawan
Tel: 429 653 4, 440 360, 448 331 Fax: 421 775

Canada
The Royal Thai Embassy, 180 Island Park Drive, Ottawa Ontario, K1Y 0A2
Tel: (613) 722-4444 Fax: (613) 722-6624

1040 Burrard Street, Vancouver, British Columbia
Tel: (1-604) 687-1143, 687-8848, 687-1661 Fax (1-604) 687-4434
Email: info@thaicongenvancover.org
http://www.thaicongenvancouver.org

China
40 Guang Hua Lu, Beijing 100600
Tel: (8610) 6532-1749, 6532-1848, 6532-2151 Fax: (8610) 6532-1748
http://203.150.20.55/beijing

White Swan Hotel
Southern Street, Shamian Island, Guangzhou
Tel: (8620) 8188-6986 ext. 3301 - 3303,- 3307 Fax: (8620) 8187-9451
Email: gzthaicg@public1.guangzhou.gd.cn

145,1st Floor, South Building—Kunming Hotel, Dong Feng Dong Road,
Kunming. Tel: (86871) 3168916, 3149296 Fax: (86871) 3166891
Email: thaikmg@public.km.yn.cn
www.mfa.go.th/web/2165.php?depid=193

China (Taiwan)
www.mfa.go.th/web/1157.php?depid=195

Finland
www.thaiembassy.fi

France
Embassy of Thailand
8, rue Greuze, 75016 Paris, France
Tel: 01.56.26.50.50 ,Fax: 01.56.26.04.46
http://203.150.20.55/paris

Hong Kong
Fairmont House—8th Floor, 8 Cotton Tree Drive
Central, Hong Kong. Tel: (852) 25216481 - 5 Fax: (852) 25218629
Email: thai-cg@hongkong.super.net
www.thai-consulate.org.hk

Germany
Ubierstrasse 65, D-53173 Bonn Tel: (0228) 956860 Fax: (0228) 363702
www.thaiembassy.de

261

Greece
23 Taigetou Street, P.O. Box 65215
Paleo Psychico 15452, Athens
Tel: (301) 6717969, 6710155 Fax: (301) 6479508

Hungary
Verecke ut.79, 025 Budapest
Tel: (36-1) 1689421, 1689422 Fax: (36-1) 2501580, 1882347

India
56-N, Nyaya Marg,, Chanakyapuri, New Delhi-110021
Tel: 611 8103, 611 8104 Fax: 687 2029
www.thaiemb.org.in

Indonesia
74, Jalan Imam Bonjol, Jakarta Pusat
Tel: 390 4225, 390 4055 Fax: 310 7469

Israel
21 Shaul Hamelech Blvd, Tel Aviv Israel
Tel: (972-3) 695-8980, 695-8984, Fax: (972-3) 695-8991
Email: thaisr@netvision.co.il
http://www.mfa.go.th/web/1315.php?depid=210

Iran
Baharestan Avenue, Park Amin-ed-Dowleh No. 4, P.O. Box 11495-111,
Tehran. Tel: +9821 753 1433, 753 7708

Italy
Via Bertoloni 26B, I-00197 Rome
Tel: +0039 6 8078379, 8081381 Fax: +0039 6 8078693

Japan
3-14-6, Kami-Osaki, Shinagawa-ku, Tokyo 141
Tel: +03 3441 1386, 1387 Fax: +03 3442 6750, 3442 6828
www.thaiembassy.jp

Bangkok Bank Building, 4th Floor, 1-9-16 Kyutaro-Machi, Oska
Tel: (81-6) 6262-9226 to 7 Fax (81-6) 6262-9228
Email: rtcg-osk@jupiter.plala.or.jp
http://www.thai-kansai.net

Kenya: Rose Avenue, off Denis Pritt Rd., P.O. Box 58349, Nairobi
Tel: +254 2·714276, 715800, Fax: +254 2 715801

Korea (South)

653-7, Hannam-dong, Yongsan-ku, Seoul
Tel: +82 2 795 3098, 795 0095 Fax: +82 2 798 3448
www.thaiembassy.or.kr

Kuwait
Surra, Area No.3, Block No.49, Ali Bin Abi-Taleb Street, Building No. 28., P.O. Box 66647 Bayan, 43757
Tel: 531 4870, 531 7530-1, 533 9243 Fax: 531 7532

Laos
Route Phonekheng, P.O. Box 128, Vientiane
Tel: 214 5813, 214 5856 Fax: +66 1 411 0017

Malaysia
206 Jalan Ampang
50450 Kuala Lumpur
Tel: +03 248 8222, 248 8350 Fax: +03 248 6527

Malaysia
No. 1, Jalan Tunku Abdul Rahman 10350 Penang
Tel. (60-4) 2268029, 2269484 Fax:(60-4) 2263121
Email: thaipg@tm.net.my

Mexico
Sierra Vertientes 1030, Lomas de Chapultepec, 11000 Mexico, D.F.
Tel: +525 596 1290, 596 8446 Fax: +525 596 8236

Morocco
11 Rue de Tiddes, Rabat, B.P. 4436
Tel: +212 7 763 365, 763 328 Fax: +212 7 763 920

Myanmar (Burma)
45, Pyay Road, Yangon
Tel: +951 35 670, 33 082, 21 567 Fax: +951 22 784

Nepal
Jyoti Kendra, Thapathali, Kathmandu
Tel: +977 1 213 910, 213 912 Fax: +977 1 226599

Netherlands
1 Buitenrustweg, 2517 KD, The Hague
Tel: +070 345 2088, 345 9703 Fax:+ 070 345 1929
www.mfa.go.th/web/1326.php?depid=227

New Zealand
2 Cook Street, P.O. Box 17-226, Karori, Wellington
Tel: +04 476 8618, 476 8619 Fax: +04 476 3677
www.thaiembassynz.org.nz

Nigeria
1 Ruxton Road, Old Ikoyi, P.O. Box 3095, Lagos
Tel: 269 0334 Fax: 269 2855

Norway
Munkedamsveien 59 B, 0270 Oslo
Tel: +47 22832517, 22832518 Fax: 22830384

Oman
Villa 33-34 Road "O", Madinat Qaboos East, Muscat

P.O. Box 60, M.Q., Postal Code 115, Muscat,

P.O. Box 3367 Ruwi, Postal Code 112, Muscat.
Tel: +09 68 602 683, 602 684
Fax: +09 68 605 714

Pakistan
4, Street No.8, Shalimar F-8/3, Islamabad
Tel: 859 130, 859 131, 859 195 | Fax: +92-51 256 730

Philippines
107 Rada Street, Legaspi Village, Makati, Metro Manila, P.O. Box 1228,
Makati Central Post Office, 1252 Makati, Metro Manila
Tel: 815 4220, 816 0696 7, 815 4219 Fax: 815 4221

Poland
ul. Staroscinska 1B m. 2-3, 02-516. Warsaw
Tel: +48 22 492 655,496 414, 494 730 Fax: +48 22 492 630

Portugal
Rua de Alcolena 12, Restelo, 1400 Lisbon
Tel: +35 11 301 4848,301 5051 Fax: +35 11 301 8181
www.mfa.go.th/web/1332.php?depid=235

Romania
44-48 Strada Mihai Eminescu, Etaj 2, Apartamentul 5, Bucharest
Tel: +40 1 210 1338, 210 3447 Fax: +40 1 210 2600

Russia
Eropkinsky Pereulok 3, Moscow 119034
Tel: +095 201 4893, 201 3989 Fax: +095 230 2004, 210 2853
www.thaiembassymoscow.com

Saudi Arabia
Diplomatic Quarter, Ibnu Banna Road, P.O. Box 94359, Riyadh 11693
Tel: +966-1) 488 1174, 488 0797 Fax: +966-1) 488 1179
http://203.150.20.55/riyadh

Senegal
10 Rue Leon G. Damas, Angle F. Fann Residence, B.P. 3721, Dakkar
Tel: +221) 243076, 243801 Fax: +221) 256360

Singapore
370 Orchard Road, Singapore 0923
Tel: +65 235 4175, 737 2158 Fax: +65 732 0778
www.thaiembsingapore.org

South Africa
840 Church Street, Eastwood, Arcadia 0083, Pretoria
Tel: +012 342 5470, 342 4516 Fax: +012 342 4805

Spain
Calle Del Segra, 29-2 A, 28002 Madrid
Tel: +91 5632903, 5637959 Fax: +91 5640033

Sri Lanka
43, Dr. C.W.W. Kannangara Mawatha, Colombo 7
Tel: 697 406, 689 045, 689 037 Fax: 697 516
www.mfa.go.th/web/1340.php?depid=244

Sweden
Floragatan 3, 114 31 Stockholm
Box 26220, 100 40 Stockholm
Tel: +08 791 73 40 Fax: +08 791 73 51

Switzerland
Kirchstrasse 56, CH-3097 Bern-Lieberfeld
Tel: +41 31 970 30 30 Fax: +41 31 970 30 35
www.thaiembassy.se

Turkey
Cankaya Cad. Kader Sok. 45/3-4 06700 Gaziosmanpasa, Ankara
Tel: +90 312 4673409, 4673059 Fax: +90 312 438 6474

United Arab Emirates
Villa No.1, Plot No. 341, West 14/1 Al Rowdah
P.O. Box 47466 Abu Dhabi
Tel: +97 12 453 991, 431 279, 432 554 Fax: +97 12 458 687

United Kingdom
29-30 Queen's Gate, London, SW7 5JB
Tel: +07 1 5890173, 5892944 Fax: +07 1 8239695
www.thaiembassyuk.org.uk

United States of America
1024 Wisconsin Avenue, N.W., Suite 401, Washington, D.C. 20007,
Tel: +202 944 3600
www.thaiembdc.org/index.htm

611 North Larchmont Boulevard, 2nd Floor, Los Angeles, CA USA
Tel: (+1-323) 9629574, 9629577 Fax (+1-323) 9622128
Email: thai-la@mindspring.com
http://www.thai-la.net

700 North Rush Street, Chicago, Illinois USA
Tel: (+1-312) 6643129 Fax (+1-312) 6643230
Email: thaichicago@ameritech.net
http://www.thaichicago.net

Vietnam
63-65 Hoang Dieu Street, Hanoi
Tel: +84 4 235 092 94 Fax: +84 4 235 088
www.mfa.go.th/web/1488.php?depid=258

United Nations (Switzerland)
28B Chemin du Pefit-Saconnex, 1209 Geneva
Tel: (4122) 734-2010, 734-2018, 734-2020 Fax: (4122) 733-3678
E-Mail: thai.gva@itu.ch

Useful Phone Numbers in Bangkok

Phone numbers and addresses were current at the time of publication of this book and may have changed.

Emergency Calls

Police—191

Fire—199

Tourist Police—1699

Tourist Service Center 1155

Bangkok Metropolitan Administration Hotline 1555

Missing Persons Bureau
02-282-1815

Ambulance (Bangkok)
02-255-1133-6

Telephone Services

Bangkok directory inquiries: 1133

Provincial directory inquiries: 183

Local/International directory assistance: 100

IDD: 001 + Country code + area code + phone number

AT&T direct service:
001-999-1111-1

Useful contact information

Immigration Office
Soi Suanphlu
Sathorn Tai Road
Bangkok 10120
Tel. 02-287-3101

Revenue Department
Chakkapong Road
Bangkok 10200
Tel. 02-282-9899

Tourist Information Counter
372 Bamrung Muang Road
Bangkok 10100
Tel. 02-226 0060, 226-0072

Tourist Assistance Center
4 Ratchadamnoen Nok Road
Bangkok, Tel. 02-281-5051

Tourism Authority of Thailand
Head Office, Le Concorde Building
202 Ratchadapisek Road
Tel. 02-694-1222
Fax 02-694-1220

Tourist Police,
Unico House,
Soi Lang Suan, Ploenchit Road,
Bangkok, Tel. 1699 or 02-652-1721

Bangkok International Airport
Phahonyothin Road, Bangkok, Tel.
02-535-1111

Departure Info 02-535-1254,
02-535-1386

266

Arrival Info 02-535-1310, 02-535-1305, 02-535-1149

Bangkok Domestic Airport
Phahonyothin Road, Bangkok, Tel. 02-535-2081

Departure Info
02-535-1192, 02-535-1277

Arrival Info 02-535-1253, 02-535-1305, 02-535-1149

Thai Airways International Plc.
89 Vibhavadi Rangsit Road
Bangkok, Tel. 02-513-0121

**Bangkok Railway Station
(Hua Lamphong)**
Rama IV Road, Bangkok 10500
Tel. 02-223 7010, 223-7020, 233-7461

**Northern & Northeastern
Bus Terminal**
Phahonyothin Road
Bangkok
Tel. 02-272 0299

Southern Bus Terminal
Boromrat Chonnani Road
Bangkok 10700, Tel. 02-435-1199, 02-434 5558

Eastern Bus Terminal
Sukhumvit Road (Ekamail
Bangkok 10110
Tel. 02-391-2504, 02-392-2521

Bangkok Local Bus Services: 184

Credit Cards
American Express: 02-235-0990, 02-236-0276

Lost cards: 02-273-0044

Diner's Club: 02-233-0313, 02-233-5775

Lost cards: 02-233-5644-5

MasterCard and Visa: 02-270-1122, 02-270-1259

Lost cards: 02-252-2712

Celebrations in Thailand
Here are some of the major celebrations in Thailand. Ones marked with an * are observed as public holidays.

New Year's Day* (January 1)
Thailand celebrates the traditional New Year's Day in grand style. Most Thai people head to their villages to take an extended holiday vacation. Exciting events take place in Bangkok and the other major cities in Thailand.

Magha Puja Day* (Religious holiday)
(On the full-moon day of the 3rd Thai lunar month, usually in February).
A holy Buddhist Holiday which marks the occasion when 1,250 disciples of the Lord Buddha spontaneously gathered to hear his preaching.

Chiang Mai Flower Festival
(First weekend in February)
Three day festival to celebrate the beautiful flowers and decorative plants of the north. Beauty contests and a parade is held featuring colorful floats decorated with live flowers, marching bands and thousands of people in traditional Thai costumes.

Chinese New Year
(Later January or early February)
Lion dancing and firecrackers make a festive event in the Chinatown area of Bangkok. The fun loving Thais use this celebration as another excuse to party and take an extended time off to visit the relatives.

Songkran Festival* (13 - 15 April)

The traditional Thai New Year exuberantly celebrated all over the Kingdom. Acts of merit making and paying honor to elders is now overshadowed by the riotous water splashing that keeps everyone cool in this the hottest month in Thailand. Notable celebrations in Bangkok and Chiang Mai where the party continues for 5 days.

Coronation Day* (5 May)
The date that King Bhumibol was crowned the 9th king of the Chakri Dynasty in 1950.

Ploughing Ceremony* (11 May)
This date marks the start of the planting season and is celebrated in Sanam Luang in Bangkok with prayers for the blessing of the upcoming rice crop. The King or a member of the royal family presides over this Bramanic ritual.

Rocket Festival (12 - 14 May)
This festival celebrated uniquely in the Northeast and most wildly in Yasothon province consists of launching rockets made of bamboo to insure the much needed rain for the rainy season. Beauty contests, a parade and rocket contests makes this the most exciting event in the Issan area of Thailand.

Visakha Puja Day*
(Religious holiday)
(On the full-moon day of the 6th Thai lunar month, usually in May)
On this day but in different years the Buddha was born, attained Enlightenment and entered Nirvana.

Asalha Puja Day*
(Religious holiday)
(On the full-moon day of the 8th Thai lunar month, usually in July)
Thais honor this date because it

marks when the Buddha gave his first sermon to his first five disciples after his Enlightenment.

Khao Phansa Day*
(Religious holiday)
(1st day of 8th waning moon, usually in July)
The day that marks the beginning of the Buddhist lent. Three months during the rainy season when it is customary for Thai men to be ordained as monks. Monks are required to remain at their resident temples during this period.

Her Majesty the Queen's Birthday*
(12 August)
This date commemorates the Queen's birthday and Mother's Day in Thailand. Elaborate celebrations are held in Bangkok in front of the Grand Palace and the Thais pay tribute their Queen with concerts and entertainment events.

Vegetarian Festival
(Late September or early October)
Mainly celebrated by people of Chinese decent in the Phuket area who make merit by not eating meat to honor an event in 1825 when an entire Chinese Opera company over-came extreme illness by eating only vegetarian food. The culmination of the celebration is a parade where participants perform self-tortures to invoke supernatural powers.

Loi Krathong
(On the full-moon day of the 12th Thai lunar month, usually in November)
This festival of light honors the water Goddess in the evening when the Thais float their Krathongs, lotus-shaped vessels decorated with flowers, a coin and a lit candle, on the rivers all over the Kingdom. The

most spectacular celebrations are held in Sukhothai and Chiang Mai.

His Majesty the King's Birthday*
(5 December)
Father's day is also celebrated on this date. The King is honored with celebrations at Sanam Luang in Bangkok and many music and singing contests are held around the country to pay tribute to the musical talents of His Majesty.

Constitution Day*
(10 December)
This date honors the day that Thailand's first Constitution was declared by King Rama VII in 1932.

New Year's Eve*
(31 December)
Elaborate celebrations, fireworks and parties until dawn are held all over Thailand counting down to the stroke of midnight.

Prices of Common Items

Prices below are rough estimates of what average Thai people in Bangkok pay. They are shown here for you to have a general idea how much the locals spend. Prices vary depending on the location, level of service, etc. The exchange rate used here is 40 baht to the dollar.

Item	Thai Baht	US Dollar
A bowl of noodles	30	$0.75
Fried rice	25	$0.62
Papaya salad	25	$0.62
Rice with two items	30	$0.75
Tom Yam Kung soup	80	$2.00
A bottle of Singha beer	50	$1.25
A bottle of Mekhong whisky	150	$3.75
A small bottle of water	10	$0.25
City bus (non air-conditioned)	8	$0.20
City bus (air-conditioned)	20	$0.50
Two kilometers tuk-tuk ride	60	$1.50
Motorcycle taxi (short ride)	10	$0.25
Minibus, Songtaew	10	$0.25
Starting fare of taxis	35	$0.87
Hair cut	80	$2.00
Pedicure	60	$1.50
Manicure	60	$1.50
Facial massage	200	$5.00
Foot massage (1 hour)	200	$5.00
Thai massage (2 hours)	250	$6.25
Swedish massage (1 hour)	800	$20.00

Gym daily . . . . 150 . . . . $3.75
Gym monthly . . . . 3000 . . . . $75.00
A bottle of 100 Tylenol pills . . . . 120 . . . . $3.00
A bottle of Thai aspirin pills . . . . .40 . . . . $1.00
4 pills of Viagra. . . . . 2000 . . . . $50.00
7 days supply of antibiotics . . . . 120 . . . . $3.00
Rhinocort spray. . . . . 440 . . . . $11.00
Housekeeper (monthly) . . . . . . 7000 . . . . . . $175.00
Driver (monthly) . . . . 8000 . . . . . . $200.00
Part-time gardener . . . . 2000 . . . . $50.00
Full-time nurse (monthly) . . . . .50000 . . . . . $1,250.00
Botox shots. . . . . 3000 . . . . . . $125.00
Teeth cleaning . . . . 400 . . . . 10.00
Nose job . . . . .10000 . . . . . . $250.00
Movie ticket . . . . 120 . . . . $3.00
Private dance lesson (one hour) . . 1000 . . . . $25.00

About The Authors

Philip Bryce is originally from England. Until 2003, he worked as a software engineer in Silicon Valley, California, fighting the traffic and slaving long hours to pay a mortgage, all the while dreaming of a life in paradise. After visiting Thailand a number of times and falling in love with the country (and the girls) he decided to move to Thailand.

Philip writes books and supports on-line customers of TabTrax, a drum music teaching program that he created. He is his own boss and lives the life he loves in Thailand. He has a beautiful house on the island of Koh Pha-Ngan overlooking the sea, a lovely Thai wife, and a steady income from his freelance work.

Sunisa Wongdee Terlecky left Thailand when she was 22 to continue her studies overseas. She has done extensive research on Thailand and given lectures to foreigners on the Thai language and culture. She has always been interested in early retirement. She is an avid traveler, scrabble player and accomplished Latin dancer. She now resides, with her husband, in San Francisco, California and Bangkok, Thailand. Sunisa enjoys living as an early semi-retiree and a part-time writer.

Glossary

amphur	district/district office
BE	Buddhist Era (calendar)
chanot	a form of land title
farang	Caucasian foreigner
jai yen	having a "cool" heart, be patient
koh, ko	island
Lanna	old northern Thailand
mai pen rai	never mind
muay Thai	Thai kick boxing
Nor Sor 3	a form of land title
Or-Bor-Tor	sub-district administration
rai	land area equal to 1,600 square meters
sanuk	fun, having fun
songtaew	pick-up truck public 'bus'
tabien baan	house registration document
takraw	Southeast Asian version of 'volleyball' played with feet and a small woven rattan ball
tuk-tuk	three-wheeled, open-sided taxi with a canopy roof
waa, wah	a Thai unit of measurement equal to 2 meters
wat	temple
yaa-baa	methamphetamine

Further Reading

Agar, Charles. *Frommer's Thailand.* NJ, USA: Wiley Publishing, Inc., 2006.

Bryce, Philip. *How to Buy Land and Build a House in Thailand.* Bangkok: Paiboon Publishing, 2006.

Cooper, Robert and Nanthapa. *Culture Shock! Thailand.* Singapore: Times Books International, 2005.

Clyatt, Bob. *Work Less, Live More - The New Way to Retire Early.* USA: Nolo, 2005.

Cummings, Joe and Konn, Morgan and Williams, China and Blond, Rebecca. *Thailand.* China: Lonely Planet Publications Pty Ltd., 2005.

Pirazzi, Chris and Vasant, Vitida. *Thailand Fever - A Road Map for Thai-Western Relationships.* Bangkok: Paiboon Publishing, 2004.

Stein, Ben and DeMuth, Phil. *Yes, You Can Still Retire Comfortably!* Carlsbad, California: New Beginnings Press, 2005.

Thongkaew, Ruengsak and Poomsan, Benjawan *Thai Law for Foreigners.* Bangkok: Paiboon Publishing, 2008

Warner, Ralph. *Get a Life - You Don't Need a Million to Retire Well.* USA: Nolo, 2004.

Wylie, Philip. *How to Establish a Successful Business in Thailand.* Bangkok: Paiboon Publishing, 2007.

Zelinski, Ernie J. *The Joy of Not Working.* Berkeley, California: Ten Speed Press, 2003.

Notes

Index

PHOTO CREDITS— pages 24, 174, 182, 196 © Douglas E. Morton,
Asia Pacific Media Services (www.asiapacificms.com).
All other photos © Paiboon Publishing.

PAIBOON

PUBLISHING

Titles from
Paiboon Publishing

Title: Thai for Beginners
Author: Benjawan Poomsan Becker ©1995
Description: Designed for either self-study or classroom use. Teaches all four language skills- speaking, listening (when used in conjunction with the cassette tapes), reading and writing. Offers clear, easy, step-by-step instruction building on what has been previously learned. Used by many Thai temples and institutes in America and Thailand. Cassettes & CD available. Paperback. 270 pages. 6" x 8.5"
Book   US$12.95   Stock # 1001B
Two CDs   US$20.00   Stock # 1001CD

Title: Thai for Travelers (Pocket Book Version)
Author: Benjawan Poomsan Becker ©2006
Description: The best Thai phrase book you can find. It contains thousands of useful words and phrases for travelers in many situations. The phrases are practical and up-to-date and can be used instantly. The CD that accompanies the book will help you improve your pronunciation and expedite your Thai language learning. You will be able to speak Thai in no time! Full version on mobile phones and PocketPC also available at www.vervata.com.
Book & CD   US$15.00   Stock # 1022BCD

Title: Thai for Intermediate Learners
Author: Benjawan Poomsan Becker ©1998
Description: The continuation of Thai for Beginners Users are expected to be able to read basic Thai language. There is transliteration when new words are introduced. Teaches reading, writing and speaking at a higher level. Keeps students interested with cultural facts about Thailand. Helps expand your Thai vocabulary in a systematic way. Paperback. 220 pages. 6" x 8.5"
Book   US$12.95   Stock # 1002B
Two CDs   US$15.00   Stock # 1002CD

Title: Thai for Advanced Readers
Author: Benjawan Poomsan Becker ©2000
Description: A book that helps students practice reading Thai at an advanced level. It contains reading exercises, short essays, newspaper articles, cultural and historical facts about Thailand and miscellaneous information about the Thai language. Students need to be able to read basic Thai. Paperback. 210 pages. 6" x 8.5"
Book   US$12.95   Stock # 1003B
Two CDs   US$15.00   Stock # 1003CD

Title: Thai-English, English-Thai Dictionary for Non-Thai Speakers
Author: Benjawan Poomsan Becker ©2002
Description: Designed to help English speakers communicate in Thai. It is equally useful for those who can read the Thai alphabet and those who can't. Most Thai-English dictionaries either use Thai script exclusively for the Thai entries (making them difficult for westerners to use) or use only phonetic transliteration (making it impossible to look up a word in Thai script). This dictionary solves these problems. You will find most of the vocabulary you are likely to need in everyday life, including basic, cultural, political and scientific terms. Paperback. 658 pages. 4.1" x 5.6"
Book   US$15.00   Stock # 1008B

Title: Improving Your Thai Pronunciation
Author: Benjawan Poomsan Becker ©2003
Description: Designed to help foreigners maximize their potential in pronouncing Thai words and enhance their Thai listening and speaking skills. Students will find that they have more confidence in speaking the language and can make themselves understood better. The book and the CDs are made to be used in combination. The course is straight forward, easy to follow and compact. Paperback. 48 pages. 5" x 7.5" + One-hour CD
Book & CD   US$15.00   Stock # 1011BCD

Title: Thai for Lovers
Author: Nit & Jack Ajee ©1999
Description: An ideal book for lovers. A short cut to romantic communication in Thailand. There are useful sentences with their Thai translations throughout the book. You won't find any Thai language book more fun and user-friendly.
Rated R! Paperback. 190 pages. 6" x 8.5"
Book   US$13.95   Stock #: 1004B
Two CDs   US$17.00   Stock #: 1004CD

Title: Thai for Gay Tourists
Author: Saksit Pakdeesiam ©2001
Description: The ultimate language guide for gay and bisexual men visiting Thailand. Lots of gay oriented language, culture, commentaries and other information. Instant sentences for convenient use by gay visitors. Fun and sexy. The best way to communicate with your Thai gay friends and partners! Rated R! Paperback. 220 pages. 6" x 8.5"
Book   US$13.95   Stock # 1007B
Two Tape Set   US$17.00   Stock # 1007T

Title: Thailand Fever
Authors: Chris Pirazzi and Vitida Vasant ©2005
Description: A road map for Thai-Western relationships. The must-have relationship guide-book which lets each of you finally express complex issues of both cultures. Thailand Fever is an astonishing, one-of-a-kind, bilingual expose of the cultural secrets that are the key to a smooth Thai-Western relationship. Paperback. 258 pages. 6" x 8.5"
Book   US$15.95   Stock # 1017B

Title: Thai-English, English-Thai Software Dictionary
for Palm OS PDAs With Search-by-Sound
Authors: Benjawan Poomsan Becker and Chris Pirazzi ©2003
Description: This software dictionary provides instant access to 21,000 English, Phonetic and Thai Palm OS PDA with large, clear fonts and everyday vocabulary. If you're not familiar with the Thai alphabet, you can also look up Thai words by their sounds. Perfect for the

casual traveller or the dedicated Thai learner. Must have a Palm OS PDA and access to the Internet in order to use this product.
Book & CD-ROM   US$39.95   Stock # 1013BCD-ROM

Title: Thai for Beginners Software
Authors: Benjawan Poomsan Becker and Dominique Mayrand ©2004
Description: Best Thai language software available in the market! Designed especially for non-romanized written Thai to help you to rapidly improve your listening and reading skills! Over 3,000 recordings of both male and female voices. The content is similar to the book Thai for Beginners, but with interactive exercises and much more instantly useful words and phrases. Multiple easy-to-read font styles and sizes. Super-crisp enhanced text with romanized transliteration which can be turned on or off for all items.
Book & CD-ROM   US$40.00   Stock # 1016BCD-ROM

Title: Lao-English, English-Lao Dictionary for Non-Lao Speakers
Authors: Benjawan Poomsan Becker & Khamphan Mingbuapha ©2003
Description: Designed to help English speakers communicate in Lao. This practical diction-ary is useful both in Laos and in Northeast Thailand. Students can use it without having to learn the Lao alphabet. However, there is a comprehensive introduction to the Lao writing system and pronunciation. The transliteration system is the same as that used in Paiboon Publishing's other books. It contains most of the vocabulary used in everyday life, including basic, cultural, political and scientific terms. Paperback. 780 pages. 4.1" x 5.6"
Book   US$15.00   Stock # 1010B

Title: Lao for Beginners
Authors: Buasawan Simmala and Benjawan Poomsan Becker ©2003
Description: Designed for either self-study or classroom use. Teaches all four language skills- speaking, listening (when used in conjunction with the audio), reading and writing. Offers clear, easy, step-by-step instruction building on what has been previously learned. Paperback. 292 pages. 6" x 8.5"
Book   US$12.95   Stock # 1012B
Three CDs   US$20.00   Stock # 1012CD

Title: Cambodian for Beginners
Authors: Richard K. Gilbert and Sovandy Hang ©2004
Description: Designed for either self-study or classroom use. Teaches all four language skills- speaking, listening (when used in conjunction with the CDs), reading and writing. Offers clear, easy, step-by-step instruction building on what has been previously learned. Paperback. 290 pages. 6" x 8.5"
Book   US$12.95   Stock # 1015B
Three CDs   US$20.00   Stock # 1015CD

Title: Burmese for Beginners
Author: Gene Mesher ©2006
Description: Designed for either self-study or classroom use. Teaches all four language skills- speaking, listening (when used in conjunction with the CDs), reading and writing. Offers clear, easy, step-by-step instruction building on what has been previously learned. Paperback. 320 pages. 6" x 8.5"
Book   US$12.95   Stock # 1019B
Three CDs   US$20.00   Stock # 1019CD

Title: Vietnamese for Beginners
Authors: Jake Catlett and Huong Nguyen ©2006
Description: Designed for either self-study or classroom use. Teaches all four language skills- speaking, listening (when used in conjunction with the CDs), reading and writing. Offers clear, easy, step-by-step instruction building on what has been previously learned. Paperback. 292 pages. 6" x 8.5"
Book   US$12.95   Stock # 1020B
Three CDs   US$20.00   Stock # 1020CD

Title: Tai Go No Kiso
Author: Benjawan Poomsan Becker ©2002
Description: Thai for Japanese speakers. Japanese version of Thai for Beginners. Paperback. 262 pages. 6" x 8.5"
Book   US$12.95   Stock # 1009B
Three Tape Set   US$20.00   Stock # 1009T

Title: Thai fuer Anfaenger
Author: Benjawan Poomsan Becker ©2000
Description: Thai for German speakers. German version of Thai for Beginners. Paperback. 245 pages. 6" x 8.5"
Book   US$13.95   Stock # 1005B
Two CDs   US$20.00   Stock # 1005CD

Title: Practical Thai Conversation DVD Volume 1
Author: Benjawan Poomsan Becker ©2005
Description: This new media for learning Thai comes with a booklet and a DVD. You will enjoy watching and listening to this program and learn the Thai language in a way you have never done before. Use it on your TV, desktop or laptop. The course is straight forward, easy to follow and compact. A must-have for all Thai learners! DVD and Paperback, 65 pages 4.8" x 7.1"
Book & DVD   US$15.00   Stock # 1018BDVD

Title: Practical Thai Conversation DVD Volume 2
Author: Benjawan Poomsan Becker ©2006
Description: Designed for intermediate Thai learners! This new media for learning Thai comes with a booklet and a DVD. You will enjoy watching and listening to this program and learn the Thai language in a way you have never done before. Use it on your TV, desktop or laptop. The course is straight forward, easy to follow and compact. DVD and Paperback, 60 pages 4.8" x 7.1"
Book & DVD   US$15.00   Stock # 1021BDVD

Title: A Chameleon's Tale - True   Stories of a Global Refugee -
Author: Mohezin Tejani ©2006
Description: A heart touching real life   Story of Mo Tejani, a global refugee who spends thirty four years searching five continents for a country he could call home. Enjoy the ride through numerous countries in Asia, Africa, North and South America. His adventurous   Stories are unique – distinctly different from other travelers' tales. Recommended item from Paiboon Publishing for avid readers worldwide. Paperback. 257 pages. 5" x 7.5"
Book   US$19.95   Stock #1024B

Title: Thai Touch
Author: Richard Rubacher ©2006
Description: The good and the bad of the Land of Smiles are told with a comic touch. The book focuses on the spiritual and mystical side of the magical kingdom as well as its dark side. The good and the bad are told with a comic touch. The Sex Baron, the Naughty & Nice Massage Parlors, the "Bangkok haircut" and Bar Girls & the Pendulum are contrasted with tales of the Thai Forrest Gump, the Spiritual Banker of Thailand and the 72-year old woman whose breasts spout miracle milk. Paperback. 220 pages. 5" x 7.5"
Book   US$19.95   Stock #1024B

Title: How to Buy Land and Build a House in Thailand
Author: Philip Bryce ©2006
Description: This book contains essential information for anyone contemplating buying or leasing land and building a house in Thailand. Subjects covered: land ownership options, land titles, taxes, permits, lawyers, architects and builders. Also includes English/Thai building words and phrases and common Thai building techniques. Learn how to build your dream house in Thailand that is well made, structurally sound and nicely finished. Paperback. 6" x 8.5"
Book   US$19.95   Stock #1025B

Title: Retiring in Thailand
Authors: Philip Bryce and Sunisa Wongdee Terlecky ©2006
Description: A very useful guide for those who are interested in retiring in Thailand. It contains critical information for retirees, such as how to get a retirement visa, banking, health care, renting and buying property, everyday life issues and other important retirement factors. It also lists Thailand's top retirement locations. It's a must for anyone considering living the good life in the Land of Smiles. 6" x 8.5"
Book   US$19.95   Stock #1026B

Title: How to Establish a Successful Business in Thailand
Author: Philip Wylie ©2007
Description: This is the perfect book for anyone thinking of starting or buying a business in Thailand. This book will save readers lots of headaches, time and money. This guide is full of information on how to run a business in Thailand including practical tips by successful foreign business people from different trades, such as guest house, bar trade, e-commerce, export and restaurant. This is an essential guide for all foreigners thinking of doing business - or improving their business - in Thailand.
Book   US$19.95   Stock #1031B

Title: Speak Like A Thai Volume 1
-Contemporary Thai Expressions-
Author: Benjawan Poomsan Becker ©2007
Description: This series of books and CDs is a collection of numerous words and expressions used by modern Thai speakers. It will help you to understand colloquial Thai and to express yourself naturally. You will not find these phases in most textbooks. It's a language course that all Thai learners have been waiting for. Impress your Thai friends with the real spoken Thai. Lots of fun. Good for students of all levels.
Book & CD   US$15.00   Stock # 1028BCD

Title: Speak Like A Thai Volume 2
-Thai Slang and Idioms-
Author: Benjawan Poomsan Becker ©2007
Description: This volume continues the fun of learning the real Thai language. It can be used independently. However, you should be comfortable speaking the Thai phrases from the first volume before you use this one. You will not find these words and phases in any textbooks. It's a language course that all Thai learners have been waiting for. Impress your Thai friends even more. Lots of fun. Good for students of all levels.
Book & CD   US$15.00   Stock # 1029BCD

Title: Speak Like A Thai Volume 3
-Thai Proverbs and Sayings-
Author: Benjawan Poomsan Becker ©2007
Description: The third volume is an excellent supplementary resource for all Thai learners. Common Thai proverbs and sayings listed in the book with the literal translations will help you understand Thai ways of thinking that are differnt from yours. You can listen to these proverbs and sayings over and over on the CD. Sprinkle them here and there in your conversation. Your Thai friend will be surprised and appreciate your insight into Thai culture. Good for intermdiate and advanced students, but beginners can use it for reference.
Book & CD   US$15.00   Stock # 1030BCD

Title: Speak Like a Thai Volume 4
-Heart Words-
Author: Benjawan Poomsan Becker ©2007
Description: "Heart" Words contains 300 common contemporary "heart" words and phrases. They are recorded on the CD and explained in the booklet with a brief translation, a literal translation and used in a sample phrase or sentence. More than a hundred bonus "heart" words are included in the booklet for your reference. Listen and learn how Thai people express their feelings and thoughts. You will gain significant insight about the Thai people and their social contexts.
Book & CD   US$15.00   Stock # 1033BCD

Title: Speak Like a Thai Volume 5
-Northeastern Dialect-
Author: Benjawan Poomsan Becker ©2007
Description: Northeastern Dialect contains 500 Isaan words and phrases which have been carefully chosen from real life situations. They are recorded on the CD and explained in the booklet with a brief translation and a literal translation when needed. Throughout the book there are also lists of many Isaan words that are different from standard Thai. This is a fun program that will bring a smile to the face of your Isaan friends.
Book & CD   US$15.00   Stock # 1034BCD

Title: Thai Law for Foreigners
Author: Ruengsak Thongkaew and Benjawan Poomsan ©2008
Description: Thai law made easy for foreigners. This unique book includes information regarding immigration, family, property, civil and criminal law used in Thailand. Very useful for both visitors and those who live in Thailand. Written by an experienced Thai trial lawyer. It contains both the Thai text and full English translation.
Book   US$19.95   Stock #1032B